MUHAMMAD
"A MERCY TO ALL THE NATIONS"

A HUMBLE OFFERING, THIS, TO THEE
O PROPHET OF GOD!
PRAY ACCEPT IT

MUHAMMAD
"A MERCY TO ALL THE NATIONS"

by

Al-Hajj Qassim Ali Jairazbhoy

Goodword
B·O·O·K·S

New Delhi

First published in 1937
© Goodword Books 2001
Reprinted 1998, 2001, 2003

Goodword Books Pvt. Ltd.
1, Nizamuddin West Market
New Delhi 110 013
Tel. 2435 5454, 2435 6666
Fax 2435 7333, 2435 7980
e-mail: info@goodwordbooks.com
Website: www.goodwordbooks.com

Printed in India

To my Father who passed away when I was ten months old
And to my Mother who "Brought me up when I was little."

"O my Lord! have mercy on my parents, as they brought me up when I was little."—THE QURAN 17 : 24.

CONTENTS

CHAPTER   PAGE

Frontispiece   *Facing Title*

FOREWORD 11

PREFACE 17

1. ARABIA BEFORE MUHAMMAD 27

2. BIRTH 36

3. YOUTH, AND FIRST FORTY YEARS OF MUHAMMAD'S LIFE 43

4. THE DIVINE CALL 48

5. THE ESSENTIALS OF THE PROPHETHOOD OF MUHAMMAD 50

6. THE FIRST MUSLIMS 57

7. THE ATROCITIES OF THE QURAYSH 69

8. THE EXILE TO ABYSSINIA 76

9. THE MECCAN PERIOD BEFORE THE HEGIRA . . 85

10. THE HEGIRA (THE FLIGHT) 98

11. THE PROPHET IN MEDINA 106

12. HOW THE SWORD WAS THRUST ON MUHAMMAD . 126
(a) THE BATTLE OF BADR
(b) THE BATTLE OF UHUD

13. TRIALS OF THE MUSLIMS AFTER THE BATTLE OF UHUD 145

14. THE BATTLE OF KHANDAQ OR AHZĀB . . . 151

15. MUSLIM WARS WITH THE JEWS OF MEDINA . . 157

16. THE MEDINITE PERIOD BEFORE THE BATTLE OF KHAYBAR 162

17. THE FALL OF KHAYBAR 176

18. THE FALL OF MECCA 181

9

MUHAMMAD : "A MERCY TO ALL THE NATIONS"

CHAPTER		PAGE
19.	THE BATTLES OF HUNAYN AND TĀ'IF	188
20.	THE BATTLE OF TABUK	197
21.	THE DEATH	208
22.	THE ACHIEVEMENT	211
23.	THE CHANGED ARAB WORLD	233
24.	"THERE SHALL BE NO PROPHET AFTER ME"	245
25.	AS EUROPEAN CRITICS SEE MUHAMMAD	256
26.	THE PERSONALITY AND CHARACTER OF MUHAMMAD	266
27.	THE PERSONAL QUALITIES OF MUHAMMAD	273
28.	MUHAMMAD, THE WORLD'S GREATEST BENEFACTOR	301
29.	POLYGAMY IN ISLAM AND THE HOLY PROPHET MUHAMMAD	320
30.	THE CONCEPTION OF THE BROTHERHOOD OF MAN IN ISLAM	337
31.	AL-ISLAM, THE TEACHINGS OF MUHAMMAD	355
32.	THE QURAN	368
33.	THE HOLY PROPHET MUHAMMAD FORETOLD IN ANCIENT SCRIPTURES	380

FOREWORD

AL-HAJJ QASSIM ALI JAIRAZBHOY, the author of this volume, who is to be congratulated on the pains he has taken in giving a faithful portrait of the simple and noble life of the Prophet of Islam, is a well-known figure in Islam and requires no introduction from me. His anxiety to render service to Islam is commendable; and I am glad that he devotes his leisure to the study of the principles for which Islam stands and explaining the true message of the Prophet of Islam to the world. The author has done well in showing the great principles of Islam and the mission of its Prophet as a true messenger of the Most High.

He has made considerable sacrifices for Islam, and his donation of one lakh and twenty-five thousand rupees for founding a chair for Science and Philosophy in the Aligarh University bears witness to his catholic charities and his love for science and philosophy. His various other charities for his co-religionists as well as his contributions to the progress of Islam show his earnest desire to be of service to humanity.

As he has pointed out, the holy Prophet of Islam is to us Muslims the last and greatest messenger from the Creator, and through him man is to find salvation in both this world and the next. Our reasons for holding firmly to this Faith (and it is essential to remember that the Prophet asked for Faith—'Īmān—and not like some other religious teachers for 'Īqān,[1] a point that should be remembered by all Muslims) are that this message is in its nature the essence of man's spiritual nature. The great religious teachers before and since Muhammad have all limited the area of truth by excluding either some or all of their predecessors. Muhammad, on the other hand, by a full recognition of all his predecessors and by admitting that no people, race, or nation had been left without some kind of divine illumination, gave his Faith universality in the past, and in fact made it coexistent with human history.

If, now, we turn from its historic background to its doctrine and to its possibility of development in the future, we will find the same potential universality. Take the central principle of "Allāh O Akbar." Here we find on one side divinity, on the other side infinity. For what is the greater—time, space, the starry heavens, intelligence, knowledge?—wherever existence goes there His greatness extends. Greaterness here, to anyone who understands the implications of the Arabic language, does not mean "greaterness" as literally translated into English. It means that everything else is within the womb of the greater—everything else is maintained and sustained by Divine Power, including the furthest spaces of imagination.

Muhammad told mankind *first* that the infinite sustainer and container of all existence had justice,

[1] 'Īqān signifies to be sure, to become certain.

mercy, and love as well; *secondly*, that man through these qualities and through gentleness and kindness, prayer, awe or wonder could get—howsoever infinitesimal proportion—direct communion with the all-embracing power in which he lived and moved and had his being.

I submit that this doctrine will have a universality that can be accepted as long as man is man and as long as intelligence as we understand it survives on earth.

The enemies of Islam have attacked its outward manifestations and constantly attempted to show that its practice (even such essentially elevating manifestations as prayer, fasting, alms, etc.) is impossible in modern and civilized conditions. Unfortunately, the " 'Ulamā"—the savants—have played into the hands of the enemies. The present practices of Islam took shape and form at the time when the schoolmen reigned supreme in East and West alike. The 'Ulamā of Islam, like the schoolmen of Europe, built up a fabric which had no relationship with reality. The Renaissance and the intellectual revolutions that followed (and are still going on) have cleared the West from such thraldom, but the Muslim East is only now starting its renaissance. Not only non-Muslims but some Muslims, appalled by the extent and variety of the non-essentials (*Furū'āt*) have almost followed the example of the man who in emptying the waste water from the tub threw the baby with it out of the window. They have almost thrown out the *'Usūlāt* (essentials). If Islam is ever to fulfil its

13

mission it must have a universality not only in space, namely, throughout the earth, but in time, namely, as long as mankind exists on this globe.

We maintain that the Prophet only ordered prayer, fasting, and gentleness in all human relations, kindliness and consideration for all beasts and animals from the smallest worm to the largest mammal. By the institution of the 'Ulu 'l-Amr—who can be interpreted as Imam and Caliph—and by placing obedience to 'Ulu 'l-Amr immediately after that to God and Prophet, he ensured that the Faith would ever remain living, extending, developing with science, knowledge, art, and industry.

Unlike some of his predecessors he has condemned repression, renunciation, torture (either self-inflicted or on others), dirt and physical corruption. Man is to go through life not indulging in an impossible code of "Resist not evil" but with patience, forbearance, argument, and kindliness—qualities which as even so unfriendly a witness as Mr. H. G. Wells in his *History of the World* admits, have always been greater in Muslim Society than in any other. They have, in fact, been the outward signs of Islamic countries. This absence of violence, this sweet reasonableness, this readiness to recognize that sex, marriage, parenthood are our highest duties and not sins that can only be legitimized by the fumblings of a priest or by idle ceremonies that invoke fire and rain and the elements to clean up something that is essentially unwholesome. In Islam this is not the attitude towards instincts which are as natural as eating and drinking. Men and women

14

should marry freely with their own choice, and that free choice is the highest and holiest of all blessings. The witnesses come only to insure the legal consequences of the marriage. And if it fails—as it must fail in some cases, given the essential nature of the instincts on which the attraction is founded—a healthy, wholesome, unashamed divorce with stain on neither man nor woman but leaving each free to seek new and happy union is the only solution. If, rightly, the Muslims have kept till now to the forms of prayer and fasting as practised at the time of the Prophet, it should not be forgotten that it is not the forms of prayer and fasting that have been commanded, but the facts, and we are entitled to adjust the forms to the facts of life as circumstances changed. It is the same Prophet who advises his followers ever to remain Ibnu 'l-Waqt (i.e. children of the time and period in which they were on earth), and it must be the natural ambition of every Muslim to practise and represent his Faith according to the standard of the Waqt or space-time.

PREFACE

"BUT We will this day deliver you with your body so that you may be a sign to those after you. And most surely the majority of the people are heedless to Our communications" (10: 92).

This passage from the Quran has reference to the death of Pharaoh near the Red Sea, while in pursuit of Moses and the Israelites, and states that his body was not lost in the sea, but cast ashore, and afterwards embalmed and that this should, in due course, be made known to generations to come.

The Bible makes no mention of it, nor do we find anything about it in any book of history. Recently, however, among the mummies in Egypt the body of Rameses II, who has been identified with the Pharaoh of Moses, has been discovered.

Here is a clear proof of the supernatural knowledge which was vouchsafed to the Prophet through the revelations of the Quran, and the possession of such a rare knowledge of the unseen itself goes far to substantiate the truly divine aspect of his mission.

The prophecies of the Bible, both in the Old Testament and in the New are all, more or less, ambiguous in these terms; but the above quotation from the Quran is precise and direct. Curiously enough, criticism of the Quran has been based upon this very verse, the critics averring that it was nothing but an ingenious story quite devoid of historical truth. The recent discovery referred to has again justified the words of God.

It is refreshing to think of the manner of man Muhammad was. He expressed his opinion directly and without fear, his views on religious and social matters being the results of thought and observation based upon Right and Justice. His Justice was tempered with mercy, but the latter never blinded the former. He knew that "God is not merciful to him who is not so to mankind."

He spoke plain truths in a plain way—with no diplomatic jugglery. His "slogan," as we might put it nowadays, was, "Say what is true, although it be bitter and displeasing to people."

So also, he had no patience with concealment or secrecy. When a follower hinted to him that he needed advice on a matter which was most secret, the Prophet's reply was, "If thou hast aught to hide, keep silence, that which is whispered to the birds is sung to the stream."

In this directness must be found the secret of his power over his followers. He was consistently direct in reply, advice, or reproof.

Thomas Carlyle, than whom was no speaker more fearless, says. "He was a man of truth and fidelity; true in what he did, in what he spoke, in what he thought; he always meant something; a man rather taciturn in speech, silent when there was nothing to be said, but pertinent, wise, sincere, when he did speak, always throwing light on the matter."

He was "A Rock in the Way," a strong man with strong convictions and one could live up to them. "A still strong man in a blatant land"; and it was not for such a one to have truck with expediency and half-hearted measures. He declared for One God at a time when idolatry, immorality, infidelity, drunkenness, and persecution were rampant, when many would have given up the task, would have been forced to give it up, and would have yielded half-way.

It was the same with him regarding drunkenness. He stood firm for total prohibition—no temperance or gradual reform. The evil must be uprooted, root and branch.

It was his steadfast conviction that man is personally responsible for all his actions, and that there is no room for a third person to interfere on his behalf. He says, "None can come between man and his Maker." There are both justice and mercy in forgiveness, without doubt, but to punish one for the sin of another is neither the way of justice nor that of mercy. Even he himself could not think of influencing God on behalf of another.

"Wouldst thou have favour from God? Thou thyself must ask it." How thoroughly rational!

There is a beautiful story told to illustrate this aspect of the Prophet. A wealthy follower of his called upon him to ask for his influence and his prayers. The Prophet replied: "I can obtain for thee nothing from God thou canst not obtain for thyself, go thou and ask by prayer." "But," said the other, "I know not how or what to ask." "Then go thou and stand before God, with thy hands clean and open, and say, 'God, thou knowest, and thy servant waiteth!' "

His soul answered to himself as directly as he did to others. He had no doubts, no stumbling "buts" and "ifs"; he approached God direct with unflinching faith. Says Carlyle:

"From of old a thousand thoughts, in his pilgrimings and wanderings, had been in this man. What am I? What is this unfathomable thing I live in which men name the universe? What is life? What is death? What am I to believe? What am I to do? The grim rock of Mount Hirā, of Mount Sinai, the stern sandy solitudes answered not, there was no answer. The man's own soul and what of God's inspiration dwelt there had to answer."

Concerning himself, the Prophet was equally plain and outspoken, leaving no room for doubt or misunderstanding. He says, "Verily God had made me a humble servant, and not a proud king. I am no more than man."

Against all blasts and storms of persecutions he stood firm and immovable for Truth and God—a monument of sincerity, perseverance, and humility. "Verily I have fulfilled my mission. I have left amongst you a plain command, to wit, the Book of God, and my 'Ahlu 'l-Bayt, my descendants, of which if ye take fast hold ye shall never go astray." With the words delivered from a hillock of the plains of 'Arafāt, the seat of pilgrimage, the Prophet concluded his last sermon in his last pilgrimage to Mecca. And he said with uplifted eyes towards Heaven, "O God! I have delivered my message and discharged my ministry." And all the people shouted, "Yea, Verily thou hast." Then the Prophet said, "Bear thou witness thereunto, O God! I beseech Thee."

To raise a people sunk in the lowest depths of degradation and vice, and to have the rare fortune of achieving success in his mission in his own lifetime, is decidedly the monumental work of a highly successful character, one to inspire mankind with action, perseverance, patience, and faith. Any other would have despaired of success, would have yielded to the pressure of utterly hostile circumstances, but the Prophet gloriously outlived all struggles, persecutions, temptations, and failures; he was confident of his mission, confident of success, and so he succeeded at last in the very place of persecution, and could confidently say, "Verily, I have fulfilled my mission." Neither Moses nor Jesus could claim this degree of success. "How often would I have gathered thy children together, even as a hen doth gather her brood under her wings, and ye would not!" (Luke xiii : 34), is what Jesus himself says regarding his work.

Nor did Ramachandra nor Krishnā nor Zoroaster leave the world with any brilliant hopes after them. Muhammad is the only model of success as a Prophet and Teacher of humanity, living ever after death, through his words and actions. So his success was classical and immortal success. "I leave amongst you the Book of God and my 'Ahlu 'l-Bayt of which if you take fast hold ye shall never go astray," are his words, and they stand true to this day.

The Quran affords practical guidance on all matters, religious, social, and moral, and the Prophet's own life and that of 'Ahlu 'l-Bayt is a translation into actual practice of the Quranic teachings. For he was himself a model for all walks of life. He was orphan, servant, trader, husband, preacher, refugee, soldier, king, and judge. So the Quran, among other things, is a suggestive text-book, as it were, on human affairs. This consistent regard for the practical is, perhaps, the secret of the Prophet's success, which sets him apart as a unique character in the world's history.

God and His Apostle Muhammad are ever the source of inexhaustible inspiration, and through such a divine urge only, through such strength, invisible and invincible, I have been able to complete this task of mine—my bounden duty as a true Muslim, and to present my humble homage and offering in this literary form to Him and His Apostle, my never-failing guide in life.

He, God, has helped me in this task as He has promised in the Quran—to help all those who strive to carry the Word of God to the people of the world. Words cannot express my deep debt of gratitude to Him for His guidance and inspiration.

Q. A. J.

"GOOLSHANABAD,"
PEDDAR ROAD, BOMBAY

MUHAMMAD
"A MERCY TO ALL THE NATIONS"

CHAPTER I

ARABIA BEFORE MUHAMMAD

> "Corruption appeared in the land
> and the sea on account of what
> the hands of men had wrought."—
> THE QURAN 30 : 41.

MUHAMMAD, the holy Prophet of Islam, was born and grew to manhood in Arabia, a land at that time considered as beyond redemption, and in something like twenty years not only had he made of the Arabs a people of outstanding excellence both in manner and men, but he had fired them with a zeal that carried them to many lands and climes. Wherever they went they revolutionized thought and life, working a change whereof the results are seen to-day in the greatness of many nations. To appreciate rightly the power of the teachings of the Prophet and the miracle which they have wrought it is necessary to describe the Arabs and Arabia in the days before Islam.

The condition of affairs in Arabia, and of the Arabs before the advent of the Prophet Muhammad was calamitous. The whole land was plunged in a sea of ignorance and darkness. Justice and Truth, the two fundamentals of civilized life, were unknown. Morality was at its lowest ebb. Religion was at its lowest depth. The lives of the people were little better than those of beasts, and the finer qualities inherent in man were dead.

Some redeeming points there still might be. Hospitality, bravery, generosity, manliness, and tribal fidelity were some of the noble traits in their character; but what were these few virtues in comparison with the general life of corruption and brutality that they were leading? These few good qualities were easily drowned in an extravagance of sin, free and open indulgence in adultery, gambling, drinking, highway robbery, uncleanness, and every kind of abomination. Not only, moreover, were these vices indulged in, but they were actually praised and made the themes of poets' songs. In place of the One True God, Invisible, Incomprehensible, they worshipped gods and goddesses made of stone. There were about four hundred such deities in all; the belief being that to each one God had delegated the discharge of certain of His functions. For everything which they desired they turned to these idols, invoking their help and blessings and in addition they regarded the sun, the moon, the stars, and the air all as gods, worshipping them and believing them to be controllers of their destinies. These people had fallen so low as even to worship stones, mud, and trees; before any shapely piece of stone on their way they would prostrate themselves. Even men of wealth and fame were considered beings worthy of worship and adoration, while their lives were fettered in vain superstitions. Before going on a journey they would first secure four roughly hewn stones, three to cook on and one to worship; if they were unable to take four, three would suffice, and at a halt, after cooking, they would take out one and worship it before continuing their travel. Their heathenism had reached such a pitch that the Ka'ba, the House of God, which was reconstructed by Abraham for the worship of the One Almighty God, became a depositary for their idols.

They divided themselves into clans, and the clans into families, and each clan and family had its own beliefs and customs; and each family had its own idols in the house. In time of sickness and famine they would prostrate themselves before the idols, offering up cattle, grain, and the like in return for their help.

But although idolatry had obtained such a firm hold on the Arab in general, there were a few here and there who were frankly atheists who believed in no religion at all and made a mock of the idolaters. There were a few who practised such religion as Christianity and the Jewish faith. The followers of the Sābī religion believed in a book, and in the prophets Sheesh bin Adam, and 'Idrīs. They said prayers seven times a day, and did half a month's fasting in a year. They also believed in the worship of the planets. The followers of the Abrahamic religion were also polytheists, circumcision, sacrifice, and the growing of

29

a beard being among the essentials of their creed. They had their own idols in the Ka'ba, including an image of Abraham and one of his son Ishmael. The idol of Ishmael had seven arrows in its hand, and each arrow had a different name, and was there for a different purpose.

The Jews had also become idolaters, and had their idols in the Ka'ba also. The Christians too had made an idol of the Virgin Mary with the child Jesus in her lap, and that also was placed in the Ka'ba. In fact, all the different religions then prevalent among the Arabs believed in the worship of idols and the Ka'ba was full of them, some belonging only to certain of the big clans, while others were for the worship of all.

Hubal was considered the greatest of the idols, and its power extended over the rains, riches, and general good. Dawar was an idol worshipped only by young women. The house of God that had been built for the worship of the One True God had thus become a great temple packed with idols; for the Arabs believed that everything could be obtained through the intercession of idols and that these idols would save their souls and send them to Heaven after death.

As for the social condition of the Arabs, it was everywhere as bad as the religious. The various clans and families were always at war with one another. Anger and hatred were their chief characteristics, and revenge their main life force. Fighting and the shedding of blood over trifles were the commonplaces of their existence. They were ignorant of every social principle and did not know what it was to lead a peaceful and settled life. They wandered from place to place with their cattle, halting when and where they chose. A few settled in villages and towns, but wherever they were there was constant fighting and bloodshed. Above all, there was no central government to enforce law and order. The whole of Arabia was divided into little states, and each state or clan was a separate political unit, with its own chief who, whenever he thought proper, would lead it to battle against another clan. There were, indeed, a few provincial governments, but these were too weak to enforce justice.

When not fighting, "Wine, Women, and Song" represented the summit of their ambitions, while gambling was their chief intellectual occupation. This was a daily pastime, and the very few who did not indulge in it were objects of derision. As to drink, it was as great a vice as gambling. Intoxicating liquors flowed like water in nearly every household. And there was not a dwelling without its goodly reserve of wine jars.

Women were in those days considered as mere chattels—things scarcely human. It was this low esteem in which they were held that established the custom of infanticide in many tribes, it being reckoned a disgrace and ignominy for a man to have a daughter. Those girls who by any chance escaped death at birth were cruelly treated. When they grew up, they were made to work like beasts of burden, and regarded as beings without a soul,

31

feelings, or even emotions. Women were entitled to no share in the property of either father or husband, and in the absence of male issue the property would go to the nearest male relation— not to a daughter.

A man had as many wives as he wished, as well as any number of mistresses. Prostitution was rife among them. Married women were forced to have other lovers beside their own husbands, and women servants were made prostitutes just to earn money for their masters. When a daughter was born, her father would bury her alive or have her killed most cruelly, and often the poor mother herself was made to kill her own daughter.

As for education, there was no such thing among the Arabs in those days. Ignorant and superstitious, they believed in all sorts of queer things, such as genii and evil spirits, charms and incantations. They believed that the soul was a special germ that got into the body of a child at birth, and went on growing, leaving the body only after death, when it assumed the form of an owl and hovered over the tomb. Their superstitions knew no bounds; if a bird crossed their path from right to left, they considered it a very bad omen. Some believed there was another life after death, and these would tie a camel to a tomb, and let it starve to death, believing that on the Last Day the deceased would mount on its back and ride to heaven. They had great faith in fortune-tellers and believed all that was told by them.

Such, then, was the degrading and most pitiable

condition of the Arabs before the coming of Islam. When ignorance and darkness had reached its height, when irreligion had become rampant, and cruelty and oppression lords of the land, then, like day after night, like rain after intense heat, God in His infinite mercy and love for the human race, made Muhammad His Prophet and sent him to lead those astray back to the right path. Like a sun to dispel darkness, a rain to shower blessings, he came and he succeeded in his mission. The Arabs, a fallen nation, wild and uncivilized, steeped in the vilest vices, underwent a change that made them the most learned and most civilized of beings. Polytheism was forgotten, and the Unity of the One and Indissoluble God became their firm belief. They who knew not God were, in a short time, so faithful to Him that they did their best to spread Islam the world over, and they did succeed in spreading that True Light, which the Prophet brought, to many climes and many people.

The holy Prophet consolidated the Arabs; from a divided people, they soon became a united nation, each and every individual working together and sympathizing with each other, instead of fighting as before. God in the Quran says:

"And remember the favour of God on you when you were [the] enemies [of one another], then He united your hearts, so by His favour you became brethren, and you were on the brink of a pit of fire, then He saved you from it" (3: 102).

He made the life and the working condition of

the slave tolerable, by enforcing the same treatment for him as for a member of the family. The Islamic brotherhood which the teachings of the Prophet brought into being did away with all social inequalities between man and man, and man and woman. He taught them to treat slaves with kindness and love, and made the manumission of a slave a meritorious deed. He insisted that no free person should by force be made a slave, and that those who were already slaves should be treated as members of the family, and granted freedom gradually. The holy Prophet made it an obligation on the part of the Islamic Government to budget annually for the allocation of a certain percentage of the revenues to the purpose of the liberation of the slaves, by paying the ransom from the Government exchequer.

The holy Prophet removed all misconceptions about women. He taught the Arabs to regard them as friends and companions, and to be kind and loving to them. He said, "A person who does not show kindness should not expect kindness from God." He taught them to regard infanticide as abominable and most displeasing to God, and thus it soon came to an end.

He had a great regard for the rights of women; since the passing away of the matriarchal form of society women were, for the first time, emancipated by the Prophet. He showed by his example the love, care, and respect that was due to them, and so woman, once deemed the lowest of the low, was raised up to a position of great dignity.

34

As has been shown, all this was achieved by the holy Prophet in face of the greatest difficulties in but a few years. Is this not enough to convince all that he was the greatest of Reformers, and the most perfect of mankind?

CHAPTER 2

BIRTH

(571 A.C.)

> "Our Lord! and raise up in them
> an Apostle from among them who
> shall recite to them Thy com-
> munications and teach them the
> Book and the wisdom and purify
> them."—THE QURAN 2 : 129.
> *Abraham's Prayer in the Quran.*

FROM time to time, both before and after
Abraham, God had raised up prophets in the
world—different prophets for different nations; for
in those days the nations dwelt in complete isola-
tion, one from another—modern conveniences of
transport and communication being then unknown
—but when, in the infinite Wisdom of God, the
time was ripe for merging all religious systems into
one, under a single and universal brotherhood, He,
as promised through the prophecies of the former
prophets, raised up the World-Prophet Muhammad.

The Quran teaches us that the advent of the
World-Prophet was foretold by all the prophets,
and in order that people might not be mistaken,
it was said that the promised one should bear
testimony to the truth of all the prophets, as the
following verse of the Quran shows: "And when

36

God made a covenant through the prophets: certainly what I have given you of Book and wisdom —then an apostle comes to you verifying that which is with you, you must believe in him, and you must aid him. . . ." (3 : 80). That the holy Prophet testified to all the previous prophets is shown by the fact that he has made a belief in them an essential of his faiths. The definition of a faithful, accordingly, as given in the Quran, runs as follows: "And who believe in that which had been revealed to you, and that which was revealed before you, and they are sure of the hereafter" (2 : 4).

The Israelites and the Ishmaelites are from a common progenitor—Abraham. In His promises to Abraham, God has clearly said that from among both Israelites and Ishmaelites prophets would be raised up. The Quran makes mention of this, and the Old Testament also records a promise to the same effect: "And I will make of thee a great nation, and I will bless thee and make thy name great, and thou shalt be a blessing" (Gen. 12: 2). There is, moreover, a reference in the same book to Ishmael: "And as for Ishmael, I have heard, Behold I have blessed him and will make him faithful, and will multiply him exceedingly" (Gen. 17: 20).

Moses uttered another prophecy from God touching the advent of the Prophet Muhammad: "I will raise them up a Prophet from among their brethren, like unto thee, and will put My words into his mouth" (Deut. 18: 18).

Here are two references which apply solely to

37

the Prophet Muhammad, the first: "from among their brethren," which means that the one Prophet would be raised from among the brethren of the Israelites, i.e. Ishmaelites, and the second: "like unto thee," which means that he should be a law-giver like Moses, and there has been no prophet, save only the Prophet Muhammad who has been also a law-giver. Our assertion is further borne out by the conversation between John the Baptist and those who asked him, "Who art thou?" And he confessed, " . . . 'I am not the Christ,' and they asked him, 'What then? Art thou Elias?' And he said, 'I am not.' 'Art thou that Prophet?' and he answered, 'No' " (John 1: 19–21). The reference to "that Prophet" clearly shows that the people were waiting for the advent of three prophets: first, Elias, who they thought would reappear in person; secondly, Jesus; and thirdly, "that prophet." The third, "that Prophet, clearly points to the holy Prophet of Islam, for the first two, according to the Israelite scriptures, had been fulfilled in the persons of John and Jesus.

There are many other prophecies by Israelite prophets, such as David, Solomon, etc., as well as that by Jesus, the last of the Israelites, which runs, "If ye love me, keep my commandments, and I will pray to the Father and He shall give you another comforter, that he may abide with you for ever; even the spirit of Truth" (John 14: 15–17). This and similar verses from the New Testament predict in clear terms the advent of another prophet after Jesus, and the words, "that he may abide with you for ever" indicate that there would be no other prophet after the promised one. This is true only of the holy Prophet Muhammad, for in the Quran he is termed "the last of the Prophets."

Ishmael, the eldest son of Abraham, had twelve sons. One of them, Kedar, settled in the Arabian province of the Hedjaz where his progeny spread, as is borne out even on the authority of the Old Testament. It is also proved that 'Adnān, to whom the genealogy of the Prophet was traced, was of the offspring of Ishmael. In the ninth generation from Adnān is Nazir bin Kināna, who founded the dynasty of the Quraysh; and further down is Qusayy, to whom was entrusted the guardianship of the Ka'ba, an office of high honour in Arabia. Thus the dynasty to which the Prophet belonged was one of the highest in honour, respect, and nobility. 'Abdu 'l-Muttalab, the grandfather of the Prophet, had ten sons, of whom one was 'Abdullāh, the father of the holy Prophet, and 'Abdullāh married 'Āmina, a lady of another reputable family. The holy Prophet never knew or saw his father, for shortly after his parents were married 'Abdullāh went on a commercial journey to Syria, and on his way back he was taken seriously ill and died at Medina. Unfortunately, his mother also died when he was only six years old, and so at this tender age he was deprived of the care of both parents.

The following table shows the descent of the holy Prophet Muhammad.

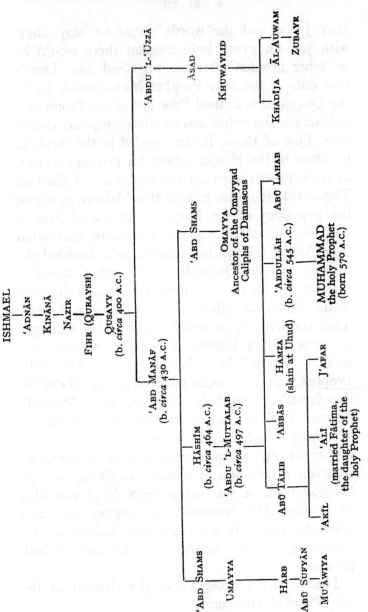

ISHMAEL
'ADNĀN
KINĀNĀ
NAZIR
FIHR (QURAYSH)
QUSAYY
(b. circa 400 A.C.)

'ABD MANĀF
(b. circa 430 A.C.)

'ABDU 'L-'UZZĀ
ASAD
KHUWAYLID
KHADĪJA
ĀL-AUWAM
ZUBAYR

'ABD SHAMS
OMAYYA
Ancestor of the Omayyad
Caliphs of Damascus

ABŪ LAHAB
'ABDULLĀH
(b. circa 545 A.C.)
MUHAMMAD
the holy Prophet
(born 570 A.C.)

HĀSHIM
(b. circa 464 A.C.)
'ABDU 'L-MUTTALAB
(b. circa 497 A.C.)

HAMZA
(slain at Uhud)
'ABBĀS
ABŪ TĀLIB
'ALĪ
(married Fātima,
the daughter of the
holy Prophet)
J'AFAR
'AKĪL

'ABD SHAMS
UMAYYA
HARB
ABŪ SUFYĀN
MU'ĀWIYA

40

The holy Prophet was born on a Monday, being the 12th day of Rabī'u 'l-Awwal (April, 571 A.C.). It was in a vision that his mother received the joyful tidings that she was to give birth to a prophet. When he was born there were the usual signs that indicate that a prophet is born, the most noteworthy of which are: abundant rainfall and the consequent disappearance of famine. Another extraordinary event that took place at the time of his birth was the destruction of an army of Christians, led by the chief of Yemen, who had marched to Mecca to demolish the Ka'ba, so that the magnificent church he had built at his capital San'ā might become the resort of the pious instead. The whole army, encamped just outside Mecca, was attacked by a most virulent form of smallpox, which caused great havoc and destroyed the major part of the forces. The rest took to flight in utter confusion; as the holy Quran says, "Hast thou not considered how thy Lord dealt with the possessors of the elephant? Did he not cause their war to end in confusion, and sent down birds in flocks (to prey) upon them, casting them against hard stones . . ." (ch. 105).

According to the custom of the Arab gentry mothers did not suckle their babies, so the Prophet was handed over to Halīma, a nurse of the tribe of Banū Sa'd. Two years later Halīma brought him back to his mother, but 'Āmina asked her to resume her charge, as Mecca at that time was stricken with an epidemic. Thus he remained in the charge of Halīma until the age of six. Although but a child, those few years spent in rural surroundings did much to mould his character; for the calm atmosphere and natural environment made him realize the presence of a Supreme Being, Who rules over and controls all. So at the age of six, when he returned to his mother, he was well on the road to Prophethood. Unfortunately, he did not enjoy the love and care of his mother for long, for soon afterwards she died on her way to Medina whither she was going to visit the tomb of her husband.

Muhammad was then taken care of by his grandfather 'Abdu 'l-Muttalab, but he died before two years had elapsed. Then at the age of eight his guardianship passed to his uncle Abū Tālib; the uncle and nephew soon became so greatly attached to each other that it became impossible for Abū Tālib to go anywhere, even on a commercial journey, without taking Muhammad with him. People were greatly impressed by his ways and manners, and once while travelling with his uncle, they met a Christian ascetic, Bāhīrā, who, beholding the boy, saw in him the marks of greatness and foretold that one day he would be a prophet.

CHAPTER 3

YOUTH, AND FIRST FORTY YEARS OF
MUHAMMAD'S LIFE

> "I have lived a life-time among
> you before it."—THE QURAN 10:16.

A NOTABLE circumstance touching the youth time of Muhammad is to be found in the fact that although his guardians took the utmost care in his upbringing, the question of education they passed over entirely. This was no fault of theirs and they cannot be blamed for it; for it was not the custom in those days and among those people to educate one's children, and especially was this true of the upper class. The Quraysh, for example, regarded reading and writing as tasks for menials only. It was, therefore, a great wonder to the world when it came to realize later the enormous depth of learning, scholarship, and philosophy to which Muhammad had obtained. According to the custom of the day, Muhammad learnt business and visited all places with which Arabs had business relations. Even at an early age, his integrity and truthfulness won him fame in Mecca and soon earned him the title of "Al-Amīn" (The Trustworthy). Anyone who had dealings with him in any connection always spoke of him with praise and respect. It is said that once when the Sacred House of Mecca

43

was to be reconstructed, the Quraysh undertook to do the work, but presently a dispute arose as to who should be given the privilege of laying the "Black Stone." Probably this would have ended in inter-tribal feuds and general bloodshed—such being the spirit of the age—had not an old man advised them to refer the whole matter to an arbitrator. Whoever, he said, should be the first to appear at the Ka'ba the next day should act as judge and settle the dispute. This was agreed to, and on the morrow, to the satisfaction of all, it was Muhammad who was the first to appear, and all welcomed him with one voice, exclaiming, "Here is the Trustworthy, here is the Trustworthy." With his great tact and understanding he soon settled the dispute and all ended peacefully.

In appearance Muhammad was pleasant yet imposing. He was of medium height and build. He had a large head and a round face; his forehead was broad; eyes dark and full of light with long lashes; his beard was dark and thick; his colour was fair. His whole appearance was comely and attractive. His bearing was dignified, and his manners charming; so charming that he won the hearts of all with whom he came in contact. Visitors were always impressed by his personal charm. Sir William Muir, the Christian critic, in describing the features of Muhammad, was compelled to write: "It is difficult to describe the feelings of those who met and talked with Muhammad. His personality was dignified, his manners were charming, his smile most winning, and his talk possessing every quality with the power to hold a person. Everyone loved and admired him because of these sterling personal qualities."

The world says, "Youth is mad, Youth is blind"; and that is right enough; for youth is both mad and blind. The intoxication of youth tends to throw the restraints of religion and morality to the winds, and indulge in what seems to youth to be pleasure. Laymen apart, even among the most learned and holy there are many who bow to the call of youth, and stray from the right path and from the strict rules of conduct. But when youth has gone, when its maddening urge has flown and old age appears, and the hair is turning grey, then do some awake from their dreams of madness and realize what they have done, and what they have missed; and in order to repent and make up for the good they have lost, become dwellers in either mosque or monastery, and henceforward goodliness and prayer become the occupation of their lives. But the best and strongest character is he who shall pass an unimpeachable and stainless life even amid the temptations and follies of youth.

A just man bows his head in reverence, when he studies the youth of the holy Prophet Muhammad. His youth was perfect, sinless, and stainless. I do not think any other such example can be found in the annals of the world. Fourteen hundred years ago, during the youth of Muhammad, ignorance and crime were in Arabia as righteousness and peace elsewhere. The people were debauchees and adulterers, and prostitution was the fashion of the

45

day. Rape and seduction were common things. Wine was the ordinary drink of the people. There were brothels and bars without number; for the Arabs were a proud race, proud even of their sins, and would boast that they led immoral and shameful lives. In such surroundings and among such people to keep one's youth pure and stainless is an achievement a little short of miraculous. Every day of the youth of Muhammad is displayed before the world in as much detail as are the latter days of his life. There is no one, even his greatest enemy, who can say that the youth of Muhammad was not good and pure. He kept himself aloof from all undesirable people and functions; he had very few friends, being of a reserved and contemplative nature, but the few he had followed his teachings and, later on, became Muslims. Thus while other young men of his age spent their youth in sin, Muhammad was seeking only ways and means to save Arabia from the pitiable state into which it had fallen.

When Muhammad was twenty-five, a rich widow Khadīja by name entrusted him with the management of her business. He was so honest in all his dealings that at last she begged him to marry her. He did not give her an immediate answer, but first went to his uncle Abū Tālib and obtained his consent. When Muhammad married her he was, as has been said, twenty-five and she forty years of age, but it was a very happy union, being blessed with four daughters and one son. Khadīja was a great help and comfort to Muhammad. He was

46

devoted to her and she willingly gave him her wealth to spend in charity. At the time of his call, he was greatly depressed and weighed down with responsibility, fearing that he would not be able to fulfil the important charge entrusted to him, but she cheered him with such words as "God will never let thee see the humiliation of failure . . ." and the like.

All who came in contact with the Prophet were devoted to him; he showed great kindness and sympathy to the poor and helpless, the orphans and the widow, and would always do his utmost to help them. Slaves loved him; and would rather remain his slaves than accept their freedom. He was kind and loving to all. He abhorred fighting and bloodshed. At the battle of "Fijār" he did nothing more than help his uncle by supplying him with arrows from time to time. From his very childhood he detested idol-worship. During his youth he often went to the cave of Hirā and prayed for hours to God to pity the fallen state of the Arabs and show them the way to the right path.

Muhammad was forty years of age when the messenger of God came to him to reveal the Word of God, and announce that he was the chosen Prophet of God.

CHAPTER 4

THE DIVINE CALL

(611 A.C.)

"Read in the name of your Lord.
He created man from a clot.
Read and your Lord is most
honourable, Who taught to write
with the pen, taught man what he
knew not."—THE QURAN 96 : 1–4.

NOT long before he attained the age of forty,
Muhammad began to see visions, most of them
while in the cave at Hirā, and during this time he
became more and more reserved and spent many
solitary hours in deep meditation. He retired more
frequently than ever to the cave of Hirā, where
he would spend days and nights in prayer and
contemplation. On a certain night during the
month of Ramazān, an angel appeared to him
and gave him a scroll, saying, "Read this."
Muhammad said, "I do not know how to read."
The angel then embraced him and again asked
him to read. Three times the request was repeated
and each time Muhammad cried, "I do not know
how to read." The angel then read out the verses
and assured Muhammad that although he was
unable to read, if he attempted it in the name of
God he would succeed. At this time he was also
made aware that he was chosen to be the Reformer
of Mankind. It was a staggering responsibility, but

Muhammad did not fear nor lose heart. When God commanded Moses to reform a nation, he was not able to do so by himself and in despair cried to God, "Give me a helper." But the holy Prophet Muhammad despaired not, nor asked for a helper. He relied only on the help of God to assist him in this great task. After the first appearance of the angel in the cave of Hirā, when it was made known to Muhammad that he was to be the World-Reformer, some time elapsed before a second visit. Some say it was a period of two or three years, but the version of Ibn 'Abbās, who states it was only a short period, is more to be relied on according to historical evidence.

No ordinary human being can ever know himself the strange phenomenon of Divine inspiration, during which the whole body is possessed by Divine Power. When the holy Prophet Muhammad first underwent this experience he perspired profusely, his whole body became heavy, his limbs turned icy cold, and he trembled from head to foot. Shivering and shaking he went home, and his wife Khadīja wrapped him up. When he told her what had happened, she implored him not to fear and assured him, that "God will never let you see the humiliation of failure. Verily you show due regard for blood ties, carry the burden of the infirm, practise virtues that are absolutely extinct, entertain guests and stand by what is righteous in the face of calamities." Muhammad received Divine inspiration many times, and each time it was accompanied with the same sensations—profuse perspiration, and heaviness of the whole body.

CHAPTER 5

THE ESSENTIALS OF THE PROPHETHOOD
OF MUHAMMAD

> "Certainly you have in the Apostle
> of God an excellent exemplar."—
> THE QURAN 33: 21.

I BELIEVE no one could deny that the spiritual advancement of mankind or the perfection of the human soul has from time immemorial been dependent on the instructions of God through His Prophets, who bring certain qualities, each of the best and perfect in itself. God could have chosen to send angels as instructors, but knowing that for human beings a human being is the best guide and teacher, He raised human beings at different times to Prophethood, to preach His word to mankind (THE QURAN 6: 8, 9).

Muslims believe that Muhammad is the last Prophet, that is to say, after whom another claimant to Prophethood cannot come. This belief is based not only upon the verses of the Quran but also upon actual facts to be met with in the life of the Prophet Muhammad.

Teaching and example are essential for a prophet; but for the last Prophet also two further things were most necessary; first that what he teaches should be perfect and complete and sufficient for all time to come, and that he should give a complete code of morals or teachings to preach to the world; secondly, that he himself by his practice should set a perfect example for the guidance of mankind.

The Quran speaks in its earlier revelations of the perfect morals of the Prophet. For example, it says, "Most surely you conform (yourself) to sublime morality" (68: 4). God also says, "So he attained completion, and he is in the highest part of the horizon" (THE QURAN 53: 6–7). The Hadith says, "I was made Prophet to perfect the highest morals." Two things were needed to perfect the morals, and the Quran says the holy Prophet possessed them. The following will make the statement plainer. It is easy for a man to be lowly and humble when he is poor, but these qualities can only be said to manifest themselves in perfection when he continues humble after he has become great and powerful. Or, let us take the case of charity. A person who is poor can also be charitable, but for the most part only in thought and intention because he has not got the money to give in charity; but to remain charitable after attaining wealth, by spending freely in charities, will mean that he has shown the quality of charitableness to perfection. The same is true of forgiveness; when a man has not power to punish one who harms him, he is compelled of necessity to overlook the offence and forgive as the safest course; but the completeness of the quality is seen in a person who is powerful and well able to deal harshly with offenders, but forgives freely those who have done their utmost to harm him.

There have been cases when a person has been perfect in one moral quality only to such an extent that other qualities have been eclipsed thereby; for example, a man may become so charitable and forgiving as to lose the quality of being just.

This height of perfection in the holy Prophet is an accepted fact such as even an enemy cannot deny or refute. The presence of all the moral qualities postulates that a person to display them must have passed through every sort and condition of experience in the course of his life; and not even a hardened critic can deny that such was the case with Muhammad. He was the only Prophet who himself followed all the principles he preached to others. Every ordinance in the Quran he himself obeyed. He is the one and only true example of this rule, that what a man teaches to the world, he must practise himself. We often have to listen to sermons and lectures by persons who have not the faintest intention of practising what they preach. Mere lip-teaching does not prove that a person possesses moral virtues. He must first convert his words into actions as did the holy Prophet, who taught the world patience and forbearance, because he himself faced the hardest trials of life. A child born after the death of his father and losing his mother within the next few years, he spent a childhood of innocence and perfection. At maturity he held all desires of the flesh at bay. From his birth to his death he passed through many difficult ordeals. At every step he was tried, but was never found wanting. When he proclaimed his Mission as Prophet, it proved one of the hardest trials of all. The whole nation turned against him. He was absolutely alone and helpless. The perfection of helplessness is seen in the event known as "Hijrat" (Flight), when alone, save for a single friend, he had to flee his native town of Mecca; when he hid in a cave and escaped to Medina, where his helpers and associates and the Jews entered into treaty relations. Then came the tortuous days of war; on all sides the Arabs gathered to kill him, but in the end he prevailed over them and became their king. In Medina he was King, Judge, Magistrate, General, Peace-maker and Law-giver, and in all these capacities he was perfect.

Again, let me emphasize that the great thing to remember is this, that all his moral qualities are of the highest degree of perfection. He knew not what it was to be avaricious; even his enemies admit that all his life through he had no desire for wealth. It had no value for him. Once the Quraysh offered him all the wealth in the land, but he refused even to consider the offer; and when he became king and the rightful owner of it he cared nothing for it and continued to live the same life of poverty in solitude. The holy Prophet expressed this quality in still greater perfection by living a life of poverty amidst the riches and luxuries of kingship.

The quality of forgiveness, too, he expressed in perfection, making no distinction between friend and enemy. When it came to forgiving he forgave all. In the battle of Uhud certain Muslims failed to obey his instructions, with disastrous result, but the holy Prophet did not court-martial or even reprimand them; he simply forgave them. His example of forgiving enemies takes its sublimest form on the occasion of the conquest of Mecca. The Meccans had been his bitterest enemies since the day he was raised to Prophethood. They did all in their power to crush Islam, and many times attempted to kill the Prophet, but he, when he entered Mecca as conqueror, forgave the chiefs when presented as captives, and granted a general amnesty. Arabia lay at his feet, and Mecca was at his mercy. He could have beheaded everyone had he wished to and he would have been justified in doing so; for they had been his greatest enemies and most cruel tormentors. But unlike many Hebrew Prophets, who severely punished their eriemies for much lesser offences, he freely forgave them. When they were all standing humble before him, awaiting their punishment, he said to them, "There shall be no reproach against you, you are free."

The Arab Chief 'Utba had been one of the greatest of the offenders and the chief instigator of the cruel persecution to which the Prophet and his companions had been subjected for many years. His daughter, Hinda, was as great an enemy of the Prophet as her father. Once in hatred, she chewed the liver of Hamza, the Prophet's uncle, when he was slain in battle; later, when she was obliged to come before the Prophet, she covered her face with a veil so that he might not recognize her, but he singled her out at once and forgave her. Abū Sufyān was another who had done his best to harm the holy Prophet. Abū Sufyān being afraid to face the Prophet, would send others to intercede for him, but the Prophet bade him have no fear and not only forgave him but declared that anyone who took refuge in his house would be safe. At the conquest of Mecca another enemy of the holy Prophet, Habbār Ibnu 'l-Aswad, who was responsible for the death of the daughter of the Prophet, was about to fly from Mecca to Persia, but knowing the compassionate nature of his enemy he decided to throw himself on his mercy. Approaching the Prophet he confessed his wrongs and prayed for mercy, and the Prophet freely forgave him. These instances stated above, and many others, prove that the holy Prophet expressed the quality of forgiveness to perfection.

In Muhammad, the holy Prophet of God, are found to perfection all qualities and morals, and the combination of all qualities and morals. With lowliness and humility he was brave, so brave that, with his companions lying dead round him, he prayed to God to guide the enemy to the right path. The example of justice set by him is equally high. Once there was dispute between a Jew and a Muslim, and on hearing the case he gave the just judgment, which was in favour of the Jew.

His reliance on God was such that he never concerned himself about personal safety, but, at the same time, his caution never relaxed, and on the slightest news of trouble he would always send men at once to deal with it. So intense was the love of God that he would spend whole nights standing in prayer before Him; he had the well-being of others so much at heart that often he used to do the marketing for the old and feeble.

The study of his life reveals that all these qualities and morals were combined in him to the highest degree of perfection, enabling him to become the sole exemplar for all generations to come.

CHAPTER 6

THE FIRST MUSLIMS

"And the foremost are the foremost; these are they who are drawn nigh to God."—THE QURAN 56: 10–11.

IN the chapter entitled "The Divine Call" I have mentioned how the word of God was first revealed to the holy Prophet. After that revelation, in the cave of Hirā, he was sure of his Mission but he did not as yet preach it openly. He taught first among the intimate circle of family and friend, and the one who embraced Islam first was his wife, Khadīja. She was the first woman to embrace Islam, and there is some controversy as to who was the first man to do so. Imām Abū Hanīfa writes: "Among men Abū Bakr, among children 'Alī, and among women Khadīja, were the first to embrace Islam." This is not a satisfactory statement for it differentiates between men, women and children, the question being who was the first man to embrace Islam. The author of the Sīrat Halabī writes: "There were three in the history of all religions who did not believe in any other God but the Real God, the first was Hizqiel, who accepted the faith and religion of Moses; the second Habīb Najjār, an inhabitant of Antākya,

57

who was the first to embrace the religion of Jesus, when he went there to preach; and the third person was 'Alī, who was the first to embrace Islam at the age of ten." Tirmizī writes, "Muhammad was made Prophet on Monday, and on Tuesday 'Alī said his prayers with him." Some of the prejudiced, who were unwilling that 'Alī should have this distinction of being the first to embrace Islam, object that as he was a mere child his conversion could hardly be considered complete and valid. This argument is very weak for the validity of an action does not require the maturity of the person acting, as the Quran says, "So they [Moses and his companion] went on until they met a boy; the companion slew him and Moses said, 'Have you slain an innocent person otherwise than for manslaughter? Certainly you have done an evil thing'" (18: 74).

Jesus Christ was made Prophet in his early childhood and said: "Surely I am a servant of God; He has given me the Book and made me a prophet; and dutiful to my mother, and He has made me blessed wherever I may be, and He has enjoined on me prayer and poor-rate so long as I live" (THE QURAN 19: 30–32).

Here we see that people who are destined to be great and worthy are placed with people of rank and dignity, even if they are mere children. This is clearly evident in the case of Jesus Christ, and it must be accepted that 'Alī was the first Muslim, in spite of his having embraced Islam when in his early teens. Mr. Émile Dermenghem, in his *Life of Mahomet* (London, 1930), thus describes the conversion of 'Alī:

"One day the young 'Alī came into the room of Khadīja unexpectedly and found Mahomet and Khadīja bowing down and reciting unknown and harmonious words.

" 'What are you doing?' asked the astonished child, 'and before whom are you bowing down?'

" 'Before God,' replied Mahomet, 'before God, whose Prophet I am and Who commands me to call men unto Him. O, son of my uncle, you also, come unto the one God. I desire you to worship the one God without a peer, and adopt the true religion chosen by Him. I request you to deny idols like El Lat and El 'Ozza who can neither harm nor help their worshippers. Say with me:

" 'God is one,

" 'And there is not anyone like unto Him.

" 'Neither slumber nor sleep seizeth Him;

" 'To Him belongeth whatsoever is in heaven, and on earth.'

" 'Never have I heard such words,' said 'Alī when he had finished. Their charm and beauty bewitched him; their strangeness dismayed him.

" 'I must consult my father,' he said. This proceeding did not please Mahomet very much, and he asked his young cousin either to do nothing or else to speak with great secrecy to Abū Tālib, and only to him.

"The child passed a very troubled night and the next morning announced to Mahomet and Khadīja his strong desire to follow them.

" 'God made me,' said he, 'without consulting Abū Tālib. Must I consult him, then, before adoring God?'

"And so 'Alī, converted in his childhood, never worshipped the idols; they called him: 'Him whose face was never sullied,' because he never bowed down before anyone but God."

As has been said, the first woman to have absolute faith in the holy Prophet's mission and to embrace Islam was his wife Khadīja. From the time of his very first revelation she had not the slightest doubt of his claim to prophethood. She was a consolation and a help to him always, especially in times of extreme depression and perplexity, a never-failing comfort and a pillar of strength. Knowing intimately and thoroughly his excellent qualities she, from the very beginning, was perfectly convinced that he and no other was the one to be chosen by God for the reformation of mankind.

I step aside to quote a few lines from Mr. Dermenghem's *The Life of Mahomet* (London, 1930), to show the unflinching nature of the belief of his wife Khadīja.

"Mahomet had given up men's companionship more and more. In the solitudes of Mt. Hirā he found greater and greater satisfaction. Spending whole weeks at a time there with a few scanty provisions, his spirit gloried in fasting, in vigils and in the search for a defined idea. He hardly knew whether it was day or night, whether he dreamed or watched. For hours at a time he remained kneeling in the darkness or lying in the sun, or he strode with long steps on the stony tracks. When he walked, it seemed as if voices came out of the rocks; when he struck a stone, it answered him. And the stones everywhere under that fiery sun seemed to greet him as 'God's Apostle.'

"On his return the good Khadīja was troubled to see him so silently elated. Sometimes he appeared to lose all consciousness of what was going on around him and lay inert on the ground, his breathing hardly perceptible. Then he would sleep, his breast rising and falling regularly with peaceful slumber. But his respiration would grow more rapid; he would pant; dream; an enormous human being as huge as the heavens over the earth and covering the whole horizon would then approach, rush towards him with extended arms ready to seize him. . . . Mahomet would wake with a start, his body covered with sweat; Khadīja would wipe his forehead and question him gently but anxiously in a voice she tried to calm. He would remain silent or evade her questions, or he would answer in words she did not understand.

"At the end of six months Mahomet's body suffered; he grew thin, his step became jerky, his hair and beard unkempt, his eyes strange. He felt hopeless. Had he become one of those madmen such as he had often met—a pathetic demoniac, a hideous plaything of the powers of darkness? Was he one of those poets inspired by a jinn?—for measured phrases often burst unconsciously from his tongue. He felt hopeless; for he had a horror of poets, playthings of every wind, who said what they did not do.

" 'I am afraid of becoming mad,' he decided to say one day to the gentle Khadīja, when he could no longer bear the weight. 'I see all the signs of madness in myself. Who would have believed that I would become a poet, or possessed by a jinn? I! By no chance speak of it to anyone."

"Khadīja wished for his confidence. She hoped and she doubted; but when she was so worried herself, how could she reassure him? But she was a woman made to give consolation and comfort; she possessed the tender firmness of a virtuous wife and a devoted mother and gave this man, younger than herself,the fullest love. In her devotion she was almost subconsciously pleased to find this strong man, her admired husband, weak and ill. How could she help reassuring him?

" 'O Abulqasim, are you not the 'amīn—for so you are called—the sincere, the trustworthy, the truthful man? How can God allow you to be deceived when you do not deceive? Are you not a pious, sober, charitable, hospitable man? Have you not respected your parents, fed the hungry, clothed the naked, helped the traveller, protected the weak? It is not possible that you are the plaything of lying demons and malicious jinns.'

" 'What, then, is this being who seeks me out again and again? What is this being who has not told me his name and from whom I cannot escape?' Mahomet was again seized with anguish. He trembled, his face grew red and then pale; his ears hummed, his eyes dilated. A strange presence had intruded itself.

" 'There he is! It is he! He is coming. . . . '

"And yet he was awake and neither asleep nor dreaming and the strange being was approaching. He was there.

"Khadīja had an inspiration:

" 'Come to me,' she said to her husband. 'Get under my cloak.' Mahomet did so. He was like a child on his mother's breast, hunting protection from all the world's dangers. Khadīja covered him with her veil, let down her hair; she seated him on her knees, embraced him closely and hid him against her flesh under her clothing and her dark hair.

" 'Well?' she asked. 'Is he still there?'

" 'I do not see nor feel him any more. He is gone.'

" 'Then he is not a lewd jinn, nor yet a demon; for he respects women's chastity. It can only be an angel of God.'

"Ramadān came. Mahomet increased his solitary watches in the passes of Mt. Hirā. Days passed; the crescent moon grew round, resplendent, then waxed thinner and thinner again. One night Mahomet was asleep in a cave. Suddenly the mysterious being who had visited him before appeared, holding a piece of silk in his hand covered with writing.

" "*Iqra*,' he said to Mahomet: 'Read.'

" 'I do not know how to read.'

"The being threw himself upon him, cast the

63

silk around his neck tight enough to almost stifle him. But letting it go he said:

" 'Read.'

" 'I do not know how to read.'

"The being again threw himself upon Mahomet to stifle him.

" 'Read,' he repeated for the third time.

" 'What shall I read?'

" 'Read,' said the being, letting him go.

" 'Read, in the name of thy Lord, Who hath created all things;

Who hath created man of congealed blood.

Read, by thy most beneficent Lord Who taught the use of the pen;

Who teacheth man that which he knoweth not' " (THE QURAN 96: 1–5).

Waraqa, a cousin of Khadīja, was the next to believe in the holy Prophet. He was a very old man, bedridden and blind. Khadīja had often heard him speak of the "Promised Prophet" of whose advent Jesus Christ had spoken. When Waraqa heard from Khadīja of the revelation received by Muhammad in the cave of Hirā, he at once proclaimed him the "Promised Prophet." Unfortunately he died shortly afterwards, during the Cessation period, without having had the opportunity of formally declaring his faith.

Abū Bakr, a Meccan, was the next to embrace Islam. The holy Prophet and he were intimate friends long before the holy Prophet received the Divine Call, but no sooner was he made aware of Muhammad's claim to prophethood than he publicly declared that he believed him to be the Prophet of God, and embraced Islam, thus being among the first men to do so.

Zayd bin Hāritha, a liberated slave of the holy Prophet, was the next. He was deeply attached to the holy Prophet, and when he was first given his freedom and had been told by Muhammad to go back with his father to his own home he refused to do so.

Thus we see that the holy Prophet's wife Khadīja, his friend Abū Bakr, his cousin 'Alī, and his liberated slave Zayd, these four, who knew his life most intimately, were the earliest believers and the first to embrace Islam. Abū Bakr, whose faith in the Prophet was as true and sincere as Khadīja's, was so profoundly convinced that Muhammad was the promised Prophet that immediately on embracing Islam he started preaching the faith to others. Soon prominent men like 'Usmān, Zubayr, 'Abdu 'r-Rahmān, Sa'd and Talha became Muslims; also Yāsir, his wife Sumayya, Bilāl, 'Abdullāh bin Mas'ūd, 'Ammār bin Yāsir and Khabbāb, who were of humbler position, and Arqam, who later gave his house to the holy Prophet for the purposes of his mission. One by one people began to follow him and within three years there were some forty converts in all. This steady progress of Islam angered and alarmed the Meccans and they did their best to oppose it; but the Muslims, in spite of all opposition, grew rapidly in numbers. As the faith spread, men of position from among the Quraysh became converts too, Hamza, an uncle of the Prophet, among them. He was a man of great importance and proved a pillar of strength to Islam. He had always been fond of Muhammad and the story of his conversion is a remarkable one. It is said that one day Abū Jahl, an uncle of the Prophet, who was bitterly opposed to the teachings of Muhammad, had met him and was ill-treating the Prophet most cruelly. A maid belonging to the house of Hamza, happening to pass by, was shocked to see this and at once reported the matter to her master. When Hamza heard this, deeply attached as he was, he was both grieved and indignant and made up his mind there and then himself to join the new faith, and aid and defend the brave little army of Muslims to the utmost of his powers.

Another remarkable conversion of a great man was that of 'Omar. He was a man of position, greatly esteemed among the Quraysh, but also well known and feared for his uncontrollable temper. From the very beginning he was bitterly against Islam, and as he heard daily that more and more were embracing the new faith, he was so enraged that one day he decided to kill Muhammad, who, he said, was the cause of all the trouble. So taking his sword he made straight for the house of the Prophet. At this time he was unaware that his own sister Fātima and her husband had become Muslims. On his way to the Prophet's house he met a man who had recently embraced Islam. Seeing the sword in 'Omar's hand this man asked him whither he was going. 'Omar replied, "To kill Muhammad." The Muslim thereupon informed him that his own sister and brother-in-law had embraced Islam. On hearing this, 'Omar's anger knew no bounds, and he decided to deal with his own relations first before putting an end to the Prophet. On reaching the house he heard one of them reciting the Quran, and this to him was the last straw. He entered wild with rage, and seizing his brother-in-law thrashed him unmercifully, while his sister in her efforts to interpose was herself injured. 'Omar, then snatching the chapters of the Quran, began reading the verses, and soon the truth and beauty of them set him thinking. Seeing him thus pensive the Muslims present took the opportunity of reasoning with him and soon the proud 'Omar joined the fold of Islam. He proceeded to the house of Arqam where the Prophet and his companions were taking shelter. The Prophet met him at the door and 'Omar proclaimed his faith to him in these words, "O Apostle of God, I declare faith in God and in His Prophet."

All this time the Muslims were compelled to carry out their religious activities in secret in the house of Arqam; for they were as yet too few in number to face their numerous opponents. But after the conversion of two such important persons as 'Omar and Hamza they were able with their help to carry on their work publicly, and say their prayers in the sacred house of the Ka'ba. Most of the early converts were from the poor class, except for the few men of wealth and position whom I have just mentioned. These poor people were forced to undergo many hardships; for they

67

had nobody to protect them and no money. The slaves who turned Muslims were put to most awful tortures. Abū Bakr was one of the rich ones who was a great help to Islam at that time; he spent much of his wealth in buying slaves from their cruel masters and setting them free.

The hatred of the Quraysh against the holy Prophet and his followers leaped up to its highest point when it was learnt that Hamza and 'Omar had also embraced Islam, for 'Omar was the chief of the Banū 'Adī tribe. Soon afterwards, a wealthy merchant belonging to the important family of Taym bin Murra embraced Islam. He was a man of clear judgment as well as energetic, honest and amenable, and a great favourite among the people. After his conversion, five others belonging to important families followed in his footsteps. The Prophet and his followers would preach to strangers coming to the city on pilgrimage and on business. But even this the Quraysh sought to prevent. When people began to arrive in the city they would post themselves at strategic points, and tell the strangers to have nothing to do with Muhammad as he was a magician and not to be trusted. This, in a way, helped the Prophet—for the strangers returning to their homes spread the tales that were told about him, and many came to see and hear the man who risked his life in telling the whole of Arabia to give up the worship of their forefathers and follow the new religion that he preached.

CHAPTER 7

THE ATROCITIES OF THE QURAYSH

> "And among men is he who says:
> We believe in God; but when
> he is persecuted in the way of
> God, he thinks the persecution
> of men as the chastisement of
> God."—THE QURAN 29: 10.

WHEN the holy Prophet began actively to preach Islam, he decided to establish a missionary headquarters, where those who wanted to embrace the faith could be instructed, and where all Muslims could gather together for prayer. He could not preach publicly, as I have already mentioned. Arqam, one of the early converts, gave his house called the "Abode of Arqam," which was situated at the foot of Safā, for the use of the mission. This house is especially famous in Islam, and is known to this day as "The Abode of Islam." In it Muhammad preached for over three years, and many people embraced Islam there.

After four years, Islam was well known and the subject of much discussion in all parts of Mecca. The Quraysh tried many ways to check it from spreading, and at last decided to resort to force. They were determined to crush the movement at any cost for many reasons. The first and the most natural one was the fear of what usually happens at the advent of a Prophet; how the people rise against him, and God proves that in spite of the power and strength of the people one single, solitary, and friendless man will succeed in establishing Truth and the Word of God. Secondly, the Quraysh thought it would be derogatory to men so proud to change their religion and depart from the ways of their forefathers. Thirdly, Mecca was the greatest temple of Arabia, and the offerings to the idols therein were a source of immense wealth. They feared lest these with the influence and power it brought would be lost. Fourthly, the chiefs of the Quraysh were apprehensive that the new religion would put an end to their prestige and a stop to their luxuries, and generally make impossible their easy and dissipated lives. So the holy Prophet was subjected to every sort of torture and atrocity. Thorns were strewn in his path, stones were thrown at his house, and dirt and rubbish at his body. He was laughed at and hooted, and once when he was at prayer, 'Uqba bin Abī Mu'īt threw his sheet round his neck and pulled it with such force that the holy Prophet fell on his face. The story of these outrages is a long and sad one. Sir William Muir, in discussing it, writes, "The people of the Quraysh had decided to extinguish this new religion from the face of the earth, and to stop its preachers from carrying on their work. Once the opposition started it gradually developed, and the hatred of the people became fierce." It was only because of the ancient and peculiar custom of the Arabs that if a man is murdered it would lead to war between the clans of the murdered and the murderer, that they stopped from killing the holy Prophet outright, and also perhaps because they were already tired of war; but all this did not stop them from doing all they could to torture the Prophet and his followers.

When the Quraysh discovered that all they did was of no avail, they sent a deputation to Abū Tālib, the chief of the tribe (and also the uncle of Muhammad) to beg him to stop Muhammad from preaching. Abū Tālib sent them away with pacifying words, but they returned again after some time to put their case before him with greater force.

The second deputation decided Abū Tālib, and he sent for the Prophet and asked him to refrain from preaching, pointing out that he could not fight the whole tribe single-handed. At this time, on account of the persistent persecution, the followers of Islam were few and weak, yet Muhammad spoke to his uncle in these words, "I would not care even if I had to lay down my life for God, but if you are afraid of your own weakness then leave me alone; my God is enough to help me. Even if these people were to give me the moon in one hand and the sun in the other, it would not stop me from doing my duty." This answer impressed and moved Abū Tālib so much that, marvelling at the courage, perseverance, and patience of Muhammad, Abū Tālib told him to go and do his duty and promised that he, Abū Tālib, would help him as much as he was able.

71

When the Quraysh found that this also had failed, they sent 'Utba, an orator, to the holy Prophet who said : "O son of my brother, thou art distinguished by thy qualities and thy descent. Now thou hast sown division among our people and cast dissension in our families; thou denouncest our gods and goddesses; thou dost tax our ancestors with impiety. We have a proposition to make to thee; think well if it will not suit thee to accept it." "Speak, O 'Utba," said the Prophet, "I listen, O son of my brother." Commenced 'Utba, "If thou wishest to acquire riches by this affair, we will collect a fortune larger than is possessed by any of us; if thou desirest honours and dignity, we shall make thee our chief, and shall not do a thing without thee; if thou desirest dominion, we shall make thee our king; and if the spirit which possesses thee cannot be overpowered, we will bring the doctors and give them riches till they cure thee." And when he had done, "Hast thou finished, O father of Walīd?" asked the Prophet. "Yes," replied 'Utba. "Then listen to me." "I listen," he said. "In the name of the most Merciful God," commenced the Prophet, "this is a revelation from the most Merciful: a book, the verses whereof are distinctly explained, an Arabic Quran, for the instruction of people who understand; bearing good tidings, and denouncing threats: but the greater part of them turn aside, and hearken not thereto. And they say, 'Our hearts are veiled from the doctrine to which thou invitest us; and there is a deafness in our ears, and a curtain between us and thee: wherefore act thou as thou shalt think fit; for we shall act according to our own sentiments.' Say, 'Verily I am only a man like you. It is revealed unto me that your God is one God: wherefore direct your way straight unto Him; and ask pardon of him for what is past.' And woe be to the idolaters, who give not the appointed alms, and believe not in the life to come. But as to those who believe and work righteousness, they shall receive an everlasting reward" (THE QURAN 41: 1–8). When the Prophet finished this recitation, he said to 'Utba, "Thou hast heard, now take the course which seemeth best to thee."

'Utba returned and told the Quraysh that it would be best to leave him to his devices, pointing out that it would be an occasion of pride if the Prophet were to succeed in his mission, "for," he said, "he belongs to our tribe, and if he fails we attain our object." But they refused to listen to his advice.

When they found that every attempt of theirs had failed they decided that each tribe should persecute in every way the Muslims of its clan, and hence starts a tale which is too painful to be told in full. Although 'Usmān was a grown-up and quite independent person, yet because he was a follower of Islam, his uncle tortured him by tying him with ropes and beating him. 'Abdullāh was unmercifully beaten in the premises of the Ka'ba itself, and other followers were beaten and tortured whenever possible. Even more cruel and ghastly

73

were the tortures meted out to the poor slaves who were the followers of the holy Prophet. Bilāl, the slave of Umayya bin Khalaf, was forced to lie down on the hot sands of the desert on his back with his face to the scorching sun and a heavy stone on the top of him, or else to be bound and dragged through the streets of the city. "You remain in the scorching sun till you are dead or you abjure Islam," his master would say. As Bilāl lay, half-stifled under the heavy weight of the stone, he would only say, "One God, One." This lasted for days until he was ransomed by Abū Bakr and set free. Zunnīra, the slave girl of Abū Jahl, was blinded, and many others were similarly treated. Abū Jahl was responsible, it is said, for the death of Sumayya, the mother of 'Ammār bin Yāsir, whom he caused to be killed in a manner unspeakably awful.

Compare these most obnoxious and cruel deeds with the courage and patience of Muhammad and his followers, and you will realize the powerful force that was in Islam, and gave them the strength to fight all the forces of the earth. These atrocities never caused one Muslim so much as even to waver. "His life," writes Ameer Ali in *The Spirit of Islam*, "is the noblest record of a work nobly and faithfully performed. He infused vitality into a dormant people; he consolidated a congeries of warring tribes into a nation inspired into action with the hope of everlasting life; he concentrated into a focus all the fragmentary and broken lights which had ever fallen on the heart of man." A

74

Christian historian says, "The preachings and examples of the holy Prophet imbibed that religiousness in his followers which was not found in the early followers of Christ. When Christ was led to the cross his followers fled and left him to die all alone, but, on the contrary, in the case of the Prophet of Arabia, his followers gathered round him whenever he was threatened, and were willing to lay down their lives for him."

The rapid growth in the numbers eager to embrace the new faith still further enhanced the alarm and consternation of the Quraysh; and they decided on organized and systematic persecution, which grew so fierce and relentless that the Prophet was obliged to advise the Muslims to migrate.

CHAPTER 8

THE EXILE TO ABYSSINIA

(615 A.C.)

> "And those who fly for God's
> sake after they are oppressed, We
> will most certainly give them a
> good abode in the world."—THE
> QURAN 16: 41.

IN the fifth year of the Prophethood (615 A.C.)
the holy Prophet had perforce to allow his
followers to migrate, because he could not bear
to see them cruelly tortured without being able to
protect themselves. The place of refuge selected was
Abyssinia, because the Prophet had heard of the
righteousness, of the tolerance, and hospitality of
its king, and a party of Muslims consisting of
eleven men and four women left in secrecy, with
no hope of ever being able to return to their
beloved motherland. All were disheartened; for to
leave their native land was, to them, the greatest
calamity possible; but their faith in God kept them
resolute. Most of these belonged to the well-to-do,
rich, and influential families, which shows that even
for such Mecca was not safe. As to the poor and
the slaves, they had neither the means nor the
opportunity to migrate. On leaving Mecca, the
emigrants travelled as far as Jeddah on foot,

whence they took ship. In the meantime, the Quraysh had learnt of this and at once sent a strong detachment to capture them and bring them back, but fortunately for the exiles the pursuers reached the port after they had sailed.

These people had a peaceful life in Abyssinia. They were neither molested nor ill-treated in any way by the Christian King Negus, and the tidings of their good reception in a foreign land induced more in Mecca to migrate. The Quraysh, of course, could not tolerate this—for to them it foretold defeat—and in consequence sent a deputation to the king to demand the fugitives back. To facilitate the accomplishment of their purpose they sent valuable presents to be given to the courtiers, and those who had the ear of the king. The deputation, which was headed by 'Abdullāh bin Rabīa, in due course reached Abyssinia,- and, by distributing the presents lavishly, found themselves in the presence of the Negus, to whom they also presented costly gifts, and begged that the offenders should be handed over to them. But the king declined to do that until he had heard the case for the other side. So the next day the Muslims in Abyssinia were sent for and the Negus inquired of them what they had to say to the demand of the deputation. Then one of the Muslims, Ja'far bin Abī Tālib, rose and addressed the king thus: "O King! we were an ignorant people given to idolatry. We used to eat corpses even of animals that died a natural death, and to do all sorts of evil and unclean things. We never made good our obligations to our relations,

77

and we ill-treated our neighbours. The strong among us would grow fat on the blood of the weak, until at last God raised up Muhammad from among us to reform us by showing us the path of righteousness. He is well known to us. We know him to be most noble, truthful, and righteous. He called us to the worship of God, and persuaded us to give up idolatry and stone worship. He enjoined on us to tell the truth, to have love for our kith and kin, to fulfil our promises, and to do good to others, teaching us to shun everything that is bad, and to cease from bloodshed. He forbade all other indecent things—telling lies, robbing and cheating orphans and widows, and bearing false witness. He taught us to keep the chastity of women sacred. So we believed in him, we followed him, and acted up to his teachings so far as in us lay. Thereupon these men began to torture us, thinking that thus we might be induced to give up our new faith and go back to idolatry. When their cruelties exceeded all bounds we came to seek peace and shelter in your country, where we trust we shall come to no harm." Thereupon the Negus wished to hear the Quran, and Ja'far recited the chapter entitled "Maryam." After this he refused to hand over the exiles to the deputation. So far foiled in their attempts they played a mean trick, and, obtaining audience of the king, told him that these Muslims held views about Jesus Christ repugnant to the king. They had thought of this plan to prejudice the king against the Muslims. The Negus sent for them again, and this time they were genuinely afraid that the deputation would succeed in effecting their extradition; for they thought that the replies that they might have would offend the king. The Negus asked them point-blank what they thought about Jesus Christ; and these truthful people, not caring for the consequences, boldly replied that they believed Jesus to be only the Prophet of God, and not the Son of God. The Negus admired this courage of theirs and entirely refused to hand them over to the deputationists, who returned in confusion to Mecca.

While the rest of the Muslims were seeking safety in far-off lands, the Prophet stuck to his post amidst every insult and outrage. The Quraysh came to him again, offering him the riches of the land, to which the Prophet replied, "I am neither desirous of riches nor am I fond of power and kingship. I am sent by God to give you glad tidings. I give you His message, and if you accept it, He will reward you both in this and the other world, but if you refuse, I leave God to judge between you and me." They then mocked at him, scoffed him, and went away. They demanded of him impossible things to prove his Prophethood. It was, in fact, the old story. The followers of Jesus Christ had insisted upon his performing miracles. As someone has remarked: "The immediate disciples of Jesus were always misunderstanding him and his work. Wanting him to call down fire from heaven; wanting him to declare himself the King of the Jews . . . ; wanting him to show them the Father, to make God visible to their eyes; wanting him to

79

do, and wanting to do themselves, anything and everything that was incompatible with His great plan. This was how they treated him until the end. When that came they all forsook him and fled." Jesus Christ always replied to them that it was evil to seek for a sign, and that, therefore, no sign should be given them. Similarly, the opponents of Muhammad wanted signs. The Prophet was asked to prove his mission. Why could he not perform miracles like Moses and Jesus? Why could he not change the hills of Safā to gold? Why not make the Book itself, of which he talked so much, fall down from heaven? Why not show them this so-called angel who came to speak with him? Why not make the dead speak? He should be able to move a mountain!

"You would do well to ask God, with whom you are on such good terms, to loosen the grip of these mountains stifling our town so disastrously," the Quraysh sniggered. "Or it would be enough to make a beautiful spring, purer than Zamzam, gush forth; for we really lack water. And as prophets can foretell the future you might as well advise about the approaching price of goods. Cannot your God disclose which articles will rise in price? We should like to know these things in order to regulate our trade and speculate with certainty."

To such as would ask for miracles the holy Prophet Muhammad would reply: "I am able neither to procure advantage unto myself, nor to avert harm from me, but as God pleaseth. If I knew the secrets of God, I should enjoy abundance of good, neither should evil befall me. I am nothing but a warner and the giver of good news to a people who believe" (THE QURAN 7: 188). "I am no more than a man like you" (THE QURAN 18: 110). The followers of Muhammad differed from those of Jesus in this that they contented themselves with the moral evidences of Muhammad's Mission. They gathered round this friendless preacher and sacrificed their all for him.

I have just said that the Prophet was left with those who were not able to migrate behind in Mecca, while the Quraysh intensified their campaign of torture. Many and various were the ways they adopted to stem the rising tide of the new faith. It was at this time that by Divine revelation (THE QURAN 15: 94, and 26: 214), the Prophet was ordered by God to proclaim God's message to the world, and he had to begin preaching in public. He climbed Mount Safā one day and called out to all the Quraysh gathered there, "Have you ever heard me tell a lie?" With one voice they replied that they had not. Upon which the Prophet said, "If I tell you that there is hidden behind this mountain a large army ready to attack you, would you believe me?" "Certainly," they all replied, "for we have never heard you tell a lie." Then the Prophet gave them the message of God, and exhorted them to give up idolatry, shun all kinds of evil, and to follow the path of righteousness.

He continued to say: "Well! I now tell you important news. O Banū 'Abdu Manāf, O Banū Taym, O Banū Makhzūm, O Banū Asad . . . O assembled Qurayshites, redeem your own souls, for I can do nothing for you in God's presence. . . . Listen to what He commanded me to tell you . . ."

Abū Lahab, the Prophet's uncle, then rose and cried: "May you be cursed for the rest of your life! Why gather us together for trifles like this?"

Muhammad, disconcerted, looked at his uncle without speaking. His face grew red and then pale; his eyes twitched; he could not breathe. Holding out his hand towards his assailant, he spoke, but it was really the angel of wrath speaking for him:

"The hands of Abū Lahab shall perish, and he
  shall perish;
His riches shall not profit him, neither that
  which he hath gained,
He shall go down to be burned into flaming fire."
(THE QURAN, chapter 110.)

This meeting made them offensive and insulting, but the Prophet was undeterred and went on delivering his messages; and more hearts warmed to his teaching and embraced Islam. This infuriated the Quraysh still further, and, when the news of the failure of the deputation to the Negus of Abyssinia came to add fuel to this fire, they decided to kill the Prophet. So they went again to Abū Tālib, this time with a handsome youth whom they wanted Abū Tālib to adopt and bring up, and give them, in return, the Prophet to be put to death. Abū Tālib declined to listen to such a ludicrous proposal, whereupon the Quraysh decided to extend a system of persecution to the whole of the Banū Hāshim family. The first they promulgated was a kind of social ban that stopped inter-marriage and commercial relations. An agreement to this effect was drawn up and hung in the Ka'ba. On learning of this the Banū Hāshim moved to the place known as Shi'b, but the Quraysh saw to it that the blockade was enforced. When someone only remotely related wanted to supply provisions the Quraysh offered obstruction, in which Abū Jahl, himself a Banū Hāshim, played the most cruel part. The whole family cheerfully suffered this ostracism for the sake of the Prophet, which they would never have done had they had no respect for him. During the ban the preaching was confined to the banned, and the Prophet took full advantage of this. Only during the days of pilgrimage, when bloodshed was sacrilegious, the Prophet would come out and preach to the people assembled from all sides.

After some time the more gentle-hearted among the Quraysh began to object to the prolonged ban, and five of them finally decided to remove it, which they did, first by tearing into shreds the scroll hung in the Ka'ba. They then went to Shi'b and brought the Hāshimites out, and sent them to their homes, nobody having the courage to stop them. The ban had lasted for three years. Immediately after this Abū Tālib, who had been such a good uncle, of over eighty years of age, and brave supporter, passed away, and shortly afterwards the Prophet's faithful wife and greatest help, Khadīja, passed away too. In Islamic history this

83

year is known as '*Āmu 'l-Huzn*, i.e. "The Year of Grief."

With the loss of these two powerful and great supporters the Prophet lost the two who were the greatest check and restraint to the cruelties of the Quraysh. As we shall see, the events following will show that the Prophet had still greater difficulties to face. In fact, these two deaths ushered in a new era of troubles. The following chapter will more than ever prove our claim that it was only through his conviction in the truth of his mission and his absolute faith in God that the Prophet was able to brave all obstacles. "His was not the communion with God," says Syed Ameer Ali, in his *Spirit of Islam*, "of those egoists who bury themselves in deserts or forests, and live a life of quietude for themselves alone. His was the hard struggle of the man who is led onward by a nobler destiny towards the liberation of his race from the bondage of idolatry."

CHAPTER 9

> "And surely they purposed to
> scare thee from the land that they
> might expel thee from it."—THE
> QURAN 17 : 76.

SO long as the Prophet had his uncle, Abū Tālib,
and his wife, Khadīja, to back him, the onslaughts
of the Quraysh were not so severe, because these
two, by reason of their influence and standing, acted
as a check upon the activities of that body. But
when they died this restraint was removed, and
the difficulties which faced the Prophet became
greater than ever. As already mentioned, it was
the threshold of a new era of persecution. Soon
after this event, when the Prophet was going out,
somebody from behind threw a handful of dust on
him. On another occasion, even when the Prophet
was within the sacred precincts of the Ka'ba, one
'Uqba, at the instigation of Abū Jahl, threw dust
at him. But these and like incidents did not deter
him from his mission. He could have migrated, as
did some others, to Abyssinia, but he chose to
remain behind and fulfil faithfully the task imposed
on him by God. He had that absolute faith in God
which gave him the conviction that whatever be
the vicissitudes of the way, the end would be

glorious. He felt that those who were foremost in obstructing his path would, in time, be the first to carry his message far and wide; and he knew that those who were now bent upon taking his life would one day be ready and eager to shed their blood for him. So he was not disheartened nor dejected, but thought it best to give a little respite to the Meccans by diverting his energies to other quarters. It was not that he did so because he was baffled by the stubbornness of the Quraysh; for he was never at a loss even in moments of greater danger.

Therefore, the holy Prophet chose to turn his attention to Tā'if, a place three miles from Mecca, whither he repaired with Zayd bin Hāritha, and invited the people to embrace Islam. But, like the Meccans, the people of Tā'if were not destined to embrace Islam at the first invitation. I think that any other man, however good, holy, and sincere, would have given up the task in despair as impossible, but the holy Prophet had so firm a faith in God and His cause that he was never disconsolate. He hoped and still hoped that success would be his, and that the greater the obstacles the more splendid would be the triumph. He was, therefore, greatly embittered when he found that the people of Tā'if not only refused to hear him but absolutely repudiated his teaching and himself. With hope still in his heart, he approached an important personage of Tā'if, and revealed to him the Word of God; but he, too, turned a deaf ear, and later on caused the people to jeer

at him in the public thoroughfares. One day they
lined the streets, and as he passed pelted him with
stones. This went on for three long miles. Yet
bleeding and exhausted he marched on until he
entered the garden of 'Utba bin Rabī'a, a nobleman
of Mecca, where he found refuge and prayed to
God thus in the shelter of the trees: "O my God,
I come to Thee alone to tell my troubles, Thou
art the Most Merciful, and the Best Protector.
I seek Thy shelter; grant it to me and peace to
others." 'Utba, who was in the garden at this time,
seeing the Prophet was filled with pity at his
condition, sent him grapes by his Christian slave
'Addās. Stretching his hands to receive the grapes,
the Prophet uttered these words, "In the name of
God." The slave, surprised at this, asked the
meaning of the phrase, and being informed, at
once embraced Islam. 'Utba, who was looking on,
warned the slave that it might lead to persecution,
but he remained staunch.

After resting in this garden for some time, the
Prophet proceeded towards Mecca, and halting at
a place called Nakhla remained there awhile.
The next halt he made at the cave Hirā, whence
he sent word to Mut'im bin 'Adī that he desired
to return to Mecca, and would do so if he agreed
to grant him protection. Mut'im, though an
unbeliever, was a gentleman who not only agreed
to do as he was desired, but called his sons, and with
them, all armed to the teeth, went to the Ka'ba,
where they remained on guard till the Prophet had
finished his obligations there.

The journey to Tā'if is an important event in the life of the Prophet; for it speaks in unequivocal terms both of his spiritual greatness and of his faith in God. Sir William Muir writes of it, "In Mahomet's journey to Tā'if his greatness is amply seen. A single man, whose own people not only looked down upon him but had expelled him, leaves the city in the cause of God, and goes to a place of unbelievers, like Jonah, and calls them to embrace Islam; which shows that he had absolute faith in his mission."

Soon after his return to Mecca came the days of pilgrimage, and the holy Prophet called on each of the clan coming from afar to perform the pilgrimage, and expounded to them the message of Islam. The Quraysh, ever ready to obstruct, so contrived by reason of their influence that none of the outsiders paid much attention to the Prophet. The consequence was that whenever he approached any tribe it contemptuously rejected him. Only two clans treated him with any respect. One said that they liked Islam but dared not give up the religion and beliefs of their forefathers, while the second promised to embrace Islam if the Prophet would agree to give them a share in the kingdom which he would realize. This event, trifling though it certainly is, yet seems to show that most of the clans and people, in their hearts, believed in the ultimate success of the Prophet's undertaking. To the condition as to sharing his kingdom, the Prophet replied, "It depends on God to bestow a kingdom and on whomsoever He likes; therefore

88

I could not and would not promise what is not in my power." If personal aggrandizement had been his purpose, as some purblind critics would have us believe, nothing would have prevented the Prophet from winning not one clan only but practically all the clans by the promise of shares in what was presently to be gained. The fact is that the achievement of temporal power was not his aim, as I shall further show in the Medina period, the events of which amply prove that the Prophet had no desire for worldly gains. Had not his own people, the Quraysh themselves, already offered him the riches of the whole of Arabia?

Tufayl bin ‘Amrū, the chief of a clan, came one day to Mecca. The Meccans, to forestall the Prophet, went to him and told him that he had come at a time when Muhammad from among them was causing a great deal of confusion and disruption by means of sorcery and magic arts, and that, therefore, to avoid being mixed up in it it would be well for him not to listen to anything Muhammad might have to say. Tufayl says that he believed the Quraysh, and was determined to be on his guard, but that one day when passing the mosque he saw the Prophet offering prayer. This, says Tufayl, impressed him so much that he decided to listen to what this man had to say, thinking that if it seemed to be trumpery he would of course have nothing further to do with it or him. With this in view he approached the Prophet, and asked him to tell him his views. Whereupon the Prophet recited to him verses from the Quran, and spoke of the theory of the Unity of God. This convinced Tufayl that the Prophet had told him the truth, and he embraced Islam. Later, when returning to his clan, he begged the Prophet to pray for him, so that he might succeed in turning the members of his tribe to Islam. On his return, however, he converted only two, his wife and his father, the rest remaining obdurate. Baffled at this he returned to the Prophet and thus addressed him, "O Apostle of God, my tribesmen have insulted me, and rejected the faith I offered. Pray that they all may be cursed." The Prophet raised his hand, and said, "My God. guide the tribe of Daus." This incident alone would place him on a pedestal of a height to which no Prophet has attained, for we see in the lives of them that they all, even including the Prince of Peace—Jesus Christ—cursed and invoked the wrath of God on those who ill-treated them. Not even fig-trees escaped.

This, then, was the state of affairs. The Prophet was surrounded on all sides by hostile forces. Every attempt of his was frustrated by the Quraysh. The only thing that kept him resolute was the conviction that in the end the cause of God must triumph. By patience, forbearance, courage, and preaching he had tried to win them over, but had so far failed in his attempts to bring about any great measure of success. Yet he did not abate his efforts, and once, preaching, he happened to meet a few men of the Khazraj clan of Medina. Having ascertained their antecedents, he preached to them the message of God and invited them to embrace

Islam. Now these people knew of and were expecting "that Prophet" as prophesied in the Scriptures. And when they heard and grasped the beauty of the teachings of the holy Prophet they believed that without doubt he was "that Prophet" (St. John 1: 19–21), and none other, and six of them there and then accepted Islam. The pledge they took was this: "We will not associate anything with God; we will not steal, nor commit adultery nor any other offence such as fornication, the killing of children, calumny, and slander; we will obey the Prophet in all that is right, and will be faithful to him."

On their return to Medina much enthusiasm prevailed there over the new faith, and the Prophet's name became a household word. The result was that a great number embraced Islam, a dozen of them going to Mecca in the following year to perform the pilgrimage. But to the Prophet the whole year was one of constant anxiety as to the fate of the converts and their efforts. So when the next year came he was seen anxiously going about looking for someone from Medina to give him the news. At last at ʿAqaba he found twelve men who received him with respect and honour. These twelve included some who had been converted the previous year. They gave all the news to the Prophet. When returning, they begged him to send with them someone who would enable them to preach and spread the faith. The Prophet sent Musʿab bin ʿUmayr, who made his headquarters with Asʿad bin Zurārah and engaged himself in the task assigned him. God was kinder to the Muslims here; and soon every house was talking about Islam, and a great number from among the Aus and Khazraj became converts. In other cases whole clans embraced Islam in a day, and here the history of Islam would have been altogether different had not the Jews taken alarm at its rapid success.

Turning from the encouraging news of Medina to the happenings at Mecca, we see that the whole year was one of great distress, trouble, and misfortune. The persecutions of the Quraysh became more severe and more ingeniously varied, and fuel was added to their enmity at every piece of good news from Medina. Save only for one very remarkable thing the whole year was disastrous. But it was during this year that the Prophet experienced his "Nocturnal Ascension," or what is called in Arabic *Mi'rāj*. There is some controversy as to whether this Ascension was bodily, or an occurrence in a vision. The Quran speaks of it thus: "Praise be to Him who carried His servant by night from the sacred temple to the temple which is more remote, whose precincts We have blessed, that We might show Him some of Our signs; for He is the Hearing and the Seeing" (17: 1). Mr. Stanley Lane-Poole, in speaking of this, writes, "It is still a grand vision full of glorious imagery, fraught with deep meaning." (*Introduction to the Selections from the Koran*). The story of the Ascension is that in the night the Angel Gabriel came to the Prophet and beckoned him to follow him to the presence of God. The Prophet in rapture went with the Angel, and passed through the seven

Heavens, where in each Heaven he met the prophets that had been raised up before him. When he reached the seventh Heaven Gabriel left him, saying that he could go no farther. Then the Prophet continued on his way alone until he reached and felt the nearness of God. It was here that the duty of prayer five times in the day was enjoined on the followers of the Prophet. He was also shown Heaven and Hell, and when he returned to his room, his bed which he had left was still warm. I, for one, see no difficulty in believing this to be a corporeal experience.

The interval which elapsed between this and the next pilgrimage was the most critical period of the Prophet's mission, and a few words of praise escape even from the pen of Sir William Muir, the hostile critic of Muhammad: "Mahomet thus holding his people at bay, waiting in the still expectation of victory, to outward appearance defenceless and with his little band, as it were, in the lion's mouth, yet trusting in His Almighty power Whose messenger he believed himself to be, resolute and unmoved . . . presents a spectacle of sublimity paralleled only in the sacred records by such scenes as that of the Prophet of Israel, when he complained to his Master, 'I, even I only, am left.' "

Next year brought seventy-two of the men of Medina to the pilgrimage. The Prophet met them one night at the same place as in the time past, but now he was accompanied by his uncle 'Abbās, who spoke to the Medinites thus: "You know the

93

position Muhammad occupies among us. So far we have been protecting him, and he is quite safe. Now you wish him to accompany you to your place. If you think you can fulfil the pledge, and are able to guard him, you are at liberty to undertake the responsibility; but if you think that you cannot, then give him up from now. Do not mistake! You are welcome to take him with you, but only on condition you guard him successfully." The Medinites, who became known as Ansārs, agreed to swear allegiance on any terms, and a fresh oath was taken. However, in spite of all precautions taken that the Quraysh might not discover this meeting, they were spied on, and by the next morning the thing was known. The Quraysh went to the camp to ascertain the truth about this meeting. But it so happened that the Medinites with whom they conversed were unbelievers. They knew nothing about the meeting. As they denied the whole thing the Quraysh returned quite satisfied. Nevertheless their fears were roused again. But as the Ansārs had left for Medina they could do nothing. They only succeeded in seizing and torturing one of them who was left behind. It was fortunate that he had a rich friend in Medina who was able to rescue him from the fury of the Quraysh.

By this time the persecution had reached its height, and all known measures of torture and obstruction were pertinaciously meted out to the Muslims. The Prophet, fearing that the situation might culminate in a general massacre, advised his followers to seek immediate safety in Medina.

This city was till then known by the name of Yasrib. Under perfect secrecy the Muslim families in twos and threes left the place and travelled to Medina, where they were warmly received. After some time the whole city began to have a look of emptiness, and 'Utba bin Rabī'a, at sight of the empty houses which were once full of life, said, "Every dwelling place, even if it has long been blessed, will one day become a prey to unhappiness and misery. And all this is the work of one among us who has scattered us, and ruined our affairs." At last all had left without any mishap, and the Prophet was alone with the devoted 'Alī and the faithful Abū Bakr. Here, again, we see the absolute faith which the Prophet had in God. The Meccans' enmity was daily growing more bitter. Their aim was frankly to kill him, yet among these deadly foes he remained behind, after having sent away all those who could have protected him. He was not careful for his own safety; he knew that God who had entrusted him with His work would never allow him to be killed before its fulfilment. But he was most solicitous about the safety of others, and dreaded any kind of bloodshed that might cast a blot on the accomplishment of his task. How unlike Jesus if the Gospel writers are correct! "Think not that I have come to send peace on earth; I came not to send peace, but a sword. For I am come to set a man at variance against his father, and the daughter against her mother, and the daughter-in-law against her mother-in-law" (Matt. 10: 34, 35). The holy Prophet of his own advent says, "I am come as a mercy to the worlds," and the Quran affirms it (21:107). If personal safety had been his aim, he could have gone on to Medina and none of the Muslims would have objected to it, but he remained, and let those whose safety was his chief consideration go and find shelter. The Meccans, thus baffled in all their attempts, decided to put an end to the Prophet by surrounding his house by night and killing him early in the morning when it was his custom to come out to say his prayers. The Prophet knew what was coming and was ready for it; for the Divine Revelation had that day told him of the plot of the Quraysh and ordered him to leave for Medina. So he had arranged with Abū Bakr to meet him at a certain distance from Mecca. How the Prophet managed to escape from the clutches of these hungry wolves will be told in the next chapter; but I should like once again to point out to my readers that the motive power in all the Prophet's ways was his conviction of the righteousness of his cause, which was that of God. It was a conviction pursued through resolute action that ultimately ended in his success. All prophets have had to face hardships, snubs, taunts, and rebukes, but those suffered by the Prophet of Arabia were more than any. We hear Jesus Christ crying out, "Eli, Eli, lama Sabachthani" (O my God, why hast Thou forsaken me?) But the Prophet of Islam in greater danger, yet never in despair, spoke to God, "O my God, to Thee I complain of the feebleness of my strength and my lack of resourcefulness. Thou art Most Merciful of all the merciful. Thou art the Lord of the weak. To whom art Thou to entrust me? To a foe who is deadly or to a friend? Not in the least do I care for anything except that I may have Thy protection. In Thee I seek shelter. May it never be that I should incur Thy wrath, or that Thou shouldst be angry with me. There is no strength, no power except that which we get through Thee." This of itself speaks volumes and this alone should be sufficient to make the critics refrain from malicious slander against such a personality. I respect all the prophets, and I believe in them, but most of all I admire and follow Muhammad; for my conscience and knowledge tell me that all that other prophets had taught has now become useless —"The old order changeth, yielding place to new."

CHAPTER 10

THE HEGIRA (THE FLIGHT)

(622 A.C.)

> "Grieve not, surely God is with us."—THE QURAN 9: 40.

THE Arabic word Hijra, when translated, means migration, and in Islamic history it stands for the migration of the Prophet from Mecca to Medina in the thirteenth year of Prophethood. European writers call it "The Flight." I have mentioned in the foregoing chapter that the Quraysh had left the Muslims no choice but to flee for their lives. Now, when they realized that the Muslims had migrated in great numbers to Medina and were achieving a considerable measure of success, their fury knew no bounds. The chiefs of all the tribes assembled at Dāru 'n-Nadwa to decide on the best course to pursue, and unanimously agreed that assassination was the only thing that could achieve their purpose. But to assassinate in those days meant, as I have already pointed out, starting a tribal feud. This seemed, at first, a difficulty, whilst Abū Jahl came forward with the plan that not one man should do the business, but that stalwarts and young men selected from all the clans should do so, and thus remove the cause for tribal bloodshed.

While the Quraysh were maturing their plans, the Word of God came to the Prophet, telling him not to sleep that night in his bed. He was also told that the time had come for him to migrate to Medina. Then the Prophet sent for the devoted 'Alī and told him to take his place in the bed, while he (the Prophet) himself would escape, and meet Abū Bakr at an appointed place. 'Alī had to be left behind because the Prophet had a trust to discharge towards certain people, and since he was leaving it was for 'Alī to undertake the duty. Abū Bakr was similarly informed and instructed to make the necessary preparations for the flight, after which the Prophet returned to his house. Soon after it was dusk, all the selected youths of the Quraysh laid siege to the house of the Prophet, so that none might come out or go in, and waited for the Prophet to appear so that they might fall upon him and kill him. I remember reading a ridiculous objection to the effect that there was no need for these youths to have waited, since they could have gone in and done the deed at any time. Perhaps they could have done so; but one must consider first that they did not because it was not ordained that they should, and secondly it was against the Arab sense of chivalry to kill a person within the four walls of his house. At dead of night the Prophet left the place, passing through this same crowd of besiegers who, in their excitement, failed to recognize him. All night they kept peeping through a hole in the door, and were quite content to see somebody sleeping in the bed. Late in the morning when

99

the youths, getting impatient and guessing that something was wrong, rushed into the house, they found 'Alī lying in bed instead of the Prophet. The Prophet himself, after leaving the house, went to the appointed place where he met Abū Bakr, and left with him for Medina, hiding themselves first in a cave called "Saur," three miles from Mecca. This cave and the cave of "Hirā" are of supreme importance in the history of Islam, for from the one the Call was received, and from the other a new life was infused into the mission of Islam.

When the Quraysh found 'Alī in bed instead of the Prophet they were first dumbfounded, and then furious, so that 'Alī did not escape severe injury. They summoned an emergency meeting and a big reward for the capture of the Prophet was proclaimed throughout the city. Not content with this they sent out tracking parties to comb the neighbourhood for the fugitive. One of these parties, actually following the footprints of the pursued, arrived at the mouth of the cave. Abū Bakr, hearing them, despaired, and said that they were lost, being but two and the enemy so many. But the Prophet replied: "We are three, for GOD is with us, and will protect us." There is surely no example in the history of the world of a man expressing such faith and displaying such calm and tranquillity as did the holy Prophet in the face of complete disaster and certain death. The enemy was at the cave's mouth, armed to the teeth, eager to kill, fierce with rage, and thirsty for blood, but the Prophet tells the only companion with him not to despair, but to take heart because GOD was with them. And it was God indeed Who saved them from certain death: it was God's Voice from above that kept his heart and head steady, and told him not to fear. God came to him to save him, for he was doing God's work.

The enemy, having reached the mouth of the cave, lost the trace of the footsteps; a sure sign to them that the fugitive whom they were pursuing so hotly was somewhere at hand. One of them suggested searching the cave, and if they had they would have succeeded both in killing the Prophet and crushing the faith that he was teaching. But God had decreed otherwise. He had ordained that His final Prophet should succeed, and, therefore, he would not be killed. Others who heard the man advising a search of the cave laughed, told him that they would not waste their time looking for him in a cave over the mouth of which a spider's web unbroken was waving in the breeze. So they turned away to hunt in other places, little dreaming that by doing so they had lost all chances of catching him. The Prophet remained three days in the cave, and was secretly supplied with food by the daughter of Abū Bakr, who was in Mecca. When the work was over and the coast was clear they came out of the cave, and with 'Abdullāh bin Urayqit, a non-Muslim, as their guide, they proceeded towards Medina. Thus, avoiding all frequented and known paths, they went on, resting for the day on account of the heat, and travelling only in the night.

The offer of the great reward had sent forth

many brave men in search of the Prophet, and
Surāqa bin Khasʻam was one of them. Soon after
the Prophet had left the cave he espied his traces,
and followed him on his Arab charger, but his
horse stumbled on the way and threw him. Hastily
remounting he continued the chase, but the horse
stumbled again, throwing him violently to a considerable distance. Again he remounted and again
the horse, this time when his rider was close to the
Prophet and was preparing to shoot an arrow,
stumbled and threw him off with great force, its
own feet sinking into the sand. "Then," says
Surāqa, "it dawned on me that it was pre-ordained
that the Prophet's cause should succeed." Renouncing all intention of murder at the behest of
this inner voice, he approached the Prophet, and
begged his forgiveness. The Prophet forgave him
with a smile, and imparted to him the happy
news that one day he would wear the gold bangles
of the rulers of Persia. This was a true prophecy
of an event which happened twenty-four years later;
for these words found fulfilment when the kingdom
of the Chosroes of Persia fell to the sword of ʻOmar,
and Surāqa was sent for and decorated with the
bangles.

The steadfastness and perfect tranquillity displayed by the Prophet in every sort of vicissitude
is attributable to the Divine revelations that came
to him from time to time. Take, for example,
"Verily, He that enjoined the Quran upon thee
shall bring thee back to Mecca" (THE QURAN 28:
85). From this verse the Prophet gathered that he

would one day return to Mecca in triumph; for he loved the city of his birth dearly, and was much grieved at leaving it. Even about the Flight the Prophet was informed through revelation long before the actual moment for it came. Therefore the Muslims knew that the success of Islam would begin from Medina. It was in the Flight that the climax of the Prophet's helplessness was reached. Therefore, the Quran says that if the Meccans did not help him, God certainly did.

One day when thus journeying to Medina they were all hungry, so when they came to a village they approached an old woman who was sitting at her door and asked her if she could give them anything to eat. The woman replied that she had nothing, not even her goats, whose milk she could have given, except one, feeble and dying, that had been left behind. The Prophet asked her to give them permission to milk the feeble and the dried goat, and on permission being given the goat gave enough milk to supply them all.

We know how the Prophet had to work in Mecca in the teeth of bitter opposition. At every step attempts were made to put an end to his teachings by force, bribery, and cruelty. But the Prophet never for a second wavered from his mission. He continued with all his spiritual and moral force; the result being that at the end of thirteen years he had succeeded in converting about three hundred people, who never for a single moment by thought, deed, or action hesitated to lay down their all for him, in whose teachings they had implicit faith.

103

Jesus Christ had only twelve disciples, and leaving aside the converts that he may have made, we see that these twelve forsook him when he was tried by Pilate, and hung on the cross. This is no doubt the greatest achievement of the Prophet, and a critic like Sir William Muir, in his *Life of Mahomet*, finds himself compelled to write about it thus: "In so short a period Mecca had, by this wonderful movement, been rent into two factions which, unmindful of the old landmarks of tribe and family, had arrayed themselves in deadly opposition one against the other. The believers bore persecution with a patient and tolerant spirit, and though it was their wisdom to do so, the credit of a magnanimous forbearance may be freely accorded. One hundred men and women, rather than abjure their precious faith, had abandoned home and sought refuge till the storm should be overpast in Abyssinian exile. And now again a large number, with the Prophet himself, were emigrating from their fondly loved city with its sacred Temple, to them the holiest spot on earth, and fleeing to Medina. There the same marvellous charm had within two or three years been preparing for them a brotherhood ready to defend the Prophet and his followers with their blood. Jewish truth had long sounded in the ears of the men of Medina, but it was not until they heard the spirit-stirring strains of the Arabian Prophet that they too awoke from slumber and sprang suddenly into a new and earnest life. The virtues of his people may be described in the words of Mahomet himself. . . ."

After eight days' journey the Prophet and Abū Bakr reached a place called Qubā, three miles from Medina. The Prophet stayed there fourteen days, in which time a mosque was built which is still frequented by Muslims from all parts of the world when they visit Medina after the pilgrimage to Mecca.

CHAPTER 11

THE PROPHET IN MEDINA

"Lo! those who believed and left
their homes and strove with their
wealth and their lives for the
cause of God, and those who took
them in and helped them."—
THE QURAN 8: 72.

MEDINA, the City of Lights, was, until the
coming of the Prophet, a place comparatively
unknown. It had originally been inhabited by
Amalekites, who were overwhelmed and destroyed
by successive colonies of Jews who, flying before
Greek, Babylonian, and Roman invaders, entered
Arabia and colonized the northern part of the
Hedjaz. The most important and powerful of these
colonies were those of Banū Nazīr at Khaybar,
Banū Qurayza at Fidak, and Banū Qaynuqā' near
Medina. These established their power and domi-
nated the surrounding country until the establishment of the two Kahtanite tribes, Aus and Khazraj,
at Medina. These, being themselves powerful, came
into constant conflict with the Jews. The people of
Aus and Khazraj had in the first place belonged to
the Yemen, whence they were compelled to move
by great floods. Their religion was idolatry, modified, later, to a great extent by Jewish influence,
which influence in fact prepared the way for

106

them to embrace Islam the more easily. These people after their conversion became known as Ansārs.

Tidings of the Prophet's departure from Mecca had reached the Ansārs, and they were eagerly expecting him. Every day they used to go out of the city to give him a grand reception, and they would return disappointed. But the Prophet, as has been mentioned, stayed at a place outside Medina, at the invitation of 'Amrū bin 'Auf, the most distinguished of the Ansārs. A number of *Muhājirīn*, the emigrants, were also there. Muslims from the neighbourhood flocked to meet the Prophet, who remained there fourteen days. 'Alī, too, had joined him after experiencing most cruel treatment when the Meccans discovered him in the bed of the holy Prophet. The first mosque in the history of Islam was built at this place for, hitherto, the Muslims in Medina as well as in Mecca used to offer their prayers in their houses. It is of this mosque that the holy Quran speaks: ". . . Certainly a mosque founded on piety from the very first day is more deserving that you should stand in it; in it are men who love that they should be purified, and God loves those who purify themselves" (9: 108). The Prophet helped the companions with his own hands in the erection of this mosque.

From this place the Prophet proceeded to Medina, and his entry into the city was a spectacle of rejoicing. Clad in their gayest attire people came out to greet him, and when he entered the city women burst out into songs from their housetops, in welcome to the noble guest. Everyone was anxious that the Prophet should stop at his house. It was a delicate question for the Prophet to decide whose invitation he should accept. So he let his camel go on, and said that he would stop wherever it should stop. Thus amidst the eager crowd the camel plodded on, and stopped in the open space in front of Abū Ayyūb's house. This piece of land belonged to two orphans and they offered it gratis to the Prophet, but he would not take it as a gift, and the orphans had to accept a price. There, as the first act of the Prophet, a mosque was built. This, then, was the second mosque built by the earliest Muslims, and presented a simplicity in design and construction that is not seen in any mosque to-day. The walls were of mud bricks, and the roof was supported by the trunks of the palm trees; while their leaves and twigs made up the roof itself. There was a platform in the courtyard for such as chose to live there and for such as had no homes. These later became known as the "residents of Suffa." Adjoining the mosque were erected two rooms for the Prophet.

Muhammad advised the emigrants to work for their livings rather than accept charity of the Ansārs. But there were some who had no family and no means of earning money. It was for these that the Prophet found a place to sleep on the raised platform in a part of the second mosque. He gave them to eat when he could. These people devoted their time to the study of religion. Of all of them Abū Hurayra is the best known for the great number of traditions of the Prophet which he collected.

Thus we see that in spite of being so many years in Mecca, and in spite of its being the birthplace of the Prophet, Muslims were not able to build a mosque of their own in their own city or say their prayers publicly, while in Medina they were able to build a mosque as their first act soon after the arrival of the Prophet. In contrast to the turbulent conditions of Mecca, Medina offered the peace that was necessary for the propagation of Islam. It has been correctly said that a new era in the life of Islam started from Medina; that there it was born again. In Mecca they were hounded from pillar to post and had no time even to say their prayers peacefully in their homes. Now that they could say them publicly the question arose as to what should be the method of calling the faithful to prayer five times a day at the fixed hours. A meeting was therefore called to discover some answer, and many suggestions were put forward. A companion who in a dream the previous night had seen and heard a man saying, "God is great, God is great," told it to the Prophet. 'Omar, too, said that he had the same dream, and the Prophet therefore adopted this formula to be called out loudly by the Muezzin at the fixed hours as the call to prayer. The formula is: "God is greatest" (repeated four times), "I bear witness that nothing deserves to be worshipped but God" (repeated twice), "I bear witness that Muhammad is the Apostle of God" (repeated twice), "Come to prayers" (repeated twice), "Come to success" (repeated twice), "God is greatest" (repeated twice), "There is no God but God." Thus we see that the Muslim call for prayers is much better than the Christian bell and the temple gong, for they neither show the essence nor speak of the greatness of prayers, while the Muslim call proclaims in words the essential Truth that God is greatest, and calls on all faithful to pray to Him and thus achieve success. Both the Christian bell and the temple gong are dumb and inarticulate. Let me divert for a while to say a few words, by way of comparison, about the institution of the bell in Christendom.

In his *Folk-lore in the Old Testament*, London, 1918, Sir James George Frazer, in discussing the origin of the bells used in religious worship, writes:

"Why should the priest in his violet robe . . . fear to die if the golden bells were not heard to jingle, both when he went into, and when he came forth from the holy place? The most probable answer seems to be that the chiming of the holy bells was thought to drive far off the envious and wicked spirits who lurked about the door of the sanctuary, ready to pounce on and carry off the richly apparelled minister as he stepped across the threshold in the discharge of his sacred office. At least this view, which has found favour with some modern scholars, is strongly supported by analogy; for it has been a common opinion, from the days of antiquity downwards, that demons and ghosts can be put to flight by the sound of metal, whether it be the musical jingle of little bells, the deep-mouthed clangor of great bells, the shrill clash of cymbals, the booming of gongs, or the simple clink and clank of plates of bronze or iron knocked together or struck with hammers or sticks. Hence, in rites of exorcism it has often been customary for the celebrant either to ring a bell which he holds in his hand, or to wear attached to some part of his person a whole nest of bells, which jingle at every movement he makes. Examples will serve to illustrate the antiquity and the wide diffusion of such beliefs and practices.

"Lucian tells us that spectres fled at the sound of bronze and iron, and he contrasts the repulsion which the clank of these metals exerted on spirits with the attraction which the chink of silver money wielded over women of a certain class. . . .

"But in Christian times the sound deemed above all others abhorrent to the ears of fiends and goblins has been the sweet and solemn music of church bells. The first Provincial Council of Cologne laid it down as an opinion of the fathers that at the sound of the bells summoning Christians to prayer demons are terrified and depart, and the spirits of the storm, the powers of the air, are laid low. . . .

". . . the service book known as the Roman Pontifical recognizes the virtue of a church bell, wherever its sound is heard, to drive far off the powers of evil, the gibbering and mowing spectres of the dead, and all the spirits of the storm. A great canonist of the thirteenth century, Durandus, in his once famous and popular treatise on the divine offices, tells us that 'bells are rung in processions that demons may fear and flee. For when they hear the trumpets of the church militant, that is, the bells, they are afraid, as any tyrant is afraid when he hears in his land the trumpets of a powerful king, his foe. And that, too, is the reason why, at the sight of a storm rising, the Church rings its bells, in order that the demons, hearing the trumpets of the eternal king, that is, the bells, may be terrified and flee away and abstain from stirring up the tempest.' . . .

"Throughout the Middle Ages and down to modern times the sound of church bells was also in great request for the purpose of routing witches and wizards, who gathered unseen in the air to play their wicked pranks on man and beast. There were certain days of the year which these wretches set apart more particularly for their unhallowed assemblies or Sabbaths, as they were called, and on such days accordingly the church bells were specially rung, sometimes the whole night long, because it was under cover of darkness that witches and warlocks were busiest at their infernal tasks. For example, in France witches were thought to scour the air most particularly on the night of St. Agatha, February 5th; hence the bells of the parish churches used to be set ringing that night to drive them away, and the same custom is said to have been observed in some parts of Spain. . . .

"In the Middle Ages, we are told, all over Germany the church bells used to be rung during thunderstorms. . . .

"The bells were solemnly consecrated and popularly supposed to be baptized by the priests; certainly they received names and were washed, blessed, and sprinkled with holy oil 'to drive away and repel evil spirits.' Inscriptions engraved on church bells often refer to the power which they were supposed to possess of dispelling storms of thunder, lightning, and hail; some boldly claim such powers for the bells themselves, others more modestly pray for deliverance from these calamities. . . ."

Having attended to the needs of the religion, the Prophet turned his attention towards the emigrants. Most of them, when in Mecca, had been comfortably off, and had had enough for their requirements. But since coming to Medina they were in great need; for they had been compelled to leave their wealth behind. The Prophet established a brotherhood between the Ansārs and the emigrants, "a brotherhood unique in the history of the world and in respect of the sincerity of the fraternization"; a brotherhood which bound its members in a relationship stronger than those of blood. Each brother took a brother - emigrant home with him, and placed half of his house at his disposal, and divided everything else equally. The Medinites were an agricultural people, and desired to divide even their farms equally, but the emigrants, being tradesmen by profession, were not used to farming. The helpers, informed of this fact, said that they would work the farms but would divide the yields equally. Not only that, but they also made arrangements that after their deaths the property should be divided likewise. It was an overwhelming scene of love and kindness. For two peoples who were till then not only alien in race, but also in culture, religion, and outlook, to join like this in a bond of brotherhood is the unequalled achievement of Islam. The history of no other religion shows anything like it. While the helpers were thus ready to share with their new brothers-in-faith, the emigrants themselves were not eager to take undue advantage of their generous offer. An emigrant named 'Abdu 'r-Rāhmān bin 'Auf was offered half of everything by his brother-helper. 'Auf expressed his gratitude and wanted to be shown the way to the market, saying that he would manage to make his own living, and in a short time he was able to develop a flourishing business. Similarly, others took to trade, or started working as potters, porters, clerks, and in other capacities.

These people not only managed to maintain themselves thus but also to contribute towards the Baytu 'l-Māl, the common fund, or the public treasury, a fund to be expended on the common welfare. This is another institution peculiar to Islam. Nowhere in the history of any other religion do we find such a thing instituted and worked so thoroughly. There was a time in their lives when they were destitute. So much so that the Prophet had to ask his companions to entertain his guest. Once he asked Abū Talha, a companion, to give hospitality to a friend. Abū Talha took the guest home and on reaching there found that there was nothing

114

worth offering, and all that was there was hardly enough even to suffice for the children at home. To avoid the awkward situation the light was put out and whatever meal there was was served to the guest. Abū Talha and his wife, who had to bear him company as hosts, took nothing, but only behaved by the movements of hands and mouths as though they were also partaking of the food. It was a time like this which was followed, by the grace of God, by the days of plenitude. But with a vast wealth at their disposal they acquitted themselves as admirably as they did when they were in dire need and utter penury. A part of their earnings went to Baytu 'l-Māl to be divided among the needy. The "residents of Suffa," from whom sprang the band of religious teachers whose energy and efforts illumined the places which they visited, were among those who were maintained from this Baytu 'l-Māl.

There is, however, one grave charge preferred against Islam, and that is that it became militant after coming to Medina. This charge it is my purpose to refute. Those who level such a charge are wantonly misrepresenting the facts, which were as follows. As we have seen, Islam in Mecca was set amid conditions entirely different from those which it found in Medina. In Mecca it had no power worth the name; the Muslims were the silent and patient sufferers. Besides, bloodshed to Islam was never to be commended and the wars to which it had to resort were purely defensive wars. Finding no peace in Mecca they left their homes to go and settle somewhere where they could have peace, but the Quraysh, who were bent upon their destruction, persisted even after the Muslims had left Mecca and come to Medina. We should not forget that in Medina the Muslims had to devise a plan for their conduct towards the other inhabitants, as also for themselves, because of their increasing numbers. If we look at the history of the evolution of society we see that rules and regulations have always been adopted according to growing needs. The fact that Islam did not approve of bloodshed is amply borne out by the fact that soon after settling their own common affairs they began to make provision for the relations that were to exist between them and other neighbouring clans. The cry that Islam was forced on others at the point of the sword is as mischievous as it is wrong. The taking up of arms was not to propagate the faith but to protect the person. So long they were in Mecca they had neither the strength nor the opportunity to exert their rights by force of arms, or to defend themselves. The instinct of self-preservation is as natural to man as the act of drawing a breath. Therefore, to fight for existence is in no sort an act of aggressive warfare—nor can it be called forcing Islam on other races at the sword-point. All religions, all governments, all people have the right to fight in self-defence. If, therefore, Islam has done the same, where lies the harm? Even Jesus Christ, called the Prince of Peace, advised his followers to buy swords. In the later history of Christianity we see that force was used not only for self-defence but for the slaughter of those whose religion was different, or whose beliefs, though the religion was the same, were at variance with those of the Church at Rome. If there is any instance in the history of Islam of a ruler forcing religion on another at the point of the sword, the blame cannot be laid at the door of Islam. Islam became militant in Medina not by way of policy but of necessity. Islam could not be militant because of policy; for the Prophet has declared, "He who is not affectionate to God's creatures and to his own children would not receive the affection of God." He taught men to be charitable in speech, deed, thought, and action. "Charity of the tongue," says Irving, "that most important and least cultivated of charities, was likewise earnestly inculcated by Mahomet." A religion that teaches us to keep the finer feelings of humanity in the forefront cannot be aggressive. Islam was supremely patient, but when the bitter animosity of the Jews, their violation of solemn engagements, their sedition, and their betrayals became dangers God ordered, "Defend yourself against your enemies, but attack them not first: God hateth the aggressor" (THE QURAN 2: 190).

The use of the sword by the Muslims was purely in self-defence, nor can the history of any other religion show any parallel to this. Muslims never used the sword for the propagation of their faith. I challenge anybody to produce one example of the Prophet using sword or force of any kind for spreading the faith. But on the other hand just picture

117

to yourself the many instances of the frightful wars waged by the Jews, the Christians, and the gentle Parsis. In the case of the Jews the force used was sanctified by their religion, and in that of the early Christians the teachings of the Prophet of Nazareth were soon forgotten in the pride of power. "From the moment Christianity became a recognized force," says an able writer, "it became aggressive and persecuting." "The name of religion," writes another, "served as the plea and justification of aggression upon weaker nations; it led to their spoliation and enslavement." Thus we see that every act of violation was sanctified by the Church, while, "in cases of extreme iniquity, absolution paved the criminal's way to heaven." From the slaughter of Charlemagne, with the sanction of the Church, to the massacre and enslavement of the weaker races of America, there is record, almost unbroken, of Christian aggressiveness. "Persecution," writes Hallam in his *History of England*, "is the deadly original sin of the Reformed Church, that which cools every honest man's zeal for their cause in proportion as his reading becomes more expansive." Thus we see that the Reformed Church, too, failed to do anything more than adopt the policy of aggression beloved of the Old Church unreformed.

In the history of religions as of individuals, with the exception of Islam only, we see that the spirit of toleration is preached and insisted upon only so long as a religion is powerless, but that it gives way to intolerance and persecution the moment

118

power is attained. Up to the time of the conversion of Constantine, Christianity was weak, and, in consequence, passive; but from that moment onwards it became safe from molestation. Then began a system of religious persecution unparalleled in conception. "From the very moment," writes Lecky, "that the Church obtained civil power under Constantine, the general principle of coercion was admitted and acted on, both against the Jews, the heretics, and pagans." Another author writes, "Father after Father wrote about the holiness of persecution. One of the greatest saints of the Church, 'a saint of the most tender and exquisite piety,' supplied arguments for the most atrocious persecution."

Later on, in the fifteenth century, the Pope apportioned the non-Christian world equally among the Portuguese and the Spaniards with absolute power to effect its conversion by whatever means they liked. History affords ample proof of the freedom with which they construed this permission and how they forthwith started an era of persecution; for had not the Master said, "Compel them to come in"? I could multiply instances to show that Christianity not only preached and sanctioned persecution, but did so in such a way that the mere thought of their instruments and devices of torture makes one's blood turn cold with horror. Yet I admire the impudence of the followers of this religion in asserting that, since its advent in Medina, Islam became militant. Yes, Islam became militant, but only in so far as it was necessary to fight for self-preservation. The spirit of tolerance which the Prophet taught he showed by example. To all conquered nations it meant freedom of worship. To proselytize by the sword was abhorrent to the holy Prophet, and expressly forbidden by the Quran. "There is no compulsion in religion" (THE QURAN 2: 258). Islam never tolerated the spirit of aggression. It was always ready to say to its enemies: "Cease hostilities, be our allies, and we shall be faithful to you; or pay tribute, and we will secure and protect you in all your rights; or adopt our religion, and you shall enjoy every privilege we ourselves possess." But this very simple and honest statement was made use of by hostile critics to prove that Islám employed force and dictated conditions that were impracticable, one writer going so far as to say that to save their lives and property people were converted to Islam. But there is nothing here that tells of insecurity of property or life. These were the terms—terms such as no foe had hitherto conceived of that Islam offered; there is absolutely no threat of compulsion, or of the taking of life, or of confiscation of property. It says in plain terms, "you cease hostility and we will be friendly neighbours; or pay us a tribute as a fee for protecting your life and property, or embrace our religion and enjoy the full rights which we enjoy." Could there be any more generous terms imaginable? Has there ever been a religion or nation before or since which offered such equitable conditions to a fallen foe? Governments to-day do not permit people of other nations to

acquire rights of citizenship until they are natural-
ized. Muslims were paying certain taxes, and
contributing otherwise to the exchequer: it would
have been great injustice to provide for others—
non-Muslims—out of this money. Similarly, it was
impossible to tax the others on the same scale.
Therefore, for them there was a special tax, in
all cases less than the usual tax, which was levied
for their protection. As to the last term, or condition,
there is absolutely no threat or coercion in it. The
Muslim Laws of war are admittedly more humane
than those of any other religion: "And fight for
the religion of God against those who fight against
you; but transgress not by attacking them first
for God loveth not the transgressors" (THE QURAN
2 : 190).

Thus we see that soon after attending to the more
urgent affairs after his arrival in Medina the holy
Prophet turned to that next in importance, namely,
the establishment of friendly relations with the
various tribes dwelling in or about Mecca. Again,
if Islam had been aggressive, it would have offered
them not friendly relations but just the bare alternative, "embrace Islam or take the consequences."
The Jews in Medina whom the Prophet himself
approached to avoid bloodshed were Banū
Qaynuqā', Banū Nazīr, and Banū Qurayza. These
being neither on friendly nor hostile terms with the
two tribes, the Aus and the Khazraj, who had now
embraced Islam, it was necessary to come to fresh
terms for a truce, and the following were offered
and concluded in a pact:

121

1. Muslims and Jews shall live as one people;
2. Each party shall keep to its own faith. Neither shall interfere with that of the other;
3. In the event of war with a third party, each is bound to come to the assistance of the other, provided the latter were the aggrieved and not the aggressors;
4. In the event of an attack on Medina both parties shall unite in defending it;
5. Peace when desirable shall be made in consultation with each other;
6. Medina shall be regarded by both as sacred, all bloodshed being forbidden there; and
7. The Prophet shall be the final court of appeal in case of dispute.

Read these terms over and over again and you will not find one word of force to be employed for the promulgation of faith as the alternative of life. The other charge often that the Muslim wars were undertaken for booty is equally wrong; for a people whose morals were so high would hardly render their wars unholy by waging them for booty instead of for the cause of God.

"Muhammad puts the religion of universal toleration into practice; he awards protection of life and property to the followers of other religions in the same way as he does in the case of a Muslim. He allows them to follow their own religion and observe their own rites. He grants concessions to Christians. 'No conquering race of faith has given to its subjects a nobler guarantee than is to be found in the following words of the Prophet: "To the Christians of Najrān and the surrounding territories the security of God and the pledge of His Prophet are extended for their lives, their religion, and their property, to the present as well as the absent, and others besides; there shall be no interference with the practice of their faith or their observances; nor any change in their rights or privileges; no bishop shall be removed from his bishopric, nor any monk from his monastery, nor any priest from his priesthood, and they shall continue to enjoy everything, great and small, as heretofore; no image or cross shall be destroyed; they shall not oppress nor be oppressed: they shall not practise the rights of blood-vengeance as in the Days of Ignorance: no tithes shall be levied from them, nor shall they be required to furnish provisions for the troops." '

"Similar concession was granted to the Zoroastrians in Arabia. I give a few extracts from the Prophet's letter to Farrukh b. Shakhsan, the head of a fire-temple:

'This is the letter from the Apostle of God (may God bless him and assoil him) to the freedman Farrukh b. Shakhsan, brother of Salman Farsi (may God be pleased with him!), and to his family and posterity that he may have, as long as they exist, regardless of which of them will turn Moslem or will remain faithful to his (original) creed. . . .

'This is my letter: Verily upon him (i.e.

Farrukh b. Shakhsan) is the protection of God, also upon his sons, with regard to their lives, property, in the lands in which they live, plains or hill; as well as freedom of use of the wells and pastures which they possess. They must not be treated unjustly or oppressed. And those to whom this my letter will be read must protect them (i.e. the Zoroastrians), leave them free, and prevent the offences from others, and not show hostility to them by insult or by using force.

'They are entirely free in their possessions of fire-temples as well as the landed and other property attached to the latter. No one also should restrict them in the use of rich dress, the use of stirrups, construction of buildings or stables, performing burials, or observing anything which is accepted in their religion or sects. They must be treated better than all other (non-Muhammadan) peoples under protection.' " (Khwaja Kamal-ud-Din, *The Ideal Prophet*, London, 1925.)

Muhammad allowed the use of arms on the following three occasions:

1. To save a house for the worship of God from destruction, be it Christian, Jew, Hindu, Buddhist, or Muslim. The holy Quran says, "Those who have been driven from their homes unjustly only because they said: 'Our Lord is God.'—For had it not been for God's repelling some men by means of others, cloisters and churches and synagogues and mosques, wherein the name of God is oft mentioned,

would assuredly have been pulled down. Verily God helpeth one who helpeth Him. Lo! God is Strong, Almighty" (22 : 40).

2. To establish freedom of conscience. Everyone, according to Quranic teaching, has the right to choose his own faith, and no one should force his religious beliefs on others by persecution or otherwise. "There is no compulsion in religion" (THE QURAN 2 : 256). And if a person does force his religious beliefs, it is the duty of a Muslim to fight against such religious persecution, irrespective of whether the aggrieved be a Jew or a Christian and the persecutor a Muslim. The holy Quran says, "Fight in the way of God against those who fight against you, but begin not hostilities. Lo! God loveth not aggressors. . . . And fight them until persecution is no more and Religion is for God. But if they desist, then-lo! God is Forgiving, Merciful" (2 : 190–192).

3. In self-defence. The holy Quran says, "Sanction is given unto those who fight because they have been wronged . . ." (22 : 39).

But in each case a Muslim should suspend hostilities whenever the oppressor shows an inclination towards peace. The Quran says, "But if the unbelievers desist, then let there be no hostility except against wrong-doers" (2 : 193).

CHAPTER 12

HOW THE SWORD WAS THRUST ON MUHAMMAD

(a) THE BATTLE OF BADR

(624 A.C.)

> "Verily God assisted you at Badr,
> while you were weak. . . ."—THE
> QURAN 3: 122.

AS previous chapters have shown, the early
Muslim history at Mecca is a melancholy one,
being for the most part a record of the violent
atrocities on the part of the people of the Quraysh.

After the boycott period the cruelties of the
Quraysh became so unbearable that gradually all
the Muslims left Mecca for Medina. Within two
months they had all gone, with the exception of
the holy Prophet, Abū Bakr, and 'Alī. There, as
I have related, the Quraysh thought was the time
to kill the Prophet, but Muhammad heard of this
in advance and, with the pursuers hot on his trail,
with the help of God continued to escape and
reach Medina in safety.

Here the Muslims were able to practise their
religion in peace without fear of molestation.
Many mosques were built wherein the people
assembled to pray five times a day; many more
converts were made to Islam, and gradually the
Muslims gained in power and influence. But while

they were at liberty in Medina, the fire of hatred and malice rose high in the hearts of the Quraysh who, when they heard of the success of the Muslims in Medina, were determined not to remain inactive.

Before the holy Prophet came to Medina, the people were thinking of making 'Abdullāh bin Ubayy, a prominent person of great influence, their overlord. But when Muhammad came they changed their minds about it, which made 'Abdullāh extremely angry. The Quraysh, knowing this, endeavoured to persuade him to expel the Muslims from Medina, but already many of his own tribe had embraced Islam, and 'Abdullāh was afraid to take such a step, since it would probably lead to his own people turning against him. Next the Quraysh, people of importance and respected by the whole of Arabia because of their being the custodians of the Ka'ba, turned to the tribes that dwelt between Mecca and Medina and did their best to excite them against the Muslims. Meanwhile, 'Abdullāh bin Ubayy had not been idle in Medina. Secretly he had engineered a deep and growing feeling of opposition, and the Muslims were once more in danger. On all sides they found themselves among enemies. They were in constant fear of being attacked any moment from within, as well as from beyond the four walls of Medina. The Quraysh, though not quite prepared, were, nevertheless, eager to come to blows with the Muslims, and anxiously on the look-out for an opportunity to pick a quarrel. They began by sending men out in small parties right out to the walls of Medina to reconnoitre the land and if possible stir up trouble. The Muslims realized that sooner or later they would have to fight the Quraysh and it was then that the holy Prophet received the Divine Revelation permitting the use of the sword in self-defence. The holy Quran proves this in the following verse: "Fight in the way of God against those who fight you, and do not transgress the limits of war" (2: 190), and also, "Permission is granted to those against whom war is waged, because they have been wronged" (22: 39).

The Prophet, now being assured that war was inevitable, decided to get some information as to the plans of the Quraysh. The Muslims, too, began to go out in small parties, in order to keep an eye on the movements of the enemy, and also to get on friendly terms with other tribes in the vicinity of Medina so that they might be a help to them in time of need. A few tribes made compacts with the Muslims, but these compacts were purely for their own safety, the terms of most of them amounting to nothing more than that they would come to the help of the Muslims on condition that, should they be attacked, the Muslims would come to their help. The Muslims continued going out in small parties to gather as much information concerning the enemy as possible. Each party that was sent out was under strict orders from the holy Prophet to seek a quarrel with no man. If the Quraysh were anxious for war, they must strike the first blow. Unfortunately, in the month of Jumādā II, 2 A.H. (624 A.C.), a few men were sent out under the leadership of 'Abdullāh bin Jahsh, with sealed orders, the contents of which were not to be read until two days had passed. After two days 'Abdullāh opened the envelope and learnt that if the party proceeded to Nakhla certain information might be obtained with regard to the plans of the Quraysh. On reaching Nakhla they came across a few Quraysh on their way back from Syria, but on seeing them 'Abdullāh bin Jahsh completely lost his head, and in flat contravention of the strict orders of the holy Prophet slew one of them, by name 'Amru bin Hazramī. On hearing of this the Prophet was grieved; for he knew that now the Quraysh had at last got the opportunity for which they were longing. In this way the battle of Badr came about. About the same time, by a most unfortunate coincidence, a trading caravan belonging to the Quraysh and led by Abu Sufyān was on its way back from Syria. Abū Sufyān sent word to Mecca that he urgently wanted protection, though he was well aware that the caravan was in no danger. On receiving his message the Quraysh in Mecca came to the conclusion that the Muslims were preparing to attack the caravan. There was, of course, no truth in this; for the caravan had already passed Medina, and was nearing its destination without having been molested in any way. But the Quraysh made this another excuse for the battle of Badr, the real cause of which was the anxiety of the Quraysh to stamp out utterly the steadily growing power of Islam.

It was in the month of Ramazān, in the year

I

2 A.H. (624 A.C.), that the Quraysh approached Medina with the view of attacking the city. The Prophet thought it best to meet the enemy outside, although this meant that he would have to do without the help of the Ansārs or Helpers; for the terms of the agreement were that they would help the Muslims within the walls of Medina. Nevertheless, when the holy Prophet propounded his plans to them, they were ready to follow his lead and help him wherever he went. Thus the tiny army of Muslims, including mere boys, with the Helpers, all poorly armed, marched out of the city of Medina to meet the Quraysh. The Muslims were in all only three hundred and thirteen, while the Quraysh were a thousand strong, all of them fully armed.

Marching until they reached Badr, where they found the enemy encamped, the Muslims were dismayed to find that they were in no way a match for the Quraysh in numbers, arms, or skill. The holy Prophet felt the greatest anxiety for his small band of Muslims and Helpers, and threw himself and his faithful followers on the mercy of God, praying to Him in these words, "O God! if Thou shouldst allow Thy small army of believers to perish, no one will be left on earth to worship Thee and carry Thy message to the world." After praying to God the holy Prophet felt greatly relieved, and, joining his followers, he recited aloud a verse from the holy Quran which reads, "Soon shall the hosts be routed and they shall turn their backs" (54: 45).

The enemy, on the other hand, were fully confident that they would wipe out the Muslims in a very short time. Now according to the instructions of the holy Prophet, Muslims must not be the first to attack. In the olden days, among the Arabs the custom was that at the commencement of a battle a few would come out from one side and call upon a like number from the opposite side. Then they would fight in single combat, man to man, until the fight became general. So after a while the Quraysh sent out three of their men, and three Muslims went to meet them. The Quraysh deemed that the day of their revenge was come at last. Conditions were all in their favour. They knew that they outnumbered the Muslim army by three to one, besides being fully equipped and skilled and well-trained soldiers, while the Muslims— some of them boys and most of them knowing nothing of warfare—were poorly armed, and many of them in tatters. To the mighty Quraysh they looked like a flock of sheep waiting to be butchered.

The three Muslims advanced to meet the Quraysh, expecting never to see their companions again, but it so happened that the three Quraysh were slain, to the astonishment of the whole Quraysh army. A few more went out and a few more were slain, and then the battle became general. It was a proof of the love the Muslims had for Islam; for father fought son and uncle fought nephew. The holy Prophet went among his men, encouraging and helping them. 'Umayr bin Abī Qās, a very young boy whom the Prophet sought to keep from the fight, said, "No, nothing can stand between me and heaven." With these words he plunged into the thickest battle and was slain.

The Quraysh fell upon the Muslims. But the scene that followed was a proof of Divine help; for the poor Muslims held their position and slew the enemy one by one. Nearly all the chiefs and prominent men among the Quraysh were slain, and the rest of the army, seeing all their leaders killed, turned and fled. The Muslims pursued them and captured seventy. In all fourteen of the Muslim army were killed, six Muslims and eight Helpers, while of the enemy seventy fell and seventy were taken prisoners. Thus ended the Battle of Badr, fight of weakness against might; but God sent Divine help to the weak and those in the right. Of this battle the holy Quran speaks in the following verse, "Indeed there was a sign for you in the two hosts which met together in encounter; one party fighting in the way of God, and the other unbelieving. . . . God strengthens with His aid whom He pleases, most surely there is in this a lesson for those who have eyes to see" (3: 12).

During the battle, when the fight was at its fiercest, the holy Prophet, with tears streaming from his eyes, prayed to God to help the poor wounded both among the enemy and among the Muslims. While Abū Jahl, at the same time but on the opposite side, was praying to God to destroy the Muslims utterly. Another interesting incident is that the Quraysh army, before leaving Mecca to attack the Muslims, went to the Sacred House of the Ka'ba and prayed that God might grant victory to those who were in the right. So assured were they of success. Thus, the battle of Badr was the judgment of God. The success of the Muslims had a startling effect on the many neighbouring tribes. How, they wondered, did the puny Muslim army manage to overpower the Quraysh? This set them thinking, and they came to the conclusion that the Muslims must have been helped by some Supreme Being, and many of these after that embraced Islam. Thus we see that as a result of the battle of Badr the strength of the Muslims was increased, while on the other hand the power of the Quraysh was greatly weakened.

The prisoners taken by the Muslims were treated with every kindness, and some of them later embraced Islam. Very often they were given the best of food to eat while the Muslims ate plain dates, and conveyances to ride in while the Muslims walked. After the very cruel manner in which they had been treated by the Quraysh here was an opportunity of paying off old scores, but, needless to say, no revenge was taken. On the receipt of a small ransom they were set free: some of those who were too poor to pay were allowed to go without payment. Those who were learned were asked to instruct ten children, and were then given their liberty. A man of position who had done his best in Mecca to injure Islam, being among the prisoners, was brought to the Prophet, and someone said, "Of all the prisoners, he at least should be punished, for he richly deserves it," but the holy Prophet

133

said, "If I disfigure him, God will disfigure me,"
so he was set free.

The Muslims returned to Medina, the victors of
the battle of Badr, but were left in peace thereafter
by the Quraysh for barely one year.

(*b*) THE BATTLE OF UHUD

(625 A.C.)

> "Thou shalt in no wise reckon
> those who have been slain in the
> cause of God, dead; nay, they
> are sustained alive with their
> Lord rejoicing for what God in
> His favour hath granted them."
> —THE QURAN 3: 163.

THE crushing defeat at Badr did not abate the hatred of the Quraysh one jot, rather did it inflame it the more; for it was a cruel blow to their pride that such a tiny mob of ill-equipped men and boys should have been able to conquer them. As they fled from the field of Badr they called out to the Muslims that next year they would come again to take vengeance for their dead, and revenge became the watchword in Mecca. Having lost all their leaders, the command was now given to Abū Sufyān, who swore he would not rest until he had had his revenge, and it was agreed that all the profits accrued to them from commerce should be spent in the preparation of the contemplated expedition.

Abū Sufyān immediately set about collecting an army. Not being content with the Quraysh alone he endeavoured to secure outside help, and by the end of the year succeeded in collecting three thousand soldiers, including two hundred cavalry, and seven hundred veterans, well armed and equipped. He also included women in his army, so that they might rouse the spirits of the soldiers by their war songs. Thus arrayed, they marched towards Medina in the year 3 A.H. (625 A.C.), and encamped three miles from the city at the foot of the hill called Uhud. Bent upon destruction, they not only cut down all the crops in the fields, but also let loose their camels and horses to graze and do as much damage as possible. When the holy Prophet heard of this, he summoned his companions to discuss the situation and decide on the best plan to adopt.

A short time previously the Prophet had had certain visions which he related to his friends. In these visions he saw that his sword was clipped. This meant some injury to himself. Again, he saw his body covered with a coat of mail. This meant that he and his companions should not venture outside the walls of Medina. In another he saw many cows being killed. This meant danger to his people. So he decided not to go outside Medina to meet the enemy as they had done at the battle of Badr, but to remain within its four walls. The elder among the companions agreed, but the youthful and hot-headed desired to go out and fight in the open. To stay within Medina, they said, would naturally give the enemy the impression that they were afraid. As the majority were of this opinion, the holy Prophet yielded to their wishes, and went to put on his armour and make preparations for their departure. He marched out of Medina at sunset, with a force of a thousand, among them there being only one hundred men properly armed, and two horsemen. They spent the night at a place not far from the city, and at dawn resumed their march. As they neared the enemy, 'Abdullāh bin Ubayy, who had embraced Islam hypocritically after the battle of Badr, deserted the Muslims with his three hundred men. 'Abdullāh bin Ubayy was the leader of a party of Medinites who, though openly with the Muslims, yet were surreptitiously trafficking with Meccans. Thus, because of the treachery of 'Abdullāh bin Ubayy, the Muslim army was left only seven hundred strong, most of them unarmed and unskilled in warfare. The only strength left them was their zeal and enthusiasm to defend the Truth at any cost; and this worked with equal force in the hearts of all, old and young alike. There was a boy who wished to enlist but, being too young, was rejected. He went before the holy Prophet and stretched himself and stood on tiptoe to look taller. He was so very eager to join that in the end the Prophet allowed him to enlist. Seeing this, another little boy came forward. He said he was very strong and he could wrestle with another bigger than himself and throw him. He was permitted to prove his assertion, and after that he, too, was allowed to enlist. A very old man came to the Prophet and said to him, "I am, O Prophet of God, on the very verge of the grave. What a blessing it would be if my life came to an end striking a blow in defence of God's Prophet."

The Prophet, as a skilled general, took up a

position with the rocks of Uhud to protect the rear. He himself arranged the ranks. Only on one side was there a gap through the rocks, and by that way was there danger of attack from the enemy. The Prophet, observing the importance of this, posted fifty archers there with strict orders not to leave the post on any account, even if the Muslims were on the point of defeat.

As to the army of the Quraysh, I have stated that Abū Sufyān was appointed leader. He split up his force into detachments, and gave the command of each to a separate person, he himself taking a central position near the camel which had on it the idol "Hubal," meaning "the greatest God." Besides the women who were there to rouse the men with their war songs, there was a Christian monk and poet, Abū 'Āmir, who also undertook to lash the spirits of the warriors. He was formerly an inhabitant of Medina, where he had wielded great power and influence owing to his spiritual and abstemious life, but later, on the arrival of the Prophet, left Medina. For it was a great blow to him to see the reverence and homage that was once given to him pass to another. He betook himself to Mecca, and thought that by appearing in the Quraysh army he would succeed in inducing the Medinites to desert the Muslims. After the army was drawn up, he stepped out and reminded the Helpers among the Muslims who he was, but he was received with contempt and forced to withdraw.

The battle of Uhud, like all other battles in those days, began with duels, in which 'Alī and

138

Hamza killed many of the enemy. After this the fighting became general and the Muslims fell upon the enemy with fury.

Again, 'Alī, Hamza, and Abū Dujāna displayed their valour and inflicted heavy losses on the foe. Each time they fell on the enemy they caused havoc among the ranks, dealing death on all sides. Hinda, the wife of Abū Sufyān was there—one of the bitterest of all the bitter enemies of the Muslims, and specially of Hamza. She bribed a negro slave to kill him at the first opportunity, which he did, taking him unawares and killing him with his javelin. She thought that with the fall of Hamza the Muslims would lose heart and the battle as well. But events proved that she was wrong; for, thereafter, the Muslims fought all the more desperately. Many of the Meccan standard-bearers fell, as well as a good number of their trained soldiers. Seeing their brave ones slain one after the other caused such utter confusion and panic among the Quraysh that they took to flight, closely pursued by the Muslims. Once more the Muslims were on the point of securing another glorious victory over the Meccans, and would assuredly have done so but for the disobedience of the archers who had been left to guard the gap in the rocks. Seeing the Meccans put to flight and believing the Muslims to be victorious they disobeyed the orders of their Commander to join in the pursuit. Khālid bin Walīd, who commanded the cavalry of the Quraysh army, observing this, turned with his two hundred men and fell upon the Muslim army in the rear.

This gave heart to the fleeing Meccans, who, seeing Khālid attack the scattered Muslims, stopped in their flight, and, turning, also pressed upon the Muslims, who were thus attacked on both sides.

The holy Prophet, who had kept behind with Talha and Sa'd, seeing Khālid sweep down on the Muslim rear through the gap deserted by the archers, at once realized the grave danger to which they were exposed. There were only two courses left to him—to fly and leave his army to its fate, or to risk his life and call out to the men to make them aware of their danger. To the Prophet the former course was out of the question. He shouted with all his might, "Rally to me, I am the Prophet of God!" Hearing the Prophet's voice, the Muslims immediately turned and perceived the danger they were in. But in warning the Prophet had made himself the target of the enemy. Deeming him the cause of all the trouble, they were determined to kill him. His faithful companions defended him from the shower of arrows as best they could. One by one they fell round him, saving his life at the cost of their own. Mus'ab bin 'Umayr, the standard-bearer of the Prophet, fell. He greatly resembled the Prophet in appearance. Someone thought he was the Prophet. The cry went up that the Prophet was slain. The news spread like wild-fire among the Muslims, causing grief and greater confusion. Some lost heart and laid down their arms, saying that there was no use fighting any longer, seeing that the Prophet was dead. Then one of the Companions said, "If our Prophet is not among us, let us at least continue to fight for the cause for which he fought and died." These words put fresh heart into them and they took up their swords and fell upon the enemy. They soon learnt, to their intense relief, that the Prophet was still alive and, clustering round him, withstood bravely the terrible attacks the enemy were making. But meanwhile the holy Prophet had received serious injuries, and unable to stand any longer, through loss of blood, he collapsed. His faithful followers made a wall round him with their own bodies. The enemy tried their best to break it, but to no purpose; for as fast as one man fell another took his place. To show how men and women, to save the life of the Prophet, exposed themselves to danger, the name of a woman, Nasība bint Ka'b, must be mentioned. She, it is said, dropped a water-jug to fight near the Prophet with her husband and sons, seized the shield of a Muslim and defended the ground step by step although she was wounded thirteen times. Her son was struck by her side. She bound his wound and sent him back to fight.

By this time order had been restored in the Muslim ranks, which, having retreated to a safe position, were now able to put up a good fight and to repulse the attacks of the enemy every time. The Quraysh soon gave up all hopes of crushing the Muslims; for they were now at a disadvantage, being entirely exposed to the shower of arrows while the Muslims themselves were sheltered from their arrows and stones. In the end they decided

141

to retreat, and with bitterness of frustration vented their hatred on the dead bodies of the Muslims.

Vile acts of barbarity were committed on the dead. Hinda, the wife of Abū Sufyān, who had hated Hamza and was the cause of his death, seeing his dead body lying, ripped it open, tore out the liver and chewed it. She then took his intestines and garlanded herself with them.

The Quraysh preferred to gratify their hatred by pillaging the dead bodies of Muslims while their women insulted the dead Muslims. They cut off their noses and ears to make necklaces, bracelets, and belts. Abū Sufyān ran about the battlefield, hoping to find the Prophet's body. He recognized the dead body of his son amongst the ranks of the Muslims. He then advanced towards the summit of Mount Uhud where the Prophet was standing with his faithful followers. "Is Muhammad with you?" Abū Sufyān cried. Muhammad forbade them to answer. "And Abū Bakr, is he there? And 'Omar?" called out Abū Sufyān. The Muslims did not speak. "Then all of them are slain; had they been alive they must have responded," said Abū Sufyān. "You lie!" called out one of the Prophet's companions, who could no longer contain himself. "In any case the victory is ours," replied Abū Sufyān. "To us alone, if God wills," said the Muslims. "All days," said Abū Sufyān, "are not alike. To-day makes up for Badr. War has its ups and downs. You will find the bodies of your dead mutilated. . . . I invite you to meet me again next year at the well of Badr so that we may measure our strength again." And Abū Sufyān began to intone a chant composed in the rajaz metre: "Be praised, O Hubal, be praised. Thy religion has triumphed." "God is the greatest and most magnificent," answered the Muslims. "We have Al-'Uzzā and you have not Al-'Uzzā," continued Abū Sufyān. And the Prophet said to his companions, "Have you no answer to that?" "What shall we say, O Prophet of God?" "Say," said Muhammad, "God is our protector and you have no protector."

It was here that while arrows were being showered on him, the Prophet addressed these words to God, "O God! forgive my countrymen; for they know not." This shows that the Prophet had a heart full of mercy even for the enemy.

Thus ended the battle of Uhud, in victory to none. The enemy were perplexed on the question of their retreat. What were they to say on their return to Mecca? Not that they had been victorious; for they had neither the spoils of victory nor the prisoners of war to show to their people. So after retreating some distance, they halted to ponder over this and decide what was to be done. Someone suggested going back to fight to the finish, but there was no response to this. For the courage and spirits of all were too low to permit them to go back and face the Muslims again. The Muslims, on the other hand, were asked by the Prophet if they would like to give chase to the enemy, and every one among them, though almost exhausted, gladly responded to the call. Meanwhile the Quraysh

143

army were still wavering over the best course to adopt, when the news reached them that the Muslims were after them. This was too much for Abū Sufyān, who gathered his men together and quickly marched off.

It has been said that the Muslims were defeated at the battle of Uhud. Such a verdict merely betrays lack of knowledge of the actual facts. It is true that the losses of the Muslims were heavy, but, nevertheless, it would be wrong to assert that they were defeated. Would it be possible, I ask, for the defeated to be the last to leave the field of battle, while the victorious march off without any prisoners or spoils of war? Or would the defeated have the courage to follow the victors a few hours after the battle, and the victors themselves decamp when they hear of the pursuit?

No doubt it could not be called a complete victory to the Muslims, yet it could not be called a defeat either. For it was the Muslims who held the field to the last and saw the enemy retreat before them. The loss of so many among them did not cause the Muslims to lose heart, although it is true that the enemy rejoiced at the large number of Muslim dead. They thought that thereby the power of Islam had been greatly reduced. But they forgot that Islam is imperishable. To quote the words of Dr. Sir Mohammad Iqbāl, the philosopher-poet of India, "Islam is like a rubber ball, that bounces the higher the harder it is hit."

CHAPTER 13

TRIALS OF THE MUSLIMS AFTER THE BATTLE OF UHUD

> "And be not infirm and be not grieving, and you shall have the upper hand if you are believers."
> —THE QURAN 3 : 138.

IN preparing for the battle of Uhud, the Quraysh had spared no pains nor expense in getting together a skilled and well-equipped army before embarking on such a gigantic expedition. Although the Quraysh were not victorious there was a deep current of unrest among all the Arab tribes. They felt sure the Quraysh would not be long in raising another and a larger army, and that soon the fate of the small band of Muslims would be sealed. With a view to have a share in the honour of having overpowered the Muslims, tribes here and there were even preparing to join the Quraysh in molesting the Muslims. Again, the Jewish tribes in Medina, who had entered into a covenant with the Muslims that they would render them help when necessary, had broken their promises, and sided with the Quraysh. Besides this, there was yet another faction known as the Hypocrites in Islamic terminology, whose existence in the Muslim camp was dangerous, because they had access to all the plans and secrets of the Muslims. These were the

K 145

men who had not the courage to offer opposition to Islam openly. They believed that they could more successfully undermine the strength of the Islamic society of Medina by joining it. The Hypocrites, too, decided to come out in the open and trouble the Muslims in every possible way. Other neighbouring tribes, seeing how the Muslims were situated, also commenced making preparations to attack them. Once more the Muslims found themselves in grave danger, both within and without the city of Medina. The holy Prophet was deeply concerned as to the welfare of those who had given up all to follow him. As their leader he was bound to take thought for the good of his people, and he found that the lives of his faithful followers were in constant danger. They were surrounded on all sides by bitter foes. It was an extremely anxious time for the Muslims. Day and night they were compelled to be armed, not knowing when they would be attacked. The stress and strain of those days soon told on them; their patience and energy were entirely exhausted. In despair they went to the holy Prophet to tell him how unbearable things had become. The Prophet did his best to cheer them. He begged them not to give up hope. He assured them that God would not desert them in their hour of need, and that they would soon be in safety and peace again.

One day at dawn there was a great uproar at the gates of the city. The Muslims, thinking that they had been attacked, quickly gathered and prepared to march out to meet the enemy. To their

146

surprise they saw the holy Prophet galloping towards them. At the beginning of the uproar he had immediately ridden out to see what the trouble was, and returned to tell his people that there was no cause for anxiety. This proved to the Muslims again the intrepidity of their Prophet. He had ridden out alone and unarmed to see what had caused the uproar, and if the enemy had indeed come to attack the Muslims they would, seeing the Prophet alone, have immediately taken the opportunity of killing him.

In spite of the grave danger, the Muslims continued their mission of conversion, although they did not meet with any great success. Preachers would commit the holy Quran to memory and try to spread the truth to members of one tribe or another. But treacherous persons, thinking this a good opportunity of doing away with a few Muslims on the sly, would invite preachers on the pretext of being instructed, and once having them at their mercy would cruelly put them to death. Once Abū Barā, the chief of certain tribes, came himself to the holy Prophet with some valuable presents. He told the Prophet that his people were inclined to embrace Islam, and asked him to send with him a few preachers. The Prophet refused the presents and told Abū Barā that he feared treachery, but Abū Barā assured the Prophet that he could be trusted and that the preachers would be quite safe with him. This convinced the Prophet, and he sent seventy. These went a short distance out of Medina with Abū Barā. Then they were met by a large army and all of them cruelly put to death, with the exception of 'Amrū Umayya, who alone managed to escape to Medina and give details of the terrible experience to the Prophet and the Muslims.

After some time the people of a place called Rajī' sent word that they had become Muslims, and wanted the Prophet to send some preachers to instruct them more fully. The holy Prophet sent ten, who met with the same sad fate as the former seventy; eight were killed and two, Zayd and Khubayb, were sold as slaves. Khubayb was executed by his master and Zayd was bought by Safwān bin Umayya for the same purpose. At his execution Abū Sufyān and other Quraysh leaders were present. Just as he was about to be beheaded, Abū Sufyān said to him, "Would you like your life to be spared on condition that Muhammad was slain instead?" and Zayd replied at the last moments of his life when the sword was ready to cut off his head: "My life is nothing compared with the holy Prophet's; I would give my life if it would save him even the prick of a thorn."

In fact, during that time, the whole of Arabia was against Islam. Idolaters, Jews, and Hypocrites, all were against the Muslims, doing their utmost to destroy them. This torturing and killing of innocent men was heart-breaking to the Prophet. He would willingly suffer any hardship himself; he would fain undergo any torture, but it was a sore grief to him to see his faithful followers thus treated. The tale of misery is too long and painful to tell in detail.

Affairs were going from bad to worse, and the holy Prophet realized that if he failed to adopt some sort of policy soon the Muslims would be compelled to flee from Medina. At this time the enemy were separate and not united. Each tribe in itself was an enemy to Islam. Therefore, in these circumstances, the only practical plan left to the Muslims was to attack these tribes quickly before they had time gradually to unite into one large army and be sufficiently strong to overthrow the Muslims completely. Being compelled to defend themselves, several small battles or skirmishes took place one after the other. The first of these was known as the battle of Badr Sughrā, and the next the battle of Badr Ākhira. Then came the battle of Dūmatu 'l-Jandal and that of Zātu 'r-Riqā', both in the year 5 A.H. (627 A C.). Two more followed in the year 6 A.H. (628 A.C.), the battle of Zū Qaradā and the battle of Banū Lihyān.

Several other such skirmishes took place. But it was in the battle of Banū Mustaliq that the Muslims completely defeated the inhabitants of Muraysī' and took six hundred of them prisoners, including the chief of the tribe, Hāris bin abī Zirār, his daughter and two sons. His daughter Juwayriya the Prophet married later at her own request. After the marriage, the six hundred prisoners belonging to her tribe were set free.

While the Muslims were thus busily engaged in several minor operations against neighbouring Arab tribes, the Quraysh in Mecca were by no means inactive. They were rapidly collecting and preparing a large army in order again to attack the Muslims in Medina. They succeeded in getting the Jewish tribes settled in Khaybar to join them, and also managed to secure the help of Bedouin tribes living in the neighbourhood of Mecca. Thus, again, the Quraysh marched towards Medina, with the determination this time to conquer the Muslims. The battle that followed was known as the battle of Khandaq.

CHAPTER 14

THE BATTLE OF KHANDAQ OR AHZĀB

(627 A.C.)

> "O you who believe! call to mind
> the favour of God to you when
> there came down upon you hosts,
> and We sent against them a strong
> wind and hosts that you saw not,
> and God sees what you do."—
> THE QURAN 33 : 9.

ABU SUFYAN, on the occasion of the retreat of the army of the Quraysh after the battle of Uhud, had said that they would return next year and inflict a most crushing defeat on the Muslims. True to his word, when next year came he left Mecca at the head of a large army, but on reaching Marru 'z-Zahrān was compelled to return owing to famine. He then busied himself in further strengthening his force, and, as I have stated before, succeeded in getting active support from the Jewish clans, and also in rousing neighbouring Bedouins against Islam. Thus it seemed that all the elements in Arabia were joined at last to inflict the final crushing blow on Islam. After mobilizing a huge army, consisting of the Quraysh themselves, the Jews, and the Bedouin tribes, they left Mecca and proceeded to Medina in the fifth year of the Hegira (627 A.C.).

The Prophet, being informed of the approach of

151

this army, hurriedly summoned the Companions together to devise means to meet the situation. It was a question of great importance; for something had to be decided upon soon to save the Muslims from being entirely wiped out. Salmān, the Persian, suggested that a deep and wide trench should be dug round the city. This was agreed to by all. The work of digging was commenced at once, as there was no time to be lost. The Prophet allocated the task among parties of ten men each, he himself taking part in the digging like the rest. Fortunately the city had on one side a natural barrier of huge rugged rocks; and on the other it was protected by the high stone walls of houses, so the digging of the trench was confined to the two remaining sides. The Muslims set to work cheerfully, and while digging recited verses from the Quran. The holy Prophet is the only example in history of a person holding spiritual and temporal power working like an ordinary labourer with others. After a time the work of one of the groups came to a standstill because of an obstruction caused by a large block of stone. They were quite exhausted in attempting to break it, and asked others to join them in breaking it. But the block would not break. The Prophet then got into the ditch and with his pickaxe struck the stone, which moved a little and gave out a spark at the same time. The Companions, seeing the spark, cried together with one voice, "God is Great," and to the Prophet it was revealed in that spark that he would be given the keys of the palace of the Syrian King. Another

stroke at the stone and it was cracked; and at the
same time another spark of fire appeared, and the
Companions shouted, "God is Great," and to
the Prophet was revealed that he would be given
the keys of the Persian Kingdom. The third time he
struck at the stone it broke into little pieces, and
the Prophet said to the Companions that he was
made aware that even the keys of the Yemen
would be his, and that his followers would have
sovereignty over all nations.

It was an extremely anxious time for the Muslims
when a huge force of nearly 24,000 strong was
almost at the very gates ready to crush them. The
whole city seemed shaken to its very foundations.
The holy Quran pictures this in the following
words: "When they came upon you from above
you and from below you, and when the eyes turned
dull and the hearts rose up to the throats, and you
began to think diverse thoughts about God . . ."
(9: 10).

As to the advance of the enemy, it must be said
it seemed like a veritable cyclone, determined to
sweep away every obstacle in its path; but in spite
of this the Muslims were full of courage, feeling
well assured that this was the last desperate attempt
of a dying foe. Having now fortified the town
against attack from without, there still remained
the danger of attack from within, as a precaution
against which the women and children were
removed to a place of safety.

The enemy approaching Medina met their first
set-back when they discovered the deep trench

which had been dug around the town. They decided to settle down to a siege which lasted a month, and caused great suffering and starvation to the Muslims, including the holy Prophet himself. But hardship and privation failed to damp the spirits of the Muslims. Knowing of the willing Helpers among them, the Prophet suggested buying help from the tribe of Ghatafān by offering them one-third of the produce of Medina. This would also weaken the strength of the enemy a great deal. But the Helpers, hearing of the plan, did not wish it to be carried out. They and the others held it was beneath their dignity to do such a thing. "Come what may, we will fight to the last," was their slogan.

In spite of all precautions the Jews and the Hypocrites were on the lookout for an opportunity to rise from within Medina. Mention of the word "Hypocrites" reminds me to deal with it more fully, for it bears a special significance in the history and phraseology of Islam. As long as the Prophet and the Muslims were in Mecca opposition towards them was open and took the form of torments and cruelties. But in Medina it was of a special and unique form. In order to undermine Islam, and bring about its fall from within, the Jews, now afraid of losing their power because of the eminence of Islam and others, started becoming Muslims in name only, 'Abdullah bin Ubayy was at the head of these. Before the arrival of the Prophet in Medina 'Abdullah wielded great power and authority and would have been made king, but the presence of the Prophet eclipsed his personality. He found it difficult to accept a second place where he had once stood first. At the outset he had offered some opposition, but the rapid growth of Islam led him to reconsider his position and adopt Hypocrisy as the best policy. He, therefore, became Muslim, but left no stone unturned in bringing trouble to Islam, and many others followed his example.

It was, therefore, natural for the Muslims to be most wary of these Hypocrites; for the danger from within was becoming as dangerous as that from without. Finally the Prophet decided to give battle, and as usual several duels were fought first in which the Muslims succeeded. 'Alī killed 'Amrū bin Wadd, who was believed to be a match for a thousand, and, indeed, had there been no 'Alī to act as the Prophet's right hand, the result would have been different.

In the end, the Quraysh made a general attack but failed to cross the deep trench. Only their arrows and stones came down in terrible showers, and had it not been for the firmness of the Muslims the enemy would have won the battle. It was, in short, their steadfastness which brought them success. The enemy became weary of the siege, and exhausted in their fruitless attempts to cross the trench. Their provisions had run short, yet they hesitated to retreat. One night a fierce storm broke over them. It blew all their tents away, and caused terrible havoc among their stores and munitions. It seemed to the Quraysh that the very elements of nature were against them. They took it as an evil omen, and next night retreated. The holy Quran alludes to this incident in the following words, "Then We sent down against them a strong wind and hosts that you could not see" (33 : 9).

This clearly shows that there was the Divine Hand at work, which frustrated all attempts of the enemy to crush the handful of Muslims.

Thus the most powerfully organized expedition against Islam failed utterly in accomplishing the task, in which at its outset it was doggedly determined to succeed.

CHAPTER 15

MUSLIM WARS WITH THE JEWS OF MEDINA

(623–627 A.C.)

> "What! whenever an Apostle came to you with that which your souls did not desire, you were insolent, some you called liars and some you slay."—THE QURAN 20: 87.

THE Jews in Medina, who formed a large portion of the population, were also the most wealthy and learned among the inhabitants. When the Prophet first arrived in Medina he entered into an agreement with them, but the steadily growing influence of Islam made them jealous and fearful lest the Muslims should soon eclipse their power in Medina. In secret they kept on friendly terms with the Hypocrites, and devised plans to cause trouble to the Muslims.

The morals of the Jews had become most degenerate, and many verses touching their immorality were revealed to the holy Prophet. As a Prophet he felt it his duty to preach to them, and teach them to depart from evil and sin, and follow the right path. Besides their resentment at the preachings of the Prophet amongst them, the principal cause that led to their antagonism towards Islam was the ever-diminishing of their influence over the Medinites, who were coming more rapidly than ever under the influence of Islam. Soon what began as jealousy turned into positive hatred, as a result of which hostilities that formerly were carried on in secret now became open. The Prophet himself was not spared. They even spoke to him with insolence. For example, instead of saying the Muslim greeting "Salāmo 'Alayk," they would go up to the Prophet and say "Assāmo 'Alayk," which meant "Death be on you," while the former meant "Peace be on you," or, while speaking to him, instead of using the word "rā'inā," which meant "listen to us," they would shorten the accent and say instead "ra'ina" meaning "you are a fool." Another method of theirs of harming Islam was to become Muslims, and shortly after to become unbelievers again; so that others might think there was something seriously amiss with the teachings of Islam. Besides, in the short time they were in the fold of Islam, they would do their best to make other Muslims follow them and apostate. They also turned their efforts to cause enmity between two important tribes of Medina, the Aus and the Khazraj. Had they succeeded in doing this, it would have broken the strength of the Muslims completely, but the timely arrival of the Prophet foiled their attempt. Gradually matters came to such a pass that the lives of the Muslims became endangered.

They made insulting insinuations against Muslim womenfolk, and even composed verses concerning them. They went so far as to molest them in the street. An incident which caused great friction, and led to a skirmish called the battle of Qaynuqā', arose because a Medinite woman went to the shop of a Jew where she was outraged. A Muslim passing heard the cries, and, going in, he was so infuriated that he slew the Jew, seeing which other Jews who had gathered there slew the Muslim. On hearing this, the holy Prophet went to the Jews and asked them to refrain from such things in future, warning them that like the Quraysh they would be punished. The Jews answered that they would prove in open fight that they were not cowards like the Quraysh. As this was an open challenge, the Prophet accepted it, and gave orders to the Muslims to make ready to fight the Jews. Having thus broken their compact with the Muslims, the Jews decided to fight. But finding the Muslims ready for battle they locked themselves up in a fort. The siege that followed lasted fifteen days. At the end of which period the Jews surrendered and agreed to accept any decision the Prophet might make. They were told to leave Medina immediately, which they did, seven hundred of them departing and settling in Syria.

The Banū Nazīr was another Jewish clan that broke its agreement with the Muslims, and was in secret on friendly terms with the Quraysh. Once the Quraysh wrote to them to do their utmost to make short work of the holy Prophet. In this they nearly succeeded. It so happened that the Prophet had occasion to visit them on business, and while conversing with them was standing under a balcony. The Jews thought that this was an excellent opportunity of carrying out their intention. Two of them went up on the balcony, one carrying a huge stone, which, if it had hit the Prophet, would have killed him instantaneously. Just in time the Prophet felt a warning impulse and moved away from his place. Later they made another attempt on his life. They sent an invitation asking the Prophet and three Companions to visit them. The Prophet agreed, but when nearing their place he was again made aware that they meant mischief, and immediately returned.

The position became so dangerous that it was decided to check the Banū Nazīr by fighting them in open battle. Like the Banū Qaynuqā', they fortified themselves in their quarters, and the Muslims besieged them. This siege also lasted for about two weeks, at the end of which time the Banū Nazīr surrendered, and asked the Prophet, as a punishment, to allow them to leave Medina as the other tribes had done. The request having been acceded to they left Medina in a great procession, taking as much of their movable property as could be taken on their camels. The procession was preceded by a band playing and women singing. The little property they left behind included weapons of warfare, and of these the Muslims took possession. Some of the Banū Nazīr settled in Khaybar. Others scattered and settled elsewhere.

The only Jewish tribe now left in Medina was the Banū Qurayza. As they had not been guilty of any treachery against the Muslims, they were allowed to renew their agreement with the Muslims. But the Banū Nazīr, although banished and scattered, were still bent on causing trouble to Islam. They roamed about the desert stirring other tribes against the Muslims. Seeing the Banū Qurayza and Muslims on friendly terms they did their best to cause a rift in this friendship. In the beginning the Banū Qurayza were by no means anxious to quarrel with the Muslims, but the Banū Nazīr informed them that all tribes, including the Quraysh, were combining forces to attack the Muslims who, they believed, had not the slightest chance of survival. The Muslims, on learning of this tribal concatenation, offered the Banū Qurayza the choice between an alliance with the Muslims and throwing in their lot with the other tribes. The Banū Qurayza chose the latter. Thus we see that the new compact made with the Muslims was broken by the Banū Qurayza during the battle of Khandaq, and that they, with the Hypocrites, were a constant danger to the Muslims within Medina; while 24,000 men on the other side of the trench just outside Medina were exerting every ounce of their strength to enter and entirely crush out the Muslims. At the conclusion of the battle of Khandaq the Muslims thought it was high time to inflict on the Banū Qurayza the punishment they so richly deserved for their treachery. They, like the other Jewish tribes, betook themselves to a fortified stronghold. A siege followed, and they were soon forced to surrender. The Banū Qurayza then asked the Prophet to allow Sa'd bin Mu'āz, a former ally of theirs, to choose what punishment they deserved. The Prophet agreed. Had it been left to the Prophet to decide the punishment they would have been exiled like the other tribes. But Sa'd was not so lenient. Their offence, he said, was too grave to be passed off with a light punishment; moreover, he wanted to make an example of them to other tribes. So the punishment he decided upon was the very same that the Banū Qurayza themselves had been wont to inflict on their fallen foes. The punishment was that every male member of the tribe should be sentenced to death, and the women and children taken prisoners, and the property confiscated.

Thus, in obedience to the verdict of Sa'd, the judge chosen by the Banū Qurayza themselves, three hundred, the whole male portion of the tribe, were put to death.

CHAPTER 16

THE MEDINITE PERIOD BEFORE THE BATTLE
OF KHAYBAR

(626 A.C.)

> "Surely He has given thee a clear
> victory."—THE QURAN 48:1.

W E have seen that in the two first battles of
Badr and Uhud, the Quraysh had tried their
best to bring about the downfall of Islam, and that
on each occasion it was nothing but the Divine
assistance that led to the rout of the enemy. The
neighbouring Jewish tribes, as well as the Bedouins,
also failed in their attempts and so did the Hypocrites in their efforts to harm Islam from within.
Each thus frustrated separately they all made
common cause to achieve jointly that which they
separately had proved themselves unable to accomplish. But here, too, the hand of God was with
the Muslims and gave them a glorious victory;
a victory so great that never again had the enemy
the courage to march on Medina. Let those who
think that Islam prevailed because of the sword
pause and study these battles of history, and I am
convinced that they will come to this conclusion:
that "Islam spread, not by the sword, but in spite
of the sword." The separate and joint attacks of
the enemy conclusively prove that these storms did

not even blight the religion which the Prophet of
Arabia had come to teach—a sure proof that Divine
help was with them.

A year after the battle of Khandaq the Prophet
saw in a vision that he, with his Companions, was
performing the pilgrimage. This led him to think
that at last the enemy had come to know the
Muslim strength, and to realize that there was some
inherent power in Islam which successfully withstood their onslaughts. Therefore, the Prophet took
the vision concerning the pilgrimage to be a sign
for him to go on pilgrimage and thus impress upon
them the spiritual greatness of Islam as well; he
also thought that as pilgrimage was a privilege
denied to none, it would not be denied to the
Muslims. With this end in view, in the 6th A.H.
(626 A.C.), with fourteen hundred Companions, he
set out for Mecca to perform the pilgrimage; but to
avoid misunderstanding, as well as to impress upon
the Quraysh the peacefulness of the Muslim intentions, the Prophet ordered that none should carry
arms, though it was then the usual thing to wear a
sword, however peaceful the conditions. So with
their sacrificial animals they started for Mecca. But
the Quraysh, whose animosity was by no means
dead, made ready to offer resistance to the Muslims.
Budayl, the chief of the tribe of Khuzā'a, though
not himself a Muslim, nevertheless, out of his
regard for Islam, informed the Prophet of the
intentions of the Quraysh, who had posted themselves outside Mecca so as to close all the approaches
and bar the entry of the Muslims. The Prophet

sent back Budayl to inform the Quraysh that the Muslims were come to perform pilgrimage and not to fight, and to suggest the Quraysh to enter into a truce with the Muslims for a certain period. The Prophet at this time was halting at a place called Hudaybiyya, till the conclusion of the terms with the Quraysh, but as the Quraysh were anxious not to let go a chance of killing a Muslim, they advanced slowly towards the Muslim camp with intent to slay any unwary Muslim who might cross their path. The wiser of the Quraysh were in favour of accepting the peace, because they knew that they could not hope to do any harm to the Muslims, especially when on every occasion of war they had failed to do so. They, therefore, agreed to depute 'Urwa as their spokesman to conclude terms of truce with the Muslims. 'Urwa came to the Prophet, but the negotiations were a fiasco, and ended in an instructive incident. 'Urwa, in the course of discussions, advised the Prophet not to place too much reliance in his followers, imputing that they were as likely as not to desert him in the hour of need. Nevertheless, he went back highly impressed with the faithfulness of the Muslims, because while he was there the time for prayer came, and when the Prophet performed the ablutions, so intense was the love of his followers towards him that they did not let even a drop of the waste water fall on the ground.

"By God!" said 'Urwa on his return to the Quraysh, "Muhammad cannot even spit but that one of his followers gathers it up to smear his face with it, and after he has washed they fight for his bath-water! I have been on embassies to princes; to the Caesar, to the Chosroes, and the Negus; but I have never seen a sovereign so well obeyed as Muhammad." Two other emissaries received the same impression.

Not disheartened by the first failure of the peace talks the Prophet sent another messenger; but he was maltreated, the camel on which he rode being killed. As a further sign of hostility a detachment of the Quraysh set out to kill as many of the Muslims as possible, but was itself taken prisoner. As the Muslims were not intent upon fighting they let them go, and this time sent 'Usman to negotiate. As soon as 'Usman arrived he was captured, and the rumour spread in the Muslim camp that he had been murdered, which led them to fear that the Quraysh were bent upon war. The Muslims were unarmed and numerically inferior. To all appearance, it was a most critical period for them, and it was only their firm faith in the Divine protection that kept their heads cool. They were unarmed, as I have said, and the enemy bent on bloodshed; in these circumstances the Prophet called on them to take a fresh oath that they would fight to the very last man, and they cheerfully took it. This is known in Muslim history as the *Bay'atu 'r-Rizwān* or "The Pledge of Rizwān." This resolve of the Muslims to shed the last drop of blood in the cause of God reached the Quraysh and brought them to their senses. They realized then that whatever their number or strength might be, they would never succeed in overthrowing this band of devotees, who fought like men endowed with supernatural strength. Their past experience told them that they had no chance against the Muslims. Realizing all their disadvantages they sent one Suhayl bin 'Amrū to come to terms with the Muslims. Thus an agreement known as the Truce of Huday biyya was drawn up. The parties agreed to maintain peace for ten years on the following conditions:—

1. The Muslims should return that year without performing the pilgrimage;
2. Next year they should perform the pilgrimage, but must not stay more than three days at Mecca;
3. They must not take back with them any Muslims then living in Mecca, nor must they stand in the way of any one of their own number who might wish to remain in Mecca;
4. They must surrender any Meccan going to settle in Medina, but if any of the Medina Muslims should go to Mecca, the Meccans would not send him back to Medina; and lastly,
5. The Arab tribes will be free to make what alliances they would with either party.

The Muslims in general were far from satisfied with these terms, which they regarded as humiliating, and an incident which occurred during the drawing up of the treaty also tended to infuriate them. But thanks to the influence of the Prophet they kept quiet. 'Alī, who was chosen to reduce the agreement into writing, began with the words, "Bismillāhi 'r-Rahmānī 'r-Rahīm," i.e. "In the name of God the Compassionate, the Merciful." But the Meccans would have none of it, and insisted on the traditional opening: "In thy name, O God!" and to this the Prophet agreed. Further on 'Alī came to the words, "This is an Agreement between Muhammad, the Apostle of God, and the Quraysh." The Meccans again objected, saying, "If we were to admit that you are the Apostle of God, why all this bloodshed?" But 'Alī refused to erase the words "Apostle of God," and the Prophet himself had to do this, bidding him put "Muhammad, son of 'Abdullāh," instead.

Soon after these terms were concluded, one Abū Jandal, a Muslim, who was in Mecca and being tortured, came over to the Muslims, thinking that by so doing he would be safe. He showed the scars on his body, which moved the Prophet to try to get an exception in his case, but Suhayl would have none of it, and demanded that the man be returned. The Prophet had to yield and hand him over to the Quraysh. 'Omar was indignant at this apparent weakness of the Prophet, and the Muslims also remonstrated, but to no purpose. The Prophet, saying that it was a great hour of trial, exhorted them to remain true to their vows, and also consoled Abū Jandal, telling him that he should fear nothing in the cause of God. I have shown that the Muslims felt this truce to be most humiliating to themselves, yet on his return to Medina the Prophet received the revelation, "Surely We have

given to you a clear victory" (THE QURAN 48: 1).
On the receipt of which the Prophet sent for
'Omar, the most indignant of all, and told him
that what he considered a defeat was really a great
victory in the eyes of God.

Events that followed amply show that this truce
was, indeed, a victory for the Muslims; for, in the
following year, on the occasion of pilgrimage there
were ten thousand men with the Prophet instead
of the fourteen hundred he had had on the occasion
of the truce. This increase in the number of Muslims was due to no other cause than the treaty
which the Muslims had thought humiliating. The
truce of Hudaybiyya, in fact, bridged the gulf that
had yawned between Muslims and non-Muslims
because of the existence of the state of warfare.
The truce went a long way to bring them together,
because the Muslims could mix freely with the
Quraysh and imbue them with their ideas and
morals. During the truce the Quraysh also could
come into contact with the Muslims and discover
that those under the influence of the Prophet were
superior in morality and unity. So long as the
barrier of warfare existed the Arabs had no time
to appreciate the moral edification brought about
by Islam. Until then, their sole aim in life had been
to devise plans for the annihilation of the Muslims.
Now they came to know that the Prophet was quite
other than the person they imagined, and soon
found out that his teachings were for the well-
being and good of mankind. They realized that
they had been led astray in their estimate of his

169

character; for now they saw that it was above reproach, kind and invigorating. It was this impression, wrought on them by the peaceful conditions brought about by the truce, that effected their conversion to the new faith.

Following the revelation referred to above comes this: "That God may rectify for you that which has gone before of the faults attributed to you and that which remains behind, and complete His favour to you, and guide you on a right way. And that God might help you with a mighty help" (THE QURAN 48: 2–3). These words were amply fulfilled by the conversion of a large number to the new faith. All the imputations that had been heaped upon him were removed by close contact, and his sterling qualities were made manifest to the Arabs. As to the words "That which remains behind," the happenings of to-day are a proof. Europe is gradually discovering, now that it is in closer contact with Muslims, that what its historians wrote of the holy Prophet is far from being true.

It is thus clear that the harsh terms of Hudaybiyya accepted by the Prophet were because of a Divine purpose, and also by reason of the peace-loving nature of the Prophet. The Muslims had defeated the Quraysh almost on all occasions, and in spite of being unarmed they could have done so this time as well; but the Prophet in his inclination towards mercy could not neglect the chance for peace, however slight it might be. The Quran, too, confirms this in its words, "And if the Quraysh incline towards peace, thou shalt also incline towards it" (8: 61).

On his return the Prophet found that with his mind at rest about war he could do much to bring about some realization of his mission. So far his efforts confined to the Arabs only, and of them only such as belonged to the Hedjaz. Now, after this truce, he sent envoys to neighbouring sovereigns inviting them to embrace Islam. Two of the embassies were especially despatched to the Emperor of the Greeks, and the Chosroes of Persia. The latter was amazed at the audacity of the fugitive of Mecca in addressing him on equal terms, and indignantly tore up the letter. When this news was brought to the Prophet, he said: "Thus shall the Kingdom of the Chosroes be torn to pieces"; and this prophecy was duly fulfilled, as history tells us. When the emissary of the Prophet reached the court of the Roman Emperor, Abū Sufyān, the arch-enemy of the Prophet and Islam, was also there, and the Emperor summoned him to his presence to enquire about the Prophet. When questioned about Muhammad, Abū Sufyān bore witness to the character of the Prophet.

"Did you make war against him?" asked the Emperor Heraclius.

"Yes," replied Abū Sufyān.

"Who was the victor?" inquired Heraclius.

"Once he was—once we were," said Abū Sufyān.

"Does he keep his word?" asked the Emperor.

"We are," said Abū Sufyān, "at the present time actually at peace with him, but we do not know how he will observe it."

"What does he believe?" asked the Emperor.

171

"He asks us," said Abū Sufyān, "to give up the faith of our fathers, to worship one God, to pay the poor-rate, to keep our word, and to abstain from fornication."

This account of Islam, and by an avowed enemy at that, impressed the Emperor highly. He called a meeting of prominent personages, and tried to win them over to his views of Islam. He told them that the adoption of Islam would increase their well-being. But they all resented this suggestion of his. To save appearances he had to say that he was only testing their integrity. He died, it is said, without making public confession of his faith.

The despatch to Persia that was torn up by the Chosroes was couched in the following terms: "In the name of God, the Beneficent and Merciful, Muhammad the Apostle of God invites you . . ." Another epistle was sent to the Negus of Abyssinia. He honoured the emissary and embraced Islam.

The emissary sent to the governor of Basra in the confines of Syria was killed at Mūta by an Arab of the tribe of the Ghassan, Christian vassals of the Emperor Heraclius. To avenge his death Muhammad sent Zayd bin Hāritha with three thousand men under orders to sweep Mūta with an invasion, but to spare women, children, the blind, and the monks and avoid the destruction of houses and trees. But the Muslims ran up against a strong army of the Ghassan and some Greeks. As they did not know how to form squares they were routed by the enemy's cavalry. Zayd was mortally wounded and gave the standard over to

Ja'far, the brother of 'Alī, as it fell from his hand. He heroically defended the emblem, having his two hands cut off before falling, with head split open and body pierced with more than ninety wounds from lances or arrows. The poet, 'Abdullāh bin Rawāha, was killed also. And in the end, Khālid bin al-Walīd, the new convert, took over the banner, rallied his troops, and had nine sabres snapped off in his hand.

Night separated the combatants. The following day Khālid, well versed in war tactics, pushed forward his troops at a number of points so that the enemy believed he had received reinforcements, and retreated.

The army returned to Medina, piously carrying the body of Ja'far. The Prophet wept for the death of his three generals. He went to call upon Ja'far's widow, and taking the martyr's little son upon his knee he caressed the child's head in such a fashion that the mother at once understood what had occurred.

"His two hands were cut off," he said, "but God has given him two wings of emeralds and with them he flies amongst the angels of Paradise."

And seeing the daughter of his faithful Zayd approach, he leaned his head upon her shoulder and wept. They were astonished, and he explained:

"I shed the tears of friendship for the loss of a friend."

The Prophet, as I have stated above, had given the command of the army to Zayd bin Hāritha, his liberated slave. The act of the Prophet in giving the command of the army to a liberated slave, and the fact that the army, though comprised of noble and proud elements, accepted his command, was an example of the holy Prophet's teachings of equality and their hold on his followers.

Those who charge the Prophet with personal aggrandizement and worldly ambition should pause and reflect, for here is something to convince them of their error in estimating this unique personality. Their charge might have had some weight if the Prophet had sent these envoys to other places after his subjugation of the whole of Arabia, but the fact that he sent them long before that proves that his purpose was neither self-aggrandizement nor worldly ambition. They should remember that only twelve months before Medina had been beseiged, and that but a few weeks previously they had been refused permission to perform the pilgrimage. In face of these circumstances the Prophet's invitation to various powerful monarchs to embrace Islam could not well be on account of self-aggrandizement. It was, in fact, on account of his absolute faith in God and supreme conviction as to the ultimate success of his mission. It was a struggle between Truth and falsehood, and as Truth does not depend on force and is potent enough to hold its own, it succeeded. Two things are borne out by this event; one that the Prophet was neither an impostor nor an imbecile, and the other that from the very beginning he had looked upon Islam as the religion of the whole world. Therefore, if he was not an impostor then he was certainly the

Prophet of God. As to the universality of religion, no religion except Islam has claimed for itself that it is a universal religion. Jesus himself put forward no such claim. Instead, he always said that he came to reclaim the lost sheep of the House of Israel; and this is amply proved by the fact that he refused to pray when once a non-Israelite came to him begging for prayers. On the other hand the Prophet of Islam, from the moment of his call, claimed to have come as the Prophet for the world, to teach to all the religion of the One God. The Quran itself says as much, and the Prophet spared no pains to accomplish it. His sending of envoys to the courts of different kings was for the furtherance of the object that was his, and which God meant to be his. It was in no way like the claim of St. Paul to the Catholicity of the religion of Jesus Christ. But that the religion of the West happens to be Christianity neither proves that Islam was not a universal religion nor affirms that it is suited only to the requirements of the East, as Christianity to those of the West. Any such assertion is ridiculous, since Christianity was born and bred in the East, and the Israelites, for the reformation of which tribe it came, were the inhabitants of the East.

CHAPTER 17

THE FALL OF KHAYBAR

(628–629 A.C.)

> "Surely deep hatred has already
> appeared from out of their mouths
> and what their breasts conceal
> is greater still."—THE QURAN 3:17.

WE have seen in previous chapters how the Jews, after being repulsed and checked in their efforts to harm Islam, went into exile for choice, and settled at Khaybar. The word Khaybar means "fortified," and the town was so called because it was studded with fortresses, the most important of which, Al-Qāmūs, was supposed to be both inaccessible and impregnable. But although they had settled down in this remote place the Jews did not desist from their machinations to bring harm to Islam. The two clans, Banū Nazīr and Banū Qurayza, on their arrival at Khaybar found strong allies in the Jews of Khaybar, and all together set to work to devise means for the destruction of Islam. The Jews of Khaybar had relations with the neighbouring Bedouins and other tribes, and they succeeded in forming a coalition for the purpose of expunging Islam and the Muslims. Their hatred incited them, after the truce of Hudaybiyya, to accelerate their efforts against Islam. 'Abdullāh bin Ubayy, the chief Hypocrite, was in secret league with them, keeping them informed of the movements of the Muslims. Now the treaty of Hudaybiyya led them to think that the Muslims were weak. They imagined that their acceptance of such humiliating terms could be due to nothing but weakness, which led them to imagine that they could at last gain their long desired victory. They, therefore, got in touch with all those tribes who had agreed to help them in their fight against the Muslims, asking them to prepare to march on Medina.

In the meantime the Prophet came to know of their schemes, and after having had the intelligence confirmed at once sent an army of sixteen hundred to advance on Khaybar. This was all he could raise in the short time at his disposal. Besides, he had to move swiftly lest the Jews should seize the chance of advancing on Medina itself. At Rajī', between Khaybar and Medina, the Prophet halted, leaving a guard to watch the route with orders not to let the neighbouring tribes go to the help of the Jews. The Ghatafān, whose help was checked, thanked their stars and kept quiet; for they had no desire to fight the Muslims and court defeat. The Prophet then continued his march towards Khaybar, thinking that the news of the blockade might dissuade the Jews from offering resistance. But on reaching Khaybar he found them prepared and ready to give battle. They had strengthened all the fortresses, including the impregnable Al-Qāmūs. The Muslims had no difficulty in capturing the smaller fortresses, each in its turn falling easily. But when they reached Al-Qāmūs, they found themselves faced with a harder nut to crack. For twenty days they tried to carry it by assault, and each day they had to return unsuccessful. The Muslims had, because of the loss of many men, became dispirited. Only the Prophet was hopeful; for he knew that the Muslims would in the end succeed. When they all went to complain to him about their successive failures, he consoled them and told them that next day he would give the standard and the command to the person who was dear to God, and to whom God was dearer, and that that person would succeed in taking Al-Qāmūs. That night was a night of eager expectation and prayers for the Muslims; for each one of them prayed hard that that honour should be his. Next morning they hurried to the Prophet, each hoping that he would be the chosen one. After all were assembled the holy Prophet beckoned 'Alī and with his own hands put the armour on him, handed him the sword and staff, and sent him forth as the Commander of the Muslim troops for that day. The Muslims had suspected that this honour would go to 'Alī because of his abilities, yet each had hoped secretly that he would be chosen. They all went forth cheerfully to fight and win that day under the command of 'Alī; for if they had been jealous of the honour bestowed on him they would easily have hindered his success that day, or for the matter of that for many days to come.

The fact that 'Alī succeeded that day in winning

the fortress shows that nobody bore him ill-will, rather that all accepted him cheerfully as their commander. They had, indeed, no time for such trivialities. If they accepted the leadership of the liberated slave Zayd, there was certainly no reason for them to object to the leadership of 'Alī, who, besides being a valiant soldier, was of the same noble family as the Prophet.

The Jews had hoped to hold their own and win the battle, and when they surrendered they came to the Prophet begging his forgiveness. Not only was this readily granted but he also returned them their possessions and restored to them their lands on condition that one-half of the produce should go to the Muslims. He knew that the Jews would not keep their word. Nevertheless, he willingly agreed to their requests and did not use his prerogative of demanding from them all their possessions, which would have rendered them destitute. Let those who aver that the spread of Islam was at the point of the sword ponder on this incident. As a victor he could have commanded the Jews to change their religion or die; but what do we see instead? Whole-hearted and wholesale forgiveness. He left to them their right to continue in their religion, promising that the Muslims should not interfere with their beliefs. He only demanded from them half the produce of their lands as a tax for their protection and by way of reparation, which was neither then nor even now against any international law.

Compare this mercy and kindness of the Prophet

with the behaviour of the Jews who, instead of being grateful to the Prophet, immediately after the settlement set about conspiring to take the Prophet's life. They instigated one, Zaynab, to invite the Prophet to dinner and give him poison. But, by Divine Providence, hardly had he lifted his hand to taste the food which was poisoned, when he desisted. But a Companion who had taken it died of its effects. Not content with this they continued to prove a source of perpetual trouble. The Prophet was most merciful to them. He would have been justified in putting them all to death for this treachery alone, but he forgave them. Only Zaynab was executed, and that was because of the death of the Companion. Further, he sought to be friends with them by liberating one Saffiyya, who came as a prisoner of war, and marrying her. But all to no purpose. No conciliating act of the Prophet, no kindness on his part could keep them from mischief.

CHAPTER 18

THE FALL OF MECCA

(630 A.C.)

> "Most surely He who has made the Quran binding on you will bring you back to the destination (Mecca)."—THE QURAN 28: 85.
>
> "Have We not raised thy reputation for thee? Verily with hardship goeth ease; with hardship goeth ease."—THE QURAN 104: 4–6.

THE Truce of Hudaybiyya had been in force for two years. It gave the Prophet the right to go to Mecca on pilgrimage which was called the "Visit of Fulfilment." The Quraysh departed, leaving the town almost deserted while the unarmed Muslims performed their devotions. The Prophet, without dismounting from his camel, made the seven rounds of the Ka'ba, each time touching the Black Stone with his staff. The Faithful made the *tawāf* on foot. When three days had expired, the Quraysh begged them to leave. The peace and quietness of those two years had been a great help to Islam, which had marvellously increased in strength.

According to the terms of the Truce, the Khuzā'a tribe were on friendly relations with the Muslims, while, on the other hand, their enemies, the Banū Bakr, had entered into an alliance with the Quraysh. Towards the end of the eighth year of the Flight (630 A.C.) the Quraysh had grown more infuriated than ever at the ever-increasing popularity of the Muslims. One night the Banū Bakr, with the help of the Quraysh attacked the Khuzā'a tribe, who, taken unawares, were forced to shelter within the precincts of the Ka'ba. According to tradition, bloodshed was forbidden within the Ka'ba, but tradition notwithstanding many of them were put to death. Upon this the Khuzā'a sent a deputation to Medina, beseeching the Prophet to take action in their defence. The Prophet, after consulting the Companions, despatched a message to the Quraysh, with three conditions, bidding them accept one of the three. The conditions were: (1) that for those slain among the Khuzā'a tribe the Quraysh were to pay blood-money; (2) that they should have nothing further to do with the Banū Bakr; (3) that they should declare the truce of Hudaybiyya null and void. The Quraysh refused to accept the first two and agreed to the last. But soon after, Abū Sufyān, realizing the danger of having broken the pact, came himself to Medina to beg the Prophet to renew it. The Prophet refused his request.

For over twenty years the Quraysh had been a constant source of trouble and misery to the Muslims. Three times had they attacked Medina with the hope of entirely crushing Islam, and three times they had failed. It was but natural, therefore, that the Muslims should think it was high time to punish those who had done their best during all those years to bring about their downfall. So the Muslims, calling together all the tribes that were in alliance with them, prepared to attack Mecca. The Quraysh were quite unaware of this, until Hātib, a Muslim, who had kinsfolk at Mecca, sent a messenger to them in secret informing them of what the Muslims intended. If the letter had reached the Quraysh they would, of course, have prepared for battle, and probably a lot of unnecessary bloodshed would have been caused. But God willed it otherwise, and by some means or other the Prophet was informed of the letter sent by Hātib. He immediately sent out men who overtook the messenger and brought back the letter. The Muslims were enraged at the treachery of Hātib and wished to punish him severely. But as he was sincerely penitent for what he had done the holy Prophet forgave him.

On the tenth of Ramazān, 8 A.H. (630 A.C.), the Prophet set out at the head of ten thousand followers. They did not encamp until they reached Marru 'z-Zahrān, a place only a few hours' journey from Mecca. The Prophet ordered huge fires to be lighted in every camp, which gave the Quraysh the impression that the strength of the Muslim army was considerably greater than it really was, and they surrendered without any resistance. The first to be carried before the Prophet was the hard-hearted leader of the Quraysh who for twenty-one long years had done his best to eradicate Islam. He was brought to the holy Prophet, and, much to

183

his own surprise, freely pardoned. The Prophet also guaranteed the safety of all those who entered his house, or the Ka'ba. For some months previously, ever since the time when the Emperor Heraclius had testified to the character of the Prophet, Abū Sufyān had been infected. Now, seeing Islam triumphant in spite of all, and observing the generous treatment of their foes by the Prophet and his followers, his heart melted and he immediately embraced Islam.

Returning to Mecca, he told the people of the safety guaranteed by the Prophet, and also informed them of the great strength of the Muslim army, and that there would be no point in attempting to resist it, for all resistance would be futile. The Muslims then advanced on the city of Mecca, and entered from many sides simultaneously. One detachment, under the leadership of Khālid, entered the town at the quarter where the most bitter enemies of the Muslims lived. They were greeted with a shower of arrows and stones. Khālid was, therefore, forced, contrary to the orders of the Prophet, to attack them. In this skirmish two Muslims were killed, and about twenty-eight of the enemy. But the Prophet when he heard was grieved and shocked to see that blood had been shed in spite of his orders. But on hearing Khālid's explanation, he realized it was necessary in self-defence. He then purified the Ka'ba. Touching each idol he recited the Quranic verse, "Say, the Truth has come and falsehood has vanished. Verily, falsehood is but evanescent" (17:81). After offering his prayers there, the Prophet returned the key of the House to the key-bearer, 'Usmān bin Talha, and told him that in future the office of key-bearer would remain with him and his descendants.

The holy Prophet then delivered a sermon, and addressed a special gathering of the Quraysh, at the end of which they were to know what punishment they were to receive. But the Quraysh were all aware of the kind and noble nature of the Prophet. They knew they had harshly treated the Prophet; they had a dark record to their credit. And when the Prophet asked them what punishment they expected him to give them, they replied: "Thou art a noble Brother, and the son of a noble Brother." And the Prophet said, "This day there is no reproof against you." On hearing his words the Quraysh were dumbfounded; for in their wildest dreams they had never expected such generous treatment. They were to be let off free, without any sort of punishment for all cruel and terrible crimes they had planned, and in some cases carried out, against Islam and the Muslims. Even 'Ikrama, who only a short time before had been at the head of those who attacked Khālid and his detachment, was forgiven. He, however, had fled for his life and was in hiding, expecting to be tracked down and slain at any moment. The Prophet, however, bade his wife tell him that he need have no fear; for that he was forgiven. Hinda, who had chewed the liver of Hamza, an uncle of the Prophet, and Wahshi, the negro who had committed the murder under the instructions from

Hinda, were pardoned. Also Habbār, who had been
the cause of the death of the Prophet's own daughter
(once going from Mecca to Medina she was stoned
by Habbār and was badly hurt, dying later of the
injuries received), was freely forgiven. In all history there is no example of generous forgiveness
like that of the holy Prophet. No wonder, then,
that he has been given titles he well deserves,
"The Perfect Man," "The Best of Humanity,"
"The Ideal Prophet," "The Mercy to all Nations,"
and a score of others.

Thus Mecca was conquered, and at last in the
hands of the Muslims. The generous treatment
allotted to the fallen foe had produced an effect
greater even than that of the conquest itself. It
won all hearts—even the hearts of those who had
been the most bitter enemies of Islam. This last
scene of Islamic magnanimity disarmed all opposition. In short, all opposition just vanished. The
Wonder and Truth of Islam impressed men and
went deep down into their hearts. They turned to
the Right Path and embraced Islam. The holy
Prophet selected a place on Mount Safā to receive
them. One after another they came, and soon there
were many hundreds who had entered into the
Muslim Brotherhood. I must emphasize the fact
that, of all these hundreds of conversions, not one
was a conversion by force. Everyone who embraced
Islam did so of his own free will. There were some
who did not wish to become Muslims. They were
not asked to do so; they were not molested in any
way, but were treated with extreme kindness by

the Muslims. Although they kept to their idolatrous creed, they were friendly with the Muslims, and fought shoulder to shoulder at the battle of Hunayn (630 A.C.).

The triumphant entry of the Prophet into Mecca was a unique occurrence; for only thirteen years before he had been compelled to leave it as a fugitive. While he was there the Quraysh had done all they could to kill him and stamp out Islam. The city where he was born, the city where he first received and preached the word of God, the city whence in the end he was driven with a heavy heart, now lay open to him. It was as great a personal triumph as it was religious; and by it the Quranic prophecy of the successful entry of the holy Prophet was fulfilled.

CHAPTER 19

THE BATTLES OF HUNAYN AND TĀ'IF

(630 A.C.)

> "Certainly God helped you on
> many battlefields, and on the day
> of Hunayn, when your great num-
> bers made you vain, but they
> availed you nothing, and the earth
> became strait to you notwith-
> standing its spaciousness, then you
> turned back retreating." — THE
> QURAN 9: 25.

THE Hawāzin were a tribe occupying territories to the east of Mecca. Some time before the conquest of Mecca they had been inciting the Bedouin and other tribes to rise against and attack the Muslims. Now, seeing that Mecca had fallen and was in the hands of the Muslims, they decided to muster a large number and strike a blow at Islam before it became too strong for them. The Hawāzin themselves were a very warlike people, brave and experienced warriors and well skilled in archery.

It was about a month after the conquest of Mecca that the holy Prophet was informed of what the Hawāzin, Bedouin, and neighbouring tribes had in mind to do. On hearing of these preparations, he at once sent a messenger to watch the movements of these tribes and find out if there was really any truth in the statement. The messenger soon returned confirming the news, and gave the holy Prophet details of what was going on.

There was no time to be lost, and the Muslims marched forth immediately to disperse the enemy. In all, the Muslim army consisted of twelve thousand, including two thousand Meccans. At the head of this great army the Prophet set out from the city of Mecca towards the valley of Hunayn where, it was reported, the Hawāzin had encamped.

I must mention here that the Muslims, at the outset of this expedition had great confidence in their powers, imagining that the Hawāzin forces had but to see them to take to immediate flight, or surrender without resistance. This was but natural, for the easy conquest of Mecca, and their victories on other occasions, had turned the heads of many of them; and, this time, the great strength of their army, together with the knowledge that they were well armed and fully equipped, made them certain of immediate success. But God wished to teach them a lesson to cure their conceit and bring down their undue pride in themselves. He wished to show them that their former successes were not due to their own strength, but to Divine help and nothing else. So, for the benefit of their own souls, when the battle of Hunayn first commenced, fortune was very much against the Muslims, and it looked as though defeat was not far off. It is with reference to this scene that the holy Quran says, "Certainly God helped you on many battlefields, and on the day of Hunayn, when your great numbers made you vain, but they availed you nothing, and the earth became strait to you notwithstanding its spaciousness, then you turned back retreating" (9 : 25).

The Hawāzin had posted their best archers in the surrounding hill. As the Muslims advanced they were met with showers of arrows from the hills on all sides, and the main portion of the army attacked them from the front. The Muslim auxiliaries were leading under the command of Khālid. They were the first to be attacked, and were compelled to fall back. Their retreat caused woeful disorder among the Muslim ranks following, detachments falling over one another in hopeless confusion. The holy Prophet, seeing the Muslims retreating, remained at his post with only a small band of men to help him. The enemy was closing in upon them from all sides, but the Prophet did not fear, nor lose heart. Calmly he called out at the top of his voice, "I am the Prophet, there is no untruth in it." This gave heart to the retreating men, and all rallying to him replied, "Here are we at thy command." They threw themselves from their camels and horses and desperately attacked the enemy, who gradually gave way. A portion of them had already taken to flight; the rest resisted for a short time, and in the end, seeing most of their leaders slain, turned tail.

Before undertaking this expedition, the Commander of the Hawāzin army had ordered that all the women and children, as well as their cattle, should accompany them. When forced to retreat they left all women, children, everything, and just took to their heels. Therefore it was a great booty that fell into the hands of the Muslims. Over six thousand men and women were taken prisoners, besides thousands of sheep, etc., as well as about five thousand ounces of silver. Placing this booty in a place of safety the Muslims went after the defeated army, a part of which had taken refuge in the fort of 'Autās, whither the Prophet sent a small detachment of Muslims to dislodge them; but the largest part of the army took shelter within the walls of the city of Tā'if, which was well fortified with battlements and strong stone walls. The Hawāzin had taken every precaution in preparing for the battle of Hunayn and had laid in provisions to last many months, as well as a great store of weapons of war, such as catapults and the like, in case of defeat, within Tā'if. The holy Prophet with his Muslim army proceeded there and besieged the town, and, the Hawāzin army being well provided, the siege dragged on for months. In the end the Muslims grew weary of it, so the holy Prophet called a meeting of all his friends to decide what was best to be done. About that time an old Bedouin Chief informed the Prophet that the Hawāzin were well provided and that it was not likely that they would surrender in a hurry. He also said that if they were left alone now they would attempt no further harm to the Muslims. The holy Prophet then ordered the siege to be raised. Someone asked him to invoke the anger

191

of God on the fallen foe, but the prayer the Prophet said was, "O Lord! grant Light to this tribe and bring them to Islam." His prayer was granted; it was these very people who later embraced Islam voluntarily.

Returning from Tā'if the Prophet set aside one-fifth of the booty for the Public Treasury and the rest he divided amongst the Muslim army. After thus distributing the spoils, he made certain grants to the Bedouin and Quraysh Chiefs. But this gave rise to a feeling of resentment among the Helpers from Medina. They grumbled among themselves, and said that the holy Prophet was partial to the Quraysh because they were his own kinsmen. The holy Prophet hearing this sent for them and spoke to them who admitted that they had given expression to those views. The Prophet then spoke very kindly to them, and explained the case, ending with these words, "O Helpers! if all the people in the world go one way while my Helpers take another, I, the Prophet of God, will tread the path of the Helpers." This outburst of the Prophet greatly moved the Helpers, and they burst into tears of joy, knowing that the Prophet cared for them more than the others and more than all the riches of the world.

In his childhood the Prophet was looked after by his nurse Halīma, for whom and her family he had a great affection. Now, among the prisoners he was surprised to see her daughter, his foster-sister, Shaymā. Recognizing her, he at once rose and spread his mantle for her to sit on, and treated her with every kindness as though she was his own sister. He even asked her to accompany him to Medina but she begged him to allow her to go back to her own people. The Prophet granted this request and also gave her many valuable presents for herself and her family.

A deputation was sent to the holy Prophet asking him to release the six thousand prisoners. Any other conqueror, knowing the nature of their mission, would have refused to see them, or would have turned a deaf ear to their pleadings and their wishes. But the holy Prophet was noble by nature; his mercy knew no bounds; and it was extended even to his most bitter enemies. The spokesman of the deputation told him how the thousands suffered being separated from their homes and their people. This melted the heart of the Prophet. Thereupon he ordered the release of those prisoners who had fallen to his own share and the share of his family. As for the rest, who had fallen to the share of others, he said he could not order their release, but would intercede with others for them. During the afternoon prayer, therefore, he addressed the Muslim congregation, exhorted them to be merciful and commended the release of the prisoners who had fallen to their share. This they willingly agreed to do. Thus through the intercession of the Prophet six thousand prisoners were set free and allowed to go back to their homes.

In the month of Zu 'l-Qa'da, 8 A.H. (630 A.C.), the Prophet visited Mecca on his return from Tā'if. He performed there the Minor Pilgrimage called 'Umra,

and returned to Medina at the end of the year.
It was at this time that the name 'Ummu 'l-Qurā
was given to Mecca, which means "the mother of
all towns." Year after year thousands of people
came there from all parts of the country during the
pilgrimage, and the people of Mecca were considered leaders in the matter of religion. Naturally,
after the conquest of Mecca by the Muslims, people
began to join the Muslim Brotherhood in large
numbers from all parts of Arabia. This is why, after
the conquest of Mecca in the year 9 A.H. (631 A.C.),
Islam was soon spreading all over Arabia, tribe after
tribe turning to the right path and embracing
Islam. It was in the selfsame year that the Prophet
established the collecting of the poor-rate from all
tribes belonging to Islam. The payment of the
poor-rate is obligatory on all Muslims, and it is
the main item that goes to replenish the Public
Treasury.

It was during the years 631 A.C. and 632 A.C. that
Islam began to take a firm foothold, and it was
during those years also that the Prophet heard that
the tribe of Banū Tay were bent on making mischief and causing more trouble to the Muslims.
At once 'Alī was sent with two hundred soldiers
to deal with the situation. Many prisoners were
taken, among them being Safāna, the daughter of
Hātim Tā'ī, a man well known for his kindness
and generosity. On hearing this the Prophet set
Sufāna free for the sake of her father, but she told
the Prophet that she did not want her freedom
unless the other prisoners of her tribe were set free

as well. Thereupon her request was granted and the prisoners released. Her brother, who had been among them, later returned and embraced Islam. During this time the famous poet, Ka'b bin Zuhayr, who had at one time been a most bitter enemy of the Muslims, also embraced Islam. It was he who composed the famous poem known as *Burda* in praise of the holy Prophet.

Soon Islam won general popularity throughout Arabia. Its triumph was carried far and wide, to all corners of the Peninsula. People coming on pilgrimage carried the news; for men had been interested for many years in the struggle between the Prophet and the Quraysh. They knew of the Flight, and of the hard times that followed for the Muslims. Also they knew how the enemies of Islam year in and year out had tried their utmost to crush and put an end to it. And now deputations poured in from all parts of Arabia. They were received with honour and instructed in the principles of Islam. They even came from the very borders of Persia and Syria, from far-away places like Bahrayn, Hazramaut, and others. Thus we see how rapidly in times of peace Islam spread, and also as long as there was war and conditions were unsettled its progress was at a standstill.

So rapidly was Islam spreading and its power growing that it seemed as if some invisible power was busy bringing hundreds upon hundreds to enter the Muslim Brotherhood. There is yet another fact which deserves to be mentioned. It is that although deputations came from perilous places asking for instructors, never did the holy Prophet send armed escorts with his preachers. He sent them alone and unarmed; for he felt convinced that no harm would befall them. Since those days "Religious freedom and peace have been favouring and ever will favour the spread of the True religion, Islam."

CHAPTER 20

THE BATTLE OF TABŪK

THE YEAR OF DEPUTATIONS

(631 A.C.)

> "When there comes the help of
> God and the victory, and thou
> seest men entering the religion
> of God in groups, then celebrate
> the praise of thy Lord and ask
> His forgiveness; surely He is ever
> ready to show mercy."—THE
> QURAN 110: 1-3.

THE neighbouring Christian States were watching the progress of Islam with grave concern. Their eyes were turned towards Medina and alert for any sign that might help them to come to some decision as to what should be their own attitude towards this new religion. It will not be out of the way here if I relate in brief the fundamental difference between Christianity and Islam. The obvious and the greatest difference is in the two opposed beliefs—the One God of the Muslims, and the Trinity of the Christians.

The founder of Christianity was Jesus Christ. The Quran says of him that he was sent by God to reclaim and bring back to the right path the lost sheep, that is, the Israelites, who were the followers of Moses, but who had strayed from his

197

path. The circumstances of the birth of Jesus are unique, for he was born to Mary, a virgin. The Quran speaks of it in the following words, "And mention Mary in the Book when she drew away from her family to an eastern place; so she took a veil (to screen herself) from themselves; then We sent to her Our Inspiration, and there appeared to her a well-made man. She said: Surely I fly for refuge from you to the Beneficent God, if you are one guarding (against evil). He said: I am only a messenger of your Lord; That I will give you a pure boy. She said: When shall I have a boy and no mortal has yet touched me, nor have I been unchaste. . . . And the throes of child-birth compelled her to betake herself to the trunk of a palm tree. . . . And she came to her people with him (child). They said: O Mary! surely you have done a strange thing. . . . But she pointed to him (child). They said how shall we speak to one who was a child in the cradle. He (child) said: Surely I am a servant of God. He has given me the Book and made me a Prophet. . . . It beseemeth not God that He should take to Himself a son, Glory be to Him; when He has decreed a matter He only says to it 'Be' and it is. . . ." (chap. 19, sec. 2.) Though this Quranic account of the conception of the nature of Jesus Christ places him in a class by himself yet it does not fail to remind us that he was no more than a prophet of God like many others, and this much the Muslims acknowledge as a part of their creed. The Quran says that Jesus Christ himself never claimed divinity or relationship with God. It was after his death that, in order to bring in the pagan Romans, the Apostle Paul, the Vicar of Christ, introduced the idea that Jesus was the son of God, conceived of the Holy Ghost, and later made it the chief article of the Christian faith. As I have said, Jesus Christ himself did not mention anything about his divinity, which statement can be borne out by the books of Chrysostom and Athanasius. Speaking of the Sonhood of Jesus Christ, Gibbon writes, "The familiar companions of Jesus of Nazareth conversed with their friend and countryman, who, in all the actions of rational and animal life, appeared of the same species with themselves. His progress from infancy to youth and manhood was marked by a regular increase in stature and wisdom; and after a painful agony of mind and body he expired on the cross. He lived and died for the service of mankind: but the life and death of Socrates had likewise been devoted to the cause of religion and justice. . . . The Prophets of the ancient days had cured diseases, raised the dead, divided the sea, stopped the sun, and ascended to Heaven in a fiery chariot. And the metaphorical style of the Hebrews might ascribe to a Saint or Martyr the adoptive title of the Son of God." Thus we see the real side expressed by a European about the divinity of Jesus Christ. Cerinthus of Asis tried to amalgamate the two views about Jesus Christ the Divine and Jesus Christ the Man into one, which later was improved and modified by Carpocrates, Basilides, and Valentine. They regarded Jesus Christ as a mere mortal, the legitimate son of Joseph and Mary, but they say that when he was baptized, the real Jesus Christ, the Son of God, Himself descended on Jesus in the form of a dove, and that Jesus Christ the immortal and the impeccable forsook his earthly tabernacle, Jesus, to suffer, to complain, and to expire. Gradually the idea of the divinity of Jesus became established, yet the Christians hesitated to pronounce that God could manifest himself in flesh, or could be confined in the womb of Mary. If we are to accept it, we shall have also to admit that he was not exempt from ignorance, and that in the end he died on the cross. How God could die Christians can only quibble in vain. These are the two entirely contrary things and they can never come together. To be both ordinary man and God at the same time is impossible. Yet this doctrine was the prevailing one of the Church in the fifth century. And it is still the greatest obstacle in the way of Christian and Muslim reconciliation.

The Muslims maintain that Jesus himself did not allow image worship. As we have said he came to reform the Israelites, and was himself subject to the Laws of Moses, which strictly forbid the worship of images. Neither were the early Christians image worshippers. Instead they had a repugnance to the use of images, and would point out to the idolaters the folly of bowing before the work of their own hands. The first symbolic worship was started three hundred years after the death of Jesus Christ, and in the beginning remained confined to the veneration of the cross and the relics.

About the inauguration of the image worship among Christians, a Christian writer says, "At first the experiment was made with caution and scruple, and venerable pictures were discreetly allowed to instruct the ignorant, to awaken the cold, and to gratify the prejudice of the heathen proselytes. By a slow though inevitable progression the honours of the original were transferred to the copy. The devout Christians prayed before the image of the Saint, and the pagan rites of genuflexion . . . and incense again stole into the Catholic Church. The few scruples they had before were rendered unnecessary by the strong evidence of vision and miracles." Vicars of Christ sanctioned idol worship to satisfy the minds of the people instead of educating them to abhor it. This I presume is enough to show that the religion of Jesus Christ as preached by him is entirely different from that held by his successors.

Another great difference between Christianity and Islam is that the former has a priesthood, while it is prominent by its absence in the latter. No Christian, it seems, can worship his Creator without the aid of a priest, whereas a Muslim does not even feel the necessity of an intermediary. This advantage over the people gave the Christian priestly class great power and at the same time made it very jealous of its power. The hardships meted out thereby to all, irrespective of rank, position, influence, and knowledge were such as to make this class especially hostile to Islam. When I said in the beginning of this chapter that the neighbouring Christian States were watching the progress of Islam, I had in mind the priestly class of Christian. It was the clergy that were watching it; for to them it meant disaster if Islam should penetrate into their respective countries. There had already been a skirmish between these two at Mūta. The news that the whole of Arabia had embraced Islam caused them intense alarm, and they began to prepare to attack the Muslims with a view to hampering the spread of Islam outside the Peninsula. News in the course of time reached the Prophet that the Emperor of the Greeks had gathered a large force to crush Islam, and that all the Christian tribes in Arabia had joined him.

The Prophet, as was his custom, first verified this information, and on the strength of it sent a strong detachment to Syria to guard the frontiers. After this the Prophet called upon all tribes to come to the help of the motherland which, he told them, was in danger of being entirely subdued by the foreigners. But there were many obstacles in the way to prevent all from making common cause. The journey was long, the heat terrific, and, besides, the crops were standing in the fields and needed attention. There were many poor who had not the means to provide themselves with camels or other means of conveyance to transport them to the frontier, neither was Islam at that time in a position to arrange for the transport of a huge army from one end of the country to another. They were thus at a loss to find some solution of the difficulty, when 'Osmān offered a thousand camels and ten thousand dinars towards the cost of the expedition. The Prophet was then able to despatch an army of thirty thousand, and went himself in person.

Midway between Medina and Damascus, at Tabūk, they encamped and waited for fresh news of the movements of the enemy, but no news came. Whereupon he pushed his way to the frontier only to find it peaceful and with no foreboding of war. It was later learnt that the Christian tribes of Arabia who had promised to help the Emperor of the Greeks had backed out at the last, for they had not forgotten that to Muslims the overwhelming number of the enemy did not imply defeat. The Emperor, too, dropped the idea of attack. He could not undertake the expedition after the defeatism of the Christian Arab tribes.

Here again was another chance for the Prophet to effect conversion by force, had such a thing been permissible in Islam. He went there to fight, but he did not fight, not because there was no enemy ready to be fought, but because the Quran had commanded him. It says clearly, "And fight in the path of God against those who fight against you, but do not exceed the limits" (2 : 190); and as such it was incumbent on the Prophet to return without fighting, though he might easily have taken the enemy unawares, defeated them, and dictated what terms he liked. He waited at the frontier for twenty days, and when he found that the enemy had no intention of giving battle he returned. Is there any example parallel to this in the history of any other religion or Government?

This failure on the part of a great power restrained the evil intentions of those who still wished to see Islam disappear, and soon after the return from this expedition deputation after deputation waited upon the Prophet. The first to arrive was from Tā'if. In the course of the battle with the Hawāzin, the Prophet had to lay siege, it will be remembered, to Tā'if, because the enemy had taken shelter there. But having been assured of the harmless intentions of the besieged he had withdrawn his troops and returned to Medina. 'Urwa, the chief of the Saqīf, went to the Yemen to qualify in the art of warfare. He had known the qualities of the Prophet, and had seen some of them as well on the occasion of the truce of Hudaybiyya. Immediately after his return from the Yemen he went to Medina and embraced Islam. From that moment it became his deep concern to see that all his people too should embrace Islam. The Prophet tried to dissuade him from attempting to do so, fearing he would be harmed, but 'Urwa said that the Prophet need not fear as he was quite confident of his influence. So he returned to Tā'if, and invited all the inhabitants to accept Islam. The event proved that the Prophet was quite correct in his apprehensions for the safety of 'Urwa. The next morning when 'Urwa gave the call to prayer, some of the Saqīf came together and killed him. This murder of 'Urwa led to a conflict between the people of Tā'if and the tribe of Hawāzin, who had by that time joined the faith. The latter, when they found Islam daily growing more powerful, decided to join it, and with this purpose a deputation consisting of six chiefs and twenty others waited upon the Prophet to inform him that they were willing to embrace Islam. Here again the magnanimity of the Prophet's character is brought out into relief, for he never so much as mentioned the murder of 'Urwa. They requested that they should be allowed to keep their chief idol at-Lāt for three years, after which period it might be destroyed. The Prophet, of course, refused to listen to such a ludicrous proposition, whereupon they requested him to let them retain their idol at least for a month. This, too, the Prophet refused to concede, saying that Islam and idolatry could not go together. Thus Islam penetrated into Tā'if, the city where the Prophet himself had been pelted with stones, the city whence he had been forced to fly for his life.

Another deputation that came this year was from the Banū Tamīm, and on the same errand. Others followed suit, including the chiefs of the Yemen, Mahra, Yamāma, and 'Ummān, which led certain of the Christian tribes also to send deputations signifying their desire to know about Islam. Of these the best known was that of Najrān, belonging to the Roman Church. These were allowed to stay at a mosque and perform their services therein according to their rites. To the invitation of the Prophet to join Islam they replied they would first consider the matter. The Prophet then expounded to them the principles of Islam, but they hesitated. Whereupon he invited them to *Mubāhala*, i.e. the calling down of a curse upon such

205

of us as is the Liar. This, too, was rejected, for they feared that they might lose and the Muslims win. The deputation returned as it came, without having embraced Islam. Nevertheless, they entered into a pact of friendship with the Prophet. As regards the Christians of Mahra and the Yemen, they, however, were converted.

So ended the year 631 A.C., and more deputations were still to come. Of these, many were from the tribes of the Yemen and embraced Islam. They were followed by two deputations from the Hazramaut tribe; whereof the chiefs, Wā'il and Ash'as, came with a great number of their men and also joined Islam. In this manner came deputations from different tribes and clans, and each, on its return, took with it a preacher.

There were yet some tribes left who had not embraced Islam, and some of them were still hoping to deal it a death-blow. Two of them conspired together to kill the Prophet. 'Āmir and Abrad undertook to do the deed. It was decided that 'Āmir should engage the Prophet in conversation, and Abrad fall on him suddenly while thus engaged, and strike him dead with his sword. Forth they went with this project in mind and chanced to meet the Prophet whom 'Āmir accordingly engaged in conversation, but his comrade Abrad had not the courage to do his share of the business. Therefore 'Āmir, when he saw that his plan was miscarrying, begged the Prophet to grant him a private interview, which the Prophet declined to grant. This offended him greatly. Inasmuch as he himself was the chief of a tribe, he warned the Prophet that he would be avenged for the insult; whereupon the Prophet prayed: "O God! protect me from 'Āmir," and, strangely enough, on his way back 'Āmir died of plague.

The period of war ended with the expedition of Tabūk, after which began the turning to Islam of many clans and tribes; and in the course of two years Islam had become the religion of the whole land, with the exception of a very few Jewish and Christian communities scattered in small numbers here and there. Thus ended the mission of the Prophet. He was the only Teacher to see the fulfilment of his mission in his own lifetime. How great and wonderful this personality was, and how the Divine power was ever at his side, can be seen from what I have said before. I cannot help but say here: "Lā 'ilāha illa 'llāh Muhammadu 'r-Rasūlu 'llāh"—there is no object worthy of worship but God and Muhammad is His messenger.

CHAPTER 21

THE DEATH

(632 A.C.)

> "And Muhammad is no more
> than an apostle; the apostles have
> already passed away before him;
> if then he dies or is killed, will
> you turn back on your heels."—
> THE QURAN 3: 143.

BY the ninth year A.H. (631 A.C.), Islam had become sufficiently strong to justify the order of the Prophet that no polytheist should be allowed to perform the pilgrimage. Till then the pilgrimages of the Prophet himself were *'Umra*, that is the minor pilgrimages, but when in the tenth year A.H. (632 A.C.), all Arabia had embraced Islam, the Prophet decided to go in person for the pilgrimage. This was a memorable day in the history of Islam, for as many as 124,000 persons from all corners of Arabia and belonging to all tribes went with him. It was the greatest success a person could achieve, for the very spot whereon he stood with the 124,000 assembled round him in suppliant devotion was the place whence he had had to flee, alone by himself.

This remarkable spectacle of the ultimate triumph of Truth seemed to tell him that, his mission on earth having been accomplished, the time had come for him to depart—a feeling still further strengthened by the verse then revealed, "This day I have perfected your religion for you, and completed My favour on you" (THE QURAN 5 : 3). This verse lays claim to perfection of religion in Islam, *no such claim being made by any other religion or book.* From the time of the revelation of this verse, the Prophet was looking forward to meeting "his Companion on High." The last time he appeared in public he addressed his followers thus, "Muslims, if I have wronged any one of you, here I am to answer for it. If I owe aught to any one, all I possess belongs to you." Upon hearing this a man got up and claimed three dirhems which he had given to a poor man at the request of the Prophet. They were immediately paid back, with the words, "Better to blush in this world than in the next."

About the end of the month of Safar, 11 A.H. (632 A.C.), he fell ill, and with the consent of all his wives stayed in the house of 'Ā'isha. The mosque being next door he used to go there to lead the prayers as usual, but was too weak to deliver sermons. One day when he was very ill he addressed the congregation and said that God had offered him the choice of life on earth and life with him, and that he had accepted the latter. Abū Bakr was the first to comprehend the meaning of these words, and tears rolled down his cheeks at the thought of the separation from the Prophet.

From that day on the Prophet grew weaker every day, and it became impossible for him to go to to the mosque. He desired Abū Bakr to lead the prayers and even when 'Ā'isha made excuses on

o   209

behalf of her father he still insisted, and Abū Bakr started leading the Muslims at the prayers. One day feeling a little better, he raised the curtain of his room and stood in the doorway watching the people at prayer. This was taken as a sign of recovery, and the people returned to their normal pursuits for a while; but it was not so, for in a short time there was a relapse, and he passed away from this life into the state that was proximate to God. The day whereon the Prophet breathed his last was Monday, the 12th of Rabī'u 'l-Awwal, 11 A.H. (632 A.C.).

The news of his death spread like wild-fire, and 'Omar, who had seen him apparently better a few hours ago, refused to believe it and with his sword unsheathed swore that he would slay anybody who said that the Prophet had passed away. Abū Bakr seeing the confusion went to the house of 'A'isha, ascertained the news, came out, and announced to the people from the pulpit: "O People! Verily, whosoever worshipped Muhammad, behold! Muhammad is indeed dead. But whosoever worshipped God, behold! God is alive, and will never die." This soothed the Muslims, and precluded all chance of schism and dissension.

CHAPTER 22

"On the day when the earth shall
be changed with a different earth
and the heavens as well."—THE
QURAN 14: 48.

BY the tenth century A.H. the mission of Muhammad was accomplished. We have seen that the nation of which he was one was steeped in ignorance, barbarisms, idolatry, and sin; we have also seen what immense difficulties he had in the infusion of his teachings, how he was badgered from pillar to post, and how successfully he braved all attacks. The success he achieved is unique, for never in the history of the world had any person till then seen in his lifetime the accomplishment of his mission. Jesus, Moses, and the rest all had their ideals, but all had to depart from this world without witnessing the realization of their hopes. His success was the greatest personal success ever achieved by man. Christianity only gained strength when Kings and Emperors came with their edicts to help it, but Muhammad had no royal disciple to come to his aid. He had God only to assist him and his work, therefore, can truthfully be called the work of God.

His life, as we have seen, is the noblest record of work nobly and faithfully done. An author, describing his achievement, writes: "His democratic thunder was the signal for the uprising of all human intellect against the tyranny of Priests and Rulers," and continues: "In that world of the wrangling creeds and oppressive institutions when the human soul was crushed under the weight of unintelligible dogmas and the human body trampled under the tyranny of vested interests, he broke down the barriers of caste and exclusive privileges. He swept away with his breath the cobwebs which self-interest had woven in the path of man to God. He abolished all exclusiveness in man's relations to his Creator." Another writer says: "His persistent and unvarying appeal to reason, his thoroughly democratic conception of Divine Government, the universality of his religious ideal, his simple humanity, all serve to differentiate him from his predecessors."

Thus he saw his task accomplished and felt that his end must be approaching, so he decided to make a farewell pilgrimage to Mecca and went thither. There from Mount 'Arafāt he addressed his people in a soul-stirring speech, the fragments of which are:

"O My people! listen to my words, for I do not think that I will have another chance of being with you. Your lives and property are sacred and inviolable amongst one another till you appear before God. . . . Remember you shall have to appear before God, Who shall demand from you an account of all your actions. . . . O People! you have rights over your wives and your wives have rights over you, treat them with kindness and love, for you have taken them on the security of God, and have made them lawful by the words of God. . . . Keep always faithful to the Trust and avoid all occasions to sin. . . . And as for your slaves, see that you feed them with what you feed yourselves and clothe them with what you clothe yourselves, and if they commit any offence which you cannot forgive them let them go, for they are the creation of God like you and not to be treated harshly.

"Listen to my words and understand them fully well. Remember that all Muslims are brothers unto one another. You are one brotherhood. Nothing which belongs to one is lawful to the other, unless freely given out of good-will. And do not commit injustice."

This was his last sermon, after which he grew weaker and weaker and finally breathed his last, but with his task completed and mission fulfilled. There is no other to be compared with him, for there are none who so withstood the fire of the world and came out unscathed. From a humble preacher he rose to be the Ruler of Arabia, but the same simplicity of spirit, and the same nobility of nature, and purity of heart, delicacy of feeling, and devotion to duty remained supreme. Says Mr. Ameer Alī in his *Spirit of Islam* (London, 1922), "A nature so pure, so tender, and so heroic inspires not only reverence, but love." Mr. Stanley Lane-Poole sums up in the following beautiful language the whole nature and essence of this wonderful person, when he writes: "There is something so tender and womanly and withal so heroic, about the man, that one is in peril of finding the judgment unconsciously blinded by the feeling of reverence, and well-nigh love that such a nature inspires. He who, standing alone braved for years the hatred of his people, is the same who was never the first to withdraw his hand from another's clasp; the beloved of children, who never passed a group of little ones without smile from his wonderful eyes and a kind word for them, sounding all the kinder in that sweet-toned voice. The frank friendship, the noble generosity, the dauntless courage and hope of the man, all tend to melt criticism into admiration. He was an enthusiast in that noblest sense when enthusiasm becomes the salt of the earth, the one thing that keeps men from rotting whilst they live. . . . He was an enthusiast when enthusiasm was the one thing needed to set the world aflame. And his enthusiasm was noble for a noble cause. He was one of those happy few who have attained the supreme joy of making one great truth their very life-spring. . . . He brought his tidings to his people with a grand dignity sprung from the conscience of his high office, together with a most sweet humility, whose roots lay in the knowledge of his own weakness."

The devotional spirit which he infused into his people can well be understood by the following prayer of 'Alī, "Thanks be to my Lord: He the adorable, and to be adored. My God the Eternal, the Ever-existing, the True Lord whose mercy and might overshadow the worlds; the Regulator of the World, the Light. He is the worshipful; to Him is due all worship. He existed before all things, and will exist after all that is living has ceased. Thou art the Adored, my God. Thou art the Master, the Loving, the Forgiving; Thou alone bestowest power and on whomsoever Thou likest; him whom Thou hast exalted none can lower; and him whom Thou hast lowered none can exalt. Thou my God art the Eternal, the Creator of all. All-Wise, All-Powerful, Thy knowledge knoweth what is in earth and Heaven; Thy Beneficence is all-pervading, and Thy Mercy all-embracing. My God! Thou art the Helper of the afflicted, the Reliever of the distressed and the Consoler of the dejected, and art present everywhere to help. Thou knowest all secrets, all thoughts. Thou art the Fulfiller of needs and Bestower of blessings. Thou art the friend of the poor and the bereaved. My God! Thou art my fortress, a shelter for all who seek Thy help. Thou art the Refuge of the weak, the Helper of the pure and true. . . . My Lord! Thou art the Creator and I am the created; Thou art the Sovereign and I am the servant. Thou art the Helper and I the beseecher. Thou art my God, Thou art my Refuge, Thou art the Forgiver and I the sinner. Merciful, All-Knowing, All-Loving God, I am groping in the dark, I seek Thy knowledge and love. Bestow, my God, all Thy knowledge and love and mercy; forgive my sins and let me approach Thee."

Such was the spirit of devotion that Islam had

engendered in the Muslims. Such was the spirit which we find in no other religion. A Muslim needs no ceremony, no secluded place in which to supplicate before his God. Wherever he is, he has just to stand and offer the outpourings of his heart. An English writer says: "It is one of the glories of Islam that its temples are not made with hands, and that its ceremonies can be performed anywhere upon God's earth or under His Heaven." This individual supplication of the heart, this direct relation between the Creator and the created was made possible in the Islam of the Prophet by the absence of a priesthood. Another able writer says: "Islam allows no monopoly of spiritual knowledge or special holiness to intervene between man and his God."

I have so far written about the teachings of the holy Prophet pertaining to the rules of human conduct. My task would be incomplete if I were to pass on without touching briefly on the influence of Islam on collective thought, and on knowledge and science.

As to the influence wrought by Islam on collective thought, it is but necessary to show the conditions of life and government then prevalent. The masses which are the backbone of power both in West and East were subjected to conditions almost too miserable to imagine. They possessed no civil rights or privileges, and, as for the law, it favoured the strong and the rich as against the weak and the poor. In Persia, the priests and landocracy enjoyed all powers and privileges, while the poorer classes and the peasantry had none. In Byzantium, the priests and courtiers were rich and powerful and treated the rest as animals or worse; in short, serfdom was the order of the day and men had to work under conditions that were inhuman, degrading, and merciless. Christianity too did nothing to alleviate their lot, as the horrors of the Middle Ages show clearly enough.

Describing the state of non-Christians under the Christian rules, a distinguished writer says: "The non-Christians, Jews, Heretics, or Pagans enjoyed under Christian domination a fitful existence. It was a matter of chance whether they would be massacred or reduced to slavery. Rights they had none; enough if they were suffered to exist." Such was the state of the masses under Christianity, and it showed no signs of abatement till the Prophet of Arabia sounded the note of freedom, abolished every privilege of caste, and broke every link of slavery.

Thus the oft-repeated charge of the Christians that the non-Muslim subjects in a Muslim state laboured under severe disabilities is entirely wrong. After the victory, the Prophet declared: "To the Christians of Najrān and neighbouring territories, the security of God and the pledge of His Apostle are extended for their lives, their religion, and their property. To the present as well as the absent and the others besides there shall be no interference with their faith or their observances, nor any change in their rights or privileges; no bishop shall be removed from his bishopric, nor any monk from

217

his monastery, nor any priest from his parish, and they shall continue to enjoy everything great and small as heretofore; no image or cross shall be destroyed; they shall not oppress or be oppressed; no tithes shall be levied from them, nor shall they be required to furnish provisions for the troops." Is there the like of this in the history of the world? Those Christians who look askance at Islam should read the history of their own religion and they would find there the terms offered by Christian conquerors to the conquered were inhuman, severe, and in the highest degree intolerant. Not only did the Muslim conquerors preserve inviolate the rights of the conquered, but also the properties dedicated to the Christian churches. A Christian Patriarch addressed the Bishop of Fars in the reign of 'Usmān, the Third Caliph, thus: "The Arabs, who have been given by God the kingdom, do not attack the Christian faith; they respect our God and our Saints, and on the contrary help our religion by bestowing gifts on our churches and monasteries." Such words from the pen of a Christian and of those times indicate full well that the treatment meted out to Christians under an Islamic Government was generous in the extreme, and it has been proved in many cases that Christianity would not have been what it is to-day had it not been for the help, support, and protection of the Muslim State.

The Hindus in India were treated kindly by the Moguls, under whom they held offices of position. The Muslim kings always bestowed their benefactions equally on the Muslims and Hindus, and

218

the Mosques and Temples. The conquest of Africa
and Spain was marked by the same clemency
on the part of the Muslims. The state of Spain
before Islam, if compared with that during and
after, shows plainly that peace and progress always
followed Islam. In short, the code it gave to the
people was a code of development. It was a flexible
constitution, based on a just appreciation of human
capacity and human duty. It limited taxation, it
made all men equal in the eye of the law, and it
made the executive subordinate to the legislature.
On this subject a writer says: "The excellence and
effectiveness of each of these principles—each
capable of immortalizing its founder—gave value
to the rest; and all combined endowed the system
which they formed with a force and energy exceed-
ing those of any other political system. Within the
lifetime of a man, though in the hands of a population, wild, ignorant, and insignificant, it spread
over a greater extent than the dominions of Rome;
while it retained its primitive character it was
irresistible."

The Muslim Government under the first four
Caliphs remained exactly as the Prophet meant it
to be—not only alive to the needs of the people,
but also popular in the truest sense of the word.
The short reign of Abū Bakr was not enough for
the promulgation of the required measures; but
soon after the enthronement of 'Omar, to quote a
writer of authority, "commenced that sleepless care
for the welfare of the subject nations which characterized the early Muslim Governments." The head

219

of the State or the Vicegerent of the Prophet, styled
by the Muslims the Caliph and by the Westerners
the Pontiff of Islam, was to be chosen by a popular
vote. Abū Bakr and 'Omar were elected to the
Caliphate in this way, but 'Omar having established the electoral college for the election of the
Caliph, the next two were chosen by the college.
The prerogatives of the head were confined within
legitimate limits; he had no power to over-rule the
established law. The courts of the Kāzī were
supreme, and the Caliph had no power to grant
pardon to those condemned by the Kāzī; for the
Kāzī was the supreme authority in the sphere of
passing judgment according to the law; the Government was merely there to enforce his decrees. The
law was equal for all, the rich and the poor alike.
The period of Abū Bakr was too short for any
settled progress, but that of 'Omar, though not
long, was marked by a series of measures that show
an ever-present solicitude for the well-being of the
masses. The Caliphate of 'Usmān was from the
beginning marred by the incident which was
instrumental in choosing him. 'Usmān had given
too much consideration to the needs of the Ummay-
yads to whom his election was due. After 'Usmān
came 'Alī, but his reign, too, was disturbed by a
series of rebellions, mostly instigated by the Ummay-
yads, who were made Governors under the reign
of 'Usmān. 'Alī had, therefore, no time to reign
in peace, and commenting on this a writer writes,
"Had 'Alī been allowed to reign in peace, his
virtues, his firmness, and his ascendancy of char-

acter would have perpetuated the old republic and its simple manners." "With 'Alī perished the truest-hearted and best Moslem of whom Muhammadan history has preserved the remembrance." With the assassination of 'Alī ended the democracy of Islam; and there was established an autocracy which later corrupted itself into despotism. We need not go into details of all that happened. But we must observe that had the principles of hereditary succession, in favour of 'Alī, been recognized at the outset, it would have prevented the rise of those disastrous pretensions which engulfed Islam in the blood of Muslims.

While in Mecca the Prophet had no time to devote his energies to the literary and scientific expansion of Muslims. But Medina, after his arrival there, soon became a centre of attraction, gathering enquirers from abroad—from Syria, Greece, and Iraq. The Prophet preached that knowledge is the most valuable, national, and personal asset, his actual words being, "Acquire knowledge, for he who acquires it in the way of God performs an act of piety." Further on the Prophet says, "Who speaks of it (knowledge) praises God; who seeks it adores God; who gives it to another, bestows alms. . . . Knowledge enables its possessors to distinguish good from bad; it lights the way to Heaven; it is our friend in the desert, and a guide to happiness. It helps us in misery, and is an ornament before friends. It is an armour against the enemies. With knowledge the servant of God rises to greater heights, and noble qualities, and attains to the perfection of happiness." The Quran also speaks of the supreme value of knowledge in more than one chapter and advises men to acquire it.

Before Islam the Arab world exhibited no signs of intellectual growth. Their tastes were all for poetry, oratory, and astrology; in science and literature they took no interest at all. It was the teaching of the Prophet that turned their attention to these studies and the nucleus thus formed in his lifetime grew into universities of which the most famous were those of Baghdad, Salerno, Cairo, and Cordova. Here are a few of the many *obiter dicta* of the Prophet on this topic: "One hour of meditation on the work created by God is better than seventy years of prayer." "To attend a lecture on science and learning is more meritorious than attendance at a thousand funerals of the martyrs, more meritorious than standing up praying for a thousand nights." "To one who goes forth in the search for knowledge God allots a high place; every step he takes is blessed, and every lesson he takes is rewarded." "The greatest ornament given is learning." "It is better than religious exercises to listen to the words of the learned and instil them in the heart." "He who dedicates his life to learning never dies." Such expressions on the part of the holy Prophet gave an impetus to his followers, and the seed that he sowed continued to grow under his successors. The early Caliphs, along with their conquests, devoted a part of their time to the spread of education. Of them 'Alī was the greatest scholar and about him a French historian says, "But for his assassination, the Moslem would have witnessed the realization of the Prophet's teachings in the actual amalgamation of reason with law." One of the greatest benefits showered on mankind by the teachings of the holy Prophet is their exhortation about education and learning. The words of the holy Prophet are, "Avoid ignorance, seek learning, and always endeavour to add to it and pray God to help you."

This was commenced in earnest again after the rise of the 'Abbasides. Mansūr, the 'Abbaside monarch, established Baghdad as his capital and gradually it developed into a seat of great learning. Of the schools and colleges in Baghdad two were of the highest repute, viz. the Nizāmiyyah and Mustansariyyah. This revival was due to the energies of Mansūr, who himself was no mean scholar. He commanded that literary and scientific works from all foreign languages be translated into Arabic. Speaking of this Von Kremer in his *Orient Under the Caliphs*, says: "It is a remarkable fact that the sovereign who makes us forget some of the darker sides of his nature by his moral and mental qualities also gave an impetus to the great intellectual movement which now commenced in the Islamic world." The successors of Mansūr, being themselves great scholars, were also the great patrons of learning. "Each great nation of the world has had its golden age—Athens had her Periclean era; Rome her Augustan age; so too had the Islamic world its epoch of Glory."

It was due to Mansūr and his immediate six successors that the Muslims became the torch-bearers to the world of civilization. That was an age of great glory ascribable especially to the 'Abbasides who collected the priceless treasures of dying Greece and Rome, of Persia, India, and China, and gave them a new lease of life, a new birth, and a new meaning.

In this revival and new life in the sphere of learning every city in the Empire tried to outbid the other. Each important city had its societies and academies whither flocked students from all parts of the world. Even Christians attended these Muslim colleges. Gerbert, who afterwards became Pope Sylvester II, was a pupil of Muslim teachers. In Cairo Al-Mu'izz, the founder of the University of Cairo, added rivalry to the patronage of the Caliphs of the House of Fatima.

In writing on the impetus which the early Muslims gave to learning and science, Dr. Sir Mohammad Iqbal in his *Reconstruction of Religious Thought in Islam*, London, 1934, makes the following observations:

"It is a mistake to suppose that the experimental method is a European discovery. Duhring tells us that Roger Bacon's conceptions of science are more just and clear than those of his celebrated namesake. And where did Roger Bacon receive his scientific training? In the Muslim universities of Spain. Indeed, Part V of his *Opus Majus*, which is devoted to 'perspective,' is practically a copy of Ibn-i-Haitham's *Optics*. Nor is the book, as a whole, lacking in evidence of Ibn-i-Hazm's influence on its author. Europe has been rather slow to recognize the Islamic origin of her scientific method. But full recognition of the fact has at last come. Let me quote one or two passages from Briffault's *Making of Humanity*.

" 'It was under their successors at the Oxford School that Roger Bacon learned Arabic and Arabic Science. Neither Roger Bacon nor his later namesake has any title to be credited with having introduced the experimental method. Roger Bacon was no more than one of the apostles of Muslim science and method to Christian Europe; and he never wearied of declaring that knowledge of Arabic and Arabic Science was for his contemporaries the only way to true knowledge. Discussions as to who was the originator of the experimental method . . . are part of the colossal misrepresentation of the origins of European civilization. The experimental method of Arabs was by Bacon's time widespread and eagerly cultivated throughout Europe' (p. 202).

" 'Science is the most momentous contribution of Arab civilization to the modern world; but its fruits were slow in ripening. Not until long after Moorish culture had sunk back into darkness did the giant to which it had given birth rise in his might. It was not science only which brought Europe back to life. Other and manifold influences from the civilization of Islam communicated its first glow to European life' (p. 202).

" 'For although there is not a single aspect of

European growth in which the decisive influence of Islamic culture is not traceable, nowhere is it so clear and momentous as in the genesis of that power which constitutes the permanent distinctive force of the modern world, and the supreme source of its victory—natural science and the scientific spirit' (p. 190).

" 'The debt of our science to that of the Arabs does not consist in startling discoveries of revolutionary theories; science owes a great deal more to Arab culture, it owes its existence. The ancient world was, as we saw, pre-scientific. The Astronomy and Mathematics of the Greeks were a foreign importation never thoroughly acclimatized in Greek culture. The Greeks systematized, generalized, and theorized, but the patient ways of investigation, the accumulation of positive knowledge, the minute methods of science, detailed and prolonged observation and experimental inquiry were altogether alien to the Greek temperament. Only in Hellenistic Alexandria was any approach to scientific work conducted in the ancient classical world. What we call science arose in Europe as a result of a new spirit of inquiry, of new methods of investigation, of the method of experiment, observation, measurement, of the development of Mathematics in a form unknown to the Greeks. That spirit and those methods were introduced into the European world by the Arabs' (p. 190)."

From the above it would have become clear that the debt which Europe owes to Islam is great. Many branches of science, for instance, certain

226

mathematical, astronomical discoveries, are the outcome of Muslim efforts solely, while there are also many others on which they have improved from Greek and other sources. In practically every case the initiative has always been Muslim, although it may have been polished and improved by others later. It was upon this strong foundation laid by the Prophet Muhammad that the structure of Islam was built, and it is because of this the world has the knowledge it has and is as learned as it is to-day. In the beginning God said, "Be," and the world was created. Later, when the world was corrupt and wellnigh lost, He created a being, the Perfect Man, Muhammad, who changed the world in the space of a few years, for the better; to use the words of a Christian writer: "Muhammad left behind a nation, a religion, and a government." Religion is principle and faith, hence it is unchangeable, as a truth is always a truth and a lie always a lie; but nations and government are subject to changes according to conditions, and the present state of Islam and Muslims generally is a phase of it.

But with Islam the peculiarity is that all is not lost; it can and will regain all its lost power and glory, if only the Muslims of to-day will make up their minds to acquire knowledge and science up to the present-day standard of the world.

The rulers of Fez, and the Moors in Spain enhanced a million-fold the cultivation of science and learning, and this period of scientific and literary renown lasted, in spite of all political and dynastic changes, right up to the capture of Baghdad by the Tartar hordes.

A comparison with the condition of science and learning in Christendom during this time would be both interesting and illuminating. Under the orthodoxy of Constantine and his successors, the doors of the schools were closed; and all the public libraries previously established were destroyed. Learning was branded as magic and punished as treason. The ecclesiastical dogma that "Ignorance is the mother of devotion" was rigidly adopted both by Church and State. It was the dogma expounded and given effect to by Pope Gregory by stopping all studies in Rome and burning the Palatine Library. He forbade the study of the Classics on pain of excommunication and death. He introduced a mythological course of study with its worship of relics and remains of Saints. Compare with this the achievement of Māmūn, rightly styled the Augustus of the Arabs. Abu 'l-Faraj speaks of him thus: "He was not ignorant that they are the elect of God, his best and most useful servants, who devote their lives to the improvement of rational faculties." Māmūn was succeeded by brilliant scholars who continued his work with zeal and energy.

Volumes would be required to give the names of all those Muslims who have made their mark in science. I will, therefore, confine myself to quoting from two European writers with a view to showing to what extent the Muslims achieved success in this field of attainment. Mr. Lane-Poole,

228

in his *The Moors in Spain*, in speaking of Cordova, writes, "Beautiful as were the gardens and palaces of Cordova, her claims to administration in higher matters were no less strong. The mind was as lovely as the body. Her professors and teachers made it the centre of European culture; students would come from all parts of Europe to study under her famous doctors, and even the nun Hrosuitha, far away in her Saxon Convents of Gaudersheim, when she told of the martydom of Eulogius, could not refrain from singing the praises of Cordova, 'the brightest splendour of the world.' Every branch of Science was seriously studied there and medicine received more and greater additions by the discoveries of the doctors and surgeons of Andulasia than it had gained during all the centuries that had elapsed since the days of Galen. Astronomy, Geography, Chemistry, Natural History, all were studied with ardour at Cordova, and as for the graces of literature there never was a time in Europe when poetry became so much the speech of everybody, when people of all ranks composed those Arabic verses which perhaps suggested models for the ballads and canzonets of the Spanish minstrels and the troubadours of Provence and Italy. No speech or address was complete without some scrap of verse, improvised on the spur of the moment by the speaker or quoted by memory from some famous poet."

Ernest Renan in his *Averroes et Averroism* says, "The taste for science and literature, by the tenth century, established, in this privileged corner of

229

the world, a toleration of which modern times hardly offer us an example. Christians, Jews, and Mussalmans spoke the same tongue, sang the same songs, participated in the same literary and scientific studies. All the barriers which separated the various peoples were effaced; and all worked with one accord in the work of a common civilization. The Mosques of Cordova, where the students could be counted by thousands, became the active centres of philosophical and scientific studies."

These two passages, taken at random from two different writers, amply testify to the scientific and literary achievements of the Muslims. That Europe was then engulfed in ignorance is amply borne out by a trivial fact that the first observatory of Europe, built by the Muslims in Cordova, was, after the expulsion of the Moors from Spain, turned into a belfry by the Christians; for they did not know what else to do with it. There is not one science upon which the Muslims did not enlarge, and there is many a discovery of which the honour is rightly theirs. The Muslims are the founders of the Physical Sciences, and Muslim scholars, students, and professors travelled far and wide in quest of knowledge. That they came to India is fact, that they penetrated into China, till then a closed barrier, is another fact. In short, wherever they went they assimilated what they could learn from different nations, and peoples, and their civilizations.

Science and learning progressed unhampered under various princes even after the disruption of the Empire. Each prince was himself a scholar of repute and worked for the enlightenment of his subjects by giving his patronage to the arts and sciences, but the blow to this enlightened era was struck by the Christians. In reality marauders, but self-styled Crusaders, they inflicted disaster on the cause of learning. They were led to this grievous rapine and slaughter by crazy priests who saw in the light of Islam a danger to their own prestige and glory. One writer pithily observes, "Christian Europe has held up to obloquy the apocryphal destruction of the Alexandrian library, which had already been burned in the time of Julius Caesar, but it has no word of blame for the crimes of her Crusaders five centuries later. The calamities inflicted by the Crusaders were lasting in their effect, and in spite of the endeavours of Saladin and his sons to restore the intellectual life of Syria, it has remained dead from that day to this."

Likewise in Architecture, Music, and the other fine arts, the superiority of the Muslims is established. The glorious remains of Saracenic art wherever the Muslims went, in the East or the West, still evoke the wonder and admiration of the whole world.

The above is but a glimpse of Muslim intellectual achievement all due to the efforts of one single man, who roused the Arabs from the depths of ignorance to enlighten and civilize the world. Everything that is in the world as the result of intellectual progress owes not only its inception but also its present form to the efforts of this one man.

231

When the rest of the world was engulfed in darkness—Christendom had tabooed all learning—this man raised up a people who became the teachers of the world. But for Islam the world would have remained in darkness even to-day.

Is it any wonder, then, that so many people follow the teachings of this Most Inspired Teacher? The day is not far off when the Quranic prophecy about the future of Islam will be fulfilled: "The unbelievers desire to put out the light of God with their mouths, but God will perfect His light, though the unbelievers may be averse. God it is who sent His Apostle Muhammad with the guidance and the true religion, that He may make it overcome the religions, all of them, though the polytheists may be averse" (THE QURAN 61 : 8–9). That fulfilment, I say advisedly, is postponed only because of the present attitude of the Muslims and their lethargy; but signs are apparent of an awakening, and we ardently hope that the future generations will not only regain the ground lost but also by fresh and renewed effort become again the beaconlight of the world.

CHAPTER 23

THE CHANGED ARAB WORLD

> "Certainly an Apostle has come
> to you from among yourselves,
> grievous to him is your falling
> into distress, excessively solicitous
> respecting you."—THE QURAN 9:
> 128.

IN this chapter it is my desire to emphasize and explain two Muslim reforms, one social and the other civic. Islam came to reform the old Laws of society which had been promulgated by different prophets before Islam. The two reforms—the Muslim Laws of Marriage and Divorce and the Muslim Theory of Government—which I am selecting are two of the many Islam enunciated.

As to the first, the first chapter of this book shows in brief the life of the Arab as he lived it before the advent of Islam. He was savage in his tastes, and brutal in his practices. Marriage as a recognized institution was a factor unknown to him. To the Arab the purpose of marriage was but the sating of animal passion. Woman he regarded as a mere chattel, an instrument for sensual gratification. She was man's possession, and considered no better than any other of his possessions. She was to him an instrument of convenience also; it was her duty to see to the cooking of his meals and the mending of his clothes. Marriage to them was just an everyday incident; there were no restrictions as to the number of wives a man could take, or in what way he might take them. The usual method was force, and there was no obligation on a husband to treat his wives well. The woman had no rights of her own; she was just the property of the man. And men might marry where they liked, except, perhaps, mothers, sisters, and aunts. As for divorce, it was the man only who had the right to divorce and without cause or reason assigned. At his sweet will, if the fancy so took him, he could divorce his woman. Before Islam, the Arabs had a great aversion to women, as is evident from the fact that they used to burn or bury alive the female children born to them. Woman was, with them, an object of no respect; in fact, according to their notions, she was deserving of no respect.

Such, generally, was the condition of affairs in Arabia, but to say that outside Arabia the status of woman was any better would be wrong. To the Persian, for example, his religion allowed any number of wives; and with the Syro-Phoenician races polygamy was degrading them into perfect bestiality. Multiplicity of wives prevailed also among the Thracians, Lydians, and Pelasgians of Europe and Western Asia, while the Athenians, the most civilized and cultured race of all, held women to be like chattels to be sold and transferred at the will of man. Among the Spartans the custom was the reverse. Here the man had the right to marry only one woman, but the woman could, if she chose, take to herself more than one husband. With the Romans, too, the plurality of marriage was a privileged custom, the prerogative of the male. In all such cases the women had no rights, and as such were nothing more than, as I have said before, a mere convenience to man. Of the Romans after the Punic triumphs Gibbon says, "The matrons of Rome aspired to the common benefits of a free and opulent republic, and their wishes were gratified by the indulgence of fathers and lovers." This helped on the system of concubinage, which soon became a privileged institution and recognized by the State. This was the time of the advent of Jesus Christ, and when he appeared he came with the firm hope that the Kingdom of Heaven would descend, and, therefore, set no great value on matrimony at all, though he did not express any such opinion. Polygamy, therefore, with the general status of women, for which it was responsible, continued right up to the time of Justinian and even after; for it flourished till the weight of the public opinion and the prohibitory Laws of the State intervened. After this it should have ceased, but it continued as a more or less secret practice, not as a thing permitted. Morganatic and "left-handed" marriages began to come into vogue. "Even the clergy, forgetting their vows of celibacy, contracted more than one legal or illegal union." I cannot but quote Gibbon at length on the latitude taken by the high clergy in this respect, for he quotes from standard works, and his statements are not merely the expression of his personal

235

opinion. "The influence of two sister prostitutes, Marozia and Theodora, was founded on their wealth and beauty, their political and their amorous intrigues: the most strenuous of their lovers were rewarded with the Roman mitre, and their reign may have suggested to the darker ages the fable of a female pope. The bastard son, the grandson, and the great-grandson of Marozia—a rare genealogy —were seated in the chair of St. Peter; and it was at the age of nineteen years that the second of these became the head of the Latin Church. His youth and manhood were of a suitable complexion, and the nations of pilgrims could bear testimony to the charges that were urged against him in a Roman Synod and in the presence of Otto the Great. As John XII had renounced the dress and decencies of his profession, the soldier may perhaps be not dishonoured by the wine which he drank, the blood that he spilt, the flames that he kindled. . . . But we read with some surprise that the worthy grandson of Marozia lived in public adultery with the matrons of Rome; that the Lateran palace was turned into a school of prostitution; and that his rapes of virgins and widows had deterred the female pilgrims from visiting the tomb of St. Peter, lest, in the devout act, they should be violated by his successor." This, then, was the attitude of the vicegerent of Jesus Christ, the Pope himself, towards licentiousness, in spite of strict vows of celibacy. If this thing were possible we should be inclined to say that those who were unfettered by any vows at all could scarcely have been more indulgent in the practices of the flesh. The prevalence of adultery, prostitution, and concubinage, as well as the chattel-like treatment accorded to women, is mainly due to the fact that men had no respect for women.

The Prophet of Arabia, as a first step towards the reform of this evil, taught men to respect women, not just because she was a woman, but because she was or should be the embodiment of all that was pure, true, virtuous, loving, and holy. He proclaimed to the bewildered Arabs, "Paradise is at the feet of your mothers," and said many other things, all extolling the virtues of women, and the kind and generous treatment that should be theirs. After first educating the public minds he laid it down that marriage is a civil contract between a man and woman to live together as husband and wife. Defining the duties of the husband, he said that mere maintenance is not all that the Law of God requires, but that the husband should treat his wife as a companion, as a help, as a guide, and as a moulder of the character of the children. Similarly, he defined the duties of the wife. But he did not stop here. He provided for divorce; the right of divorce that had hitherto been exclusively man's he bestowed on the woman too. Divorce he did not like; for he often said, "Nothing displeases God more than divorce," yet he allowed it, as a necessary evil, subject to formalities which allow a revocation of hurried or not well-considered resolution. Three successive declarations at a month's interval are necessary in order to make the divorce irrevocable. Another thorny subject, and one which has evoked much criticism against Islam is that of its permission of polygamy. But it must be remembered that Islam did not adopt or legalize polygamy; it found it already flourishing at its advent. All it did was to restrain polygamy by limiting the number of wives to four. On this point the Quran says, "You may take unto you two, three, or four wives, but not more. But if you could not deal equitably and justly with all, you shall marry only one" (5: 3). The word for equity used in the Quran is *Adl*, which means not only equality of treatment in matters of clothing, lodging, and the like, but also complete equality in love, affection, and regard. As absolute justice in matters of feeling is impossible, the Quranic prescription amounted in reality to a prohibition. It is nothing but frivolous obstinacy on the part of critics to say that the Muslim laws of marriage and divorce are abhorrent, and that Islam gave no status to women; for the Islamic laws of marriage and divorce are based on the study and knowledge of human psychology. The countries where they are practised are free from immorality; they have no Foundling Homes to support, no war babies to maintain; while as to the position of women in Islam I can only repeat that Islam has made them absolutely equal with men in respect of law, privileges, and actions. She was allowed by Islam for the first time in the history of the world to inherit, possess, and dispose of her property in her own right, subject only to the general conditions laid down for all.

As to the Muslim theory of government, it is embodied in two verses of the Quran, "Consult with your companions in conduct of affairs" (3: 159); "The way of the Companions of the Prophet to govern their affairs is by counsel" (42: 38). These verses lay down for all time the guiding principle of government. In these words Islam has laid the basis of government by parliaments and the ideal found a clear practical expression in the early Caliphate when the Khalifa had to refer every affair to a "Council of Counsellors." During the days of Islamic Democracy not only were the Caliphs assisted by a Council of the Companions of the Prophet, but the Provincial governors had similar advisory bodies. It is strange indeed to be told by the critics of Islam that government by parliament is foreign to the teachings of the Quran and unsuited for Muslim people.

As to the political ideal of Islam, one could quote instances from Islamic history to show the absolute equality of all men in Islam, the head of the State, the Caliph, not excepted. In some countries the king is above law. This conception of justice which differentiates between the subject and the ruler is repugnant to the Muslim. To the Quran both the servant and the master, the slave and the king, have equal legal status. Dr. Sir Muhammad Iqbāl has given full expression to the Islamic concept of equality in his *Asrār-i-Khudī*, translated by Professor R. A. Nicholson. He relates that a certain mason had built a palace for the king, who was so pleased with the work

239

that, being afraid that the mason might produce the like of it somewhere else, wantonly ordered the severing of the hand of the mason. The mason repaired to the Judge with his hand bleeding. He laid the case before the judge and demanded justice in a court of Law. He showed the judge his bleeding hand. He produced witnesses. The judge, moved by the pitiful story of the mason, issued orders for the king to attend the court and answer the charge. The king appeared before the judge and pleaded guilty. He put out his hand to be cut in the same manner. The plaintiff, realizing that justice had been given to his plaint, that the honour of the Law of the Quran was upheld and supreme, forswore his right to inflict the equivalent punishment on the king. Dr. Iqbāl winds up thus:

"*Peshi Qurān Banda o Maulā yakest Boryā o Masnadi dībā yakest.*" ("To the Quran the master and the servant are the same, to it the sackcloth and the velveted throne make no difference.")

I cite instances from the Life of Sultān Saladin, the king of Egypt and Syria (A.C. 1137–1193) to further illustrate the political ideal of Islam. It is said that whenever a petitioner applied to him, the sultan would stop to listen, to receive his complaint, and to inquire into the rights of the matter. A man of Damascus named Ibn Zubayr delivered a complaint against Taqi'u 'd-Dīn, the sultan's nephew, demanding justice. Although Taqi'u 'd-Dīn was high in the affection and esteem of his uncle, the sultan would not spare him in a matter

240

where justice was at stake, and caused him to appear before the tribunal.

Here is another incident still more remarkable' and significant than the foregoing, which likewise shows the great sense of justice inspired by the teachings of the Quran. Once a man by the name of 'Omar al-Khalātī came to the holy city of Jerusalem and appeared before the court of justice. He was a merchant and a native of Khalāt. This man placed in the hands of the judge a certified memorandum, and begged him to read its contents. The judge asked him who was his adversary, and he replied, "My affair is with the sultan; this is the seat of justice and I have heard that here you make no distinction of persons." "Why," the judge said, "do you bring a suit against the sultan?" He replied, "I have a slave named Sonkor el-Khalātī, who remained in my possession until his death. At that time he had several large sums of money in hand, all of which belonged to me. He died, leaving these sums; the sultan took possession of them, and I lay claim to them as my property." The judge remarked, "Why have you delayed so long before making your claim?" and el-Khalātī replied, "One does not forfeit one's rights by delaying to claim them, and here I have a certified document proving that the slave remained in my possession until his death." The judge took the paper, and having read it through, saw it contained a description of Sonkor el-Khalātī, with a note that his master had bought him of a merchant of Arjish (in Armenia) on a certain day of a certain

month in a certain year, when he escaped by
flight, and that the witnesses named in the document
had never understood that the man had ceased to
be the property of his master in any manner whatever. The instrument was in legal form—nothing
was wanting. Wondering very much at this affair,
the judge said to the plaintiff, "It is not meet to
adjudge a claim in the absence of the party sued:
I will inform the sultan, and will let you know
what he says in the matter." The sultan thought
the claim utterly absurd, and asked if the document
had been examined. The sultan was informed that
the document had been taken to Damascus, and
laid before the judge there, who had examined the
document officially, and appended a certificate to
that effect, which was witnessed by the signatures
of various well-known persons. "Very well," the
sultan replied, "we will let the man appear, and
I will defend myself against him, and conform to
all the regulations prescribed by law. Appoint an
attorney to act in my name, and then receive the
depositions of witnesses; do not open the document
until the plaintiff appears in the court of justice."
The sultan, placing himself in front of the man,
called upon him to state his case. He accordingly
set forth his claim in the manner related above, and
the sultan replied in these words, "This Sonkor
was a slave of mine; he never ceased to be my
property till the time when I gave him his freedom;
he is dead, and his heirs have entered upon the
inheritance he left." Then the man answered and
said, "I hold in my hand an instrument that will

prove the truth of what I state. Please to open it, that its contents may be known." The judge opened the document and found that it bore out the statements of the complainant. The sultan, having informed himself of the date of the paper, replied, "I have witnesses to prove that at the said date Sonkor was in my possession and at Cairo; the year previous I had bought him with eight others, and he remained in my possession till he received his freedom." He then summoned several of his chief military officers who bore witness that the facts were in accordance with the statements of the sultan, and declared that the date he had given was exact. The plaintiff was confounded, and the judge said to the sultan, "My lord! the man has done this only that he may obtain mercy at my lord's hands, being in your presence; and it will not be meet to let him depart disappointed." "Oh," said the sultan, "that is quite another matter." He then ordered a robe of honour to be given to the man, and a sum of money, which was ample to cover his expenses. Observe the rare and admirable qualities shown by the sultan in this matter, his condescension, his submission to the regulations prescribed by the law of Islam, the putting aside of his pride, and the generosity he displayed at a time when he might justly have inflicted a punishment.

But no democracy can be complete and aspire to be permanent unless it is accompanied by the spiritual emancipation of the individual to-day. Even Europe has begun to wonder as to whether democracy should lose ground before the rising tide of dictatorship and oligarchy. Islam, in order to stabilize democracy and make it part and parcel of human society, first emancipates everyone by inculcating that there is no mediator between man and his Creator. Islam starts from within, emancipates us spiritually and aims at building up a social system rooted in the conviction that between man and man there is no difference, that socially, morally, spiritually, all are equal. Europe, and the rest of the world with it, are still mentally, spiritually in the shackles of priestcraft. It also places in our hands a complete code of ethics which guides us in the right use of the emancipation it rains upon us. It is one thing to emancipate an individual; it is another thing to enable him to use his newly won birthright properly and justly.

CHAPTER 24

"THERE SHALL BE NO PROPHET AFTER ME"

> "Muhammad . . . is the Apostle of God and the seal of the Prophets."—THE QURAN 33 : 40.

WHEN God creates man for some special purpose, then it is natural to suppose that He should give instructions to these men to attain the purpose for which they have been created. It was for this that He sent among all nations from time to time prophets, to reveal to them His wishes, and to instruct them so that they might be guided into the right path that leads to the fulfilment of the true purpose of creation. Because the God of all mankind is One, therefore the injunctions revealed to different nations through various prophets were identical, except that they varied in detail according to national and geographical conditions. Otherwise the fundamentals of all were the same.

In the early days of our forefathers the life of man was simple and plain, entirely free from present-day complications of society and State. In consequence the intelligence of man in those days was not fully developed to the extent of understanding and fathoming the mysteries of religion; and the instructions revealed to him correspondingly simple.

The purpose of the early revelations was but to prove in simple language that the God of all creation is One; that human beings and other things created are of His creation alone; that there is a form for praying to God; and that there is a life after death, wherein the deeds of all will be judged. "And what they had done they shall find present there; and your Lord does not deal unjustly with anyone" (THE QURAN 28: 49). "On the day that every soul shall find present what it has done of good and what it has done of evil" (THE QURAN 3: 29). As humanity advanced in evolutionary progress and as the complications of life became greater, the laws of religion and its canons increased in their scope. And thus it was necessary that, from time to time, prophets should be raised up, who should add to, and improve on the old instructions, as God deemed necessary, to suit the changing conditions.

In early days the nations of the world lived in more or less complete seclusion one from another, because of the lack or, rather, absence of means of communication and transportation. They were economically and spiritually self-sufficing units. Each nation had its own prophets and books. A prophet of one nation had no intercourse with the prophet of another nation. The result was that each nation regarded itself as the chosen nation of God, and His blessings as their exclusive privilege. Later, the means of communication which had brought them closer to one another led some nations to regard all others as the despised of God, and they

246

themselves as the chosen ones. Thus the gulf went on widening, peace and tranquillity becoming ever more impossible. It was necessary, therefore, to remedy this diseased outlook so that all nations might be brought to "dwell together in unity."

When God decided that the time had come for all nations to coalesce into one large family under one religion, he sent a world religion, so that all differences and disputes between nations might be brought to an end; and one and all be fused into one fraternity under a common bond of Faith. This also struck at the root of the racial, national, and other barriers, by bringing all to the worship of the One God. To reveal this universal religion to the whole of mankind God selected the Prophet of Arabia. This was in accordance with Scriptural prophecies in which He revealed and promised to Abraham that He would raise from his sons prophets in the future (Genesis 12 : 2-3). Before, prophethood had been confined to the issue of Abraham through Isaac. Now it was transferred to the descendants of Abraham from Ishmael. Arabia, from which God chose the Last Prophet, was of all countries that most plunged in idolatry and sin. Moreover, in that country no prophet had hitherto appeared. Even the preachings of the Jewish faith, and later of Christianity, had failed to have the slightest effect on it.

Both Judaism and Christianity had strayed woefully from the teaching of their prophets. The latter had itself established idolatry by making images of Jesus Christ and his mother and worshipping them

247

as diviuities, and as to the former there is ample
evidence to prove the manipulation of the "Torah"
—the Old Testament—by human hands. The
Jewish priests had supreme authority. They con-
trolled religion and the religious books, introducing
changes and additions to suit their own ends.
These were the religions that had not been very
long in the world, but had already come to such
a phase as to become absolutely the appanage of
the clergy; and they remain to this day, religions
of the clergy, not the religion of God. Take, for
example, the Christian form of worship, the Mass
said or sung in the Catholic churches and the
services held in others; they are all for the worship
of Jesus Christ alone. But the God of all, and,
according to the Christian beliefs, the Father,
Who should be considered greater than the son, is,
comparatively speaking, forgotten. Such is the
condition of these revealed religions to-day; and
their condition in ages gone by, as the history
of the deeds of the Church and the clergy shows,
was not materially different.

Such was the state of the world when an illiterate
man from Arabia arose, and was made Prophet
to redeem it. He was illiterate; for there were no
schools or colleges or universities in the land in
those days, where he could have acquired an
education. The people from whom he came were
sunk deep in sin of every sort, and idolatry was
firmly established in their hearts. The holy Quran
says, "On land and sea men had forgotten God, and
were sunk into sin" (30: 41). The lands surrounding

248

Arabia, and those whither he used to go in connection with business, presented much the same degrading spectacle. The priests themselves were selfish and there was nothing much to choose between them and the rest of the people. But the worst place of all was his own country, Arabia.

From early childhood these things had set him pondering. He was hard put to it to seek a solution to put an end to immorality and godlessness; failing which he was convinced that some dreadful calamity must befall and destroy the whole people. To undertake the task God chose him—Muhammad, the Perfect Man—and made him the Last Prophet.

As I have shown in the previous chapters, the holy Prophet Muhammad, on being raised to the Prophethood, wrought a complete transformation in his people and his environment. Ungodly and unclean, the people were changed into clean and godly. He also did not hesitate to bring home to the followers of other scriptures the grave errors into which they had fallen, and invited them to tread in the right path to God. It was a transformation, acknowledged by the whole world, from bad to good, from ugly to beautiful, and from filthy to sublime. It was a light from Heaven that infused his being and illuminated all. It would take volumes to do justice to the reformation brought about by Islam which had chosen for its inception a place wherein no book had been revealed before. A cursory glance at the pages of history will show that Islam appeared at a period when the age of isolationism had passed. The time had come

249

for the foundation of a world-religion. There could be no more appropriate a place for its growth and culture than Arabia, chosen for the birthplace of Islam because it was not encumbered by religious limitations.

The true purpose of religion is to teach human beings to follow the right path according to the Divine teaching. But before asking them to follow a teaching, it is necessary to tell them what and whose the teaching is; secondly, to explain who had been chosen to preach it; and finally, to make clear the great benefit that will be derived by following that teaching. These are the fundamentals on which religions are based.

Of all the revealed books only the Old Testament shows that a part of it really is a revelation. As for the others, previous to the Old Testament, it is not even known what their names were or in what language they were written or what has become of them. About the New Testament European Christians themselves have proved by research that save for a few sentences which are revelations, the rest is a biography neither authoritative nor authentic. The study of the Old Testament, the Jewish Book, discloses three things: 1, that God is One; 2, that none can be associated with Him; and 3, that He is the God of the Israelites alone, which means that He is a local and national God. The story of Jacob wrestling with God has given rise to the conception that He has a body, and it is quite probable that the Christian conception of the Divinity, namely, that Jesus Christ is the Son of God, may be due to the metaphors of the Old Testament.

For the true significance of the conception of God in Islam the study of the holy Quran will be the best guide. The Catholic Bishop Lefroy, in speaking of the Muslim conception of God says, "Not so much that God is One, as that God is—that His existence is the ultimate fact of the universe—that His will is supreme, His sovereignty absolute, His power limitless." (*Mankind and the Church.*) The attributes of God in Islam are to be seen in the everyday existence of all life, and the mere understanding of it fills the heart with reverence and adoration.

The theory of the Unity of God is not only that no one else can be associated with Him, but that in obedience to His orders, no other consideration should take precedence of His Will. Whatever it be, whether another being, or just a wish of the heart, it must be got rid of, if it interferes in any way with the communion of the soul with God. This injunction is to be found in no other religious book but the holy Quran.

By repudiating the conception of a local God Islam preached that the One God is the God of the whole world, and thus laid the foundation-stone of the world-religion. On the subject of other prophets and their messages, nearly all religious books are silent. In the Bible itself the Son of God has declared previous prophets to be thieves and robbers; and all the Old Testament shows is that the nation to which it belongs is the only one beloved

251

by God. Moreover, not one of the books explains the standard by which the prophets could be believed and judged. Only the holy Quran has thrown light on this point. It was revealed in Arabia, and nothing has been added to, or subtracted from, it. The holy Prophet Muhammad came to redeem the whole world, because his God is the God of the whole world. He, Muhammad himself, gave proof of his prophethood, and did not depend on others for it. He set up a criterion for the recognition of other prophets; and one of the first things he proclaimed was that there were many prophets raised before from among many nations, and that all former prophets were equally the elect of God. By the constant changes made in the Old Testament, the characters of former Prophets became in course of time besmirched; but the holy Prophet of Islam cleared their names, confuted all false charges made against them, and testified to their impeccability. The second foundation-stone of the world religion was that the holy Prophet preached the brotherhood of mankind, and invited all—not those of his own nations, but all—to join in the world fraternity under the One True God.

Another important subject left very much to the imagination by all religious books except the holy Quran is that of the life after death. We are told in general terms that there is such a life, and that in it all deeds will be judged. The holy Quran, on the other hand, explains all this in detail. In the first place it divides the life after death into two sections; one from the time of death to the day of judgment; and the other from the day of judgment to infinity. In the second place it describes men's deeds and their philosophy, and then explains the real conception of Heaven and Hell.

Such questions as: What are Angels? What relations have they with God and human beings? are solved by the holy Quran alone which tells us at length all about the angels, their position, station, and relation with God and humanity.

Why was the world created? What purpose had God in creating human beings? To what length can human beings be tied by the hands of Fate? To what extent can man utilize nature in his development? These are problems arising from the question of fate, and, again, no other book except the Quran explains them.

The tenets of Islam are two: first, our duty to God, and second, our duty to our fellow men. The philosophy of *'Ibādat*—duty to God—is expressed in two words *La'allakum tattaqūn*—which means, "to become Godly by establishing communion with God." Islamic prayer is not a ritual, but a simple means of expressing homage and devotion to God. At the time of prayer the Brotherhood in Islam is well seen, when all, irrespective of colour, race, and position stand side by side and offer their prayers to God. To pray without knowing the significance of prayer is otiose, and Islam teaches the value of prayer by explaining it in detail. In Islam, be it remembered, there is no intermediary between man and God.

253

On the subject of the duties of man towards his fellow beings, the teaching of Islam is more thorough than that of all other religions; for by bringing it into the sphere of politics it has by its social and political code made possible and practical the theory of democracy and clearly shown the interdependence of one on the other. The civil and criminal fundamentals of these codes are on a world basis. The laws of previous religions have been modified by Islam to apply to, and to encompass, world conditions. To illustrate my point I will refer to the conception of justice in Islam. The basic principle of all legislation is justice. Islam modifies punishment, when such a course is not detrimental to the offender, according to the exigencies of the case, so as to make him again a useful member of society.

From the foregoing it may have become clear that Islam claims to be the most perfect and that the holy Prophet was the last of the race of the prophets, which is borne out not only by Muslim literature, the Quran, and world events, but also by the Christian and Hebrew Scriptures.

I append some extracts from the Traditions of the Prophet himself to show that he was the Last Prophet, and that no prophet would be raised up after him. Abū Hurayra, a companion of the holy Prophet, quotes this saying of the Prophet, "The Israelite prophets attended to the affairs of Israel, and when a prophet died another was raised up to take his place. After me there will be raised up no prophets to succeed me, but, instead, there will be my vicegerents." Tirmizī[1] writes that the Prophet said, "With me the prophethood has ended, and there will be raised up no prophet after me." Another saying of the Prophet, as quoted by Tirmizī, states, ". . . There will be some among my followers who will claim to be prophets but the truth is that I am the Last Prophet, and there shall be no prophet raised up in the world after me," while Bukhārī[1] and Muslim[1] have a saying to the effect, "I have got many names; I am Muhammad; I am Ahmad; . . . I am Hāshir, . . . and I am 'Āqib, after which there will be no prophet."

---

[1] Names of authorities on, and compilers of, the traditions of the holy Prophet Muhammad. They flourished in the 9th century A.C.

CHAPTER 25

AS EUROPEAN CRITICS SEE MUHAMMAD

> "By the pen and that which they
> write therewith, thou art not for
> thy Lord's favour a madman."
> —THE ,QURAN 68: 1–2.

I HAVE read many works by European writers on Muhammad. The majority of them, as a rule, are prejudiced. It is, therefore, refreshing to come across such writers as are capable of appreciating the personality of Muhammad, who is the most misunderstood of all religious personages—Moses, Jesus, Buddha, and Confucius. One of such writers is Major Arthur Glyn Leonard. In his *Islam: her Moral and Spiritual Value*, he has tried to allay the antagonistic attitude of Christendom towards Islam, and entreated the Christian West to approach Islam by divesting itself of all prejudices.

In the opening chapter he speaks of the attitude of Europe towards Islam, and traces the cause to the narrow mentality of Europe. The "Moslem Menace," as the author puts it, is nothing more than the "Yellow Peril" that obsessed Europe and America some time ago. In his book he says: "It is with the moral and spiritual utility of the soul of Islam that I am now about to deal." Proclaiming that Islam has a soul, he continues to say, "For

Islam, believe me . . . has a sincere and earnest soul . . . a great and profound soul that is worth knowing." For the achievement of this purpose, he says, "I have consulted no works on either Muhammad or Islam, but have gone straight to the source or fountain-head . . . to Muhammad himself"; for, he asserts, "It is here, in the man and his work, that the true soul of Islam is to be found." I raise my hat to Major Leonard for his brave attempt to speak for Islam when 99 per cent of his compatriots and probably co-religionists are decrying it. In common with his countrymen Mr. Leonard is not altogether free from preconceptions or inherited notions about Islam. For example, he refuses to believe that the Quran is the very word of God, and maintains that it is the result of the Prophet's communion with nature.

Mr. Leonard has given expression to a profound truth when he writes, "If ever man on this earth found God; if ever man devoted his life to God's service with a good and great motive, it is certain that the Prophet of Arabia was that man." In this sentence, besides speaking the truth, the author has summed up the value of the great Prophet. That Mr. Leonard comes to these conclusions is ample proof that, given the opportunity to approach in the proper manner, the personality of Muhammad will never fail to impress the seeker with its worth and greatness. He says, "Not only great; but of the greatest, i.e. truest, man that humanity has ever produced." Speaking of Islam he says, "He [the seeker] will thus acknowledge that Islam is a profound and true cult, which strives to uplift its votaries from the depths of human darkness upwards into the higher realms of Light and Truth." If this be the purpose of Islam, and if this be the finding of a European, then the day is not far distant when people of goodwill shall come to the self-same conclusion about Islam and its promulgator.

As mentioned elsewhere in these pages the Prophet was of a contemplative temperament and accustomed to spend his hours in thought and meditation. That his meditation was on God is a fact proved beyond doubt. He felt that above idols, sons of God, and the like, there was yet a greater Being who is the Ruler of all, and endeavoured to find Him. And having found Him, thereafter everywhere and in everything he saw God. Major Leonard alludes to this thus, "In the grim silence of the desert, in the vastness of the Heavens, in the great infinity of space, in the scintillation of the stars, in every fibre of his own consciousness, God was with him"; and again, "To Muhammad God was not a personal Being, but the God and Maker of the Universe and all Mankind. With him the entire theme and volume of his stream of thought was God and His religion." Also he writes, "God and the Truth was the rich, strong wine which coursed through every vein and fibre of his mental organism, stimulating and spurring him onwards."

Having exhausted all ugly epithets they could think of wherewith to decry the Prophet, the European writers dubbed him insane. Of this the

258

author says, "If ever a man was *sane* and healthy, it was he." The acceptance of the Prophet as the Apostle of God cannot be better described than in the words of Major Leonard, "His absorption of God ended in God's absorption of him." "Men," said Victor Hugo, "talk to themselves," and the author comments upon this, "The great reality as I have shown that obsessed Muhammad was God. Though invisible in person, or even in spirit, God was none the less visible and palpable to him as much in the finest speck of sand as in the consuming glory of the sun. In the mocking spectres of the night, as well as in the shifting shadows of the morning, the might and majesty of Allah was supreme. In the dead silence of human solitude the grand tumult within him was only grand and tumultuous because God talked to him and he to God in the suppressed sibilance of hushed and awesome whisperings." Truly diamonds are found in the darkness of the earth, Truths are only found in the depths of thought! This sentiment the author translates thus: "The brilliant which Muhammad searched for was the Truth . . . the greatest brilliant of all! The Truth that he found as it appeared to him was God."

Yet Christendom felt it its duty to paint this Prophet in the blackest of colours, and is still afraid lest Islam succeed in its ideals. And if it does? What harm? Can the followers of such a man be condemned?

Speaking of an average Muslim the author says, ' Not only, however, is he fervid and in downright earnest, but he is, above all, constant, faithful to, and consistent in, the principles of his creed. Thus, although there is no fatherhood about Allah, there is for all that a true and real brotherhood in Islam which contrasts very favourably with the professed brotherhood of Christendom." If it is so, would it not be better that humanity in earnest should study Islam?

Not being able to comprehend the marvellous and complex personality of Muhammad some of his European biographers have come to form a theory that Muhammad was a psychopath. Well, if a psychopath has the power to give a fresh direction to the course of human history, it is a point of the highest psychological interest to search his original experience which has turned slaves into leaders of men, and has inspired the conduct and shaped the career of whole races of mankind. To rebut this I will quote Mr. Emile Dermenghem, from his *Life of Mahomet* (London, 1930). I make no apology for these rather lengthy quotations in view of the popularity which this theory has gained and has deterred many from forming a just estimate of Muhammad. Mr. Dermenghem writes:

"To-day we cannot question his sincerity. His whole life in spite of his faults (and he did not deny having faults), proves that he believed profoundly in his mission and that he accepted it heroically as a burden of which he was to bear the heaviest portion. His creative ability and the vastness of his genius, his great intelligence, his sense of the practical, his will, his prudence, his self-control and his activity—in short, the life he led—make it impossible to take this inspired mystic for a visionary epileptic. He never for an instant asked himself whether his chances of convincing people would not be greater if he adjusted his words to the mentality of his audience. It was certainly not with soft words that he made converts, but in presenting his brilliant message in all its vigour, simple and sharp as the edge of a sword, a message which he carefully distinguished from his personal views. If at Medina he was no longer the humble and patient Prophet of Mecca it is because the circumstances were no longer the same; had he remained the same outwardly, his essential character would have had to change. The man may have been sometimes blameworthy or weak, for action is a difficult test of purity, but the Prophet remained sincere and unchanged. He may have sinned,[1] but he did not lie. How can we imagine a man in whose eyes success appeared only as a divine confirmation suddenly becoming a liar (and surely there can be no question of his sincerity at the beginning of his career)? And how could he have dared to debase his mission at the very moment when he believed it to be confirmed?

"The very faults of the Prophet prove that his unique and real grandeur came from God, from his supernatural inspiration. Without God he felt himself alone and weak. . . .

---

[1] The Prophet never sinned. He was born sinless and died sinless like all other Prophets of God. He made mistakes. The difference between sin and mistake is vast and obvious.—THE AUTHOR.

"Muhammad records in the Koran the faults with which God reproached him. Once he turned his back on a poor blind man (80: 1–11), and there were divine reproofs when he was weak with his wives, etc. . . .

"The theories of epilepsy, auto-suggestion or an excited imagination elaborated by psychiatrists do not take into account the camp-life of the desert and the ingenuity required to retain a place as a simple chief of a band of Bedouins. Until he felt the call, his life had been normal and perfectly balanced and, his revelations apart, it never ceased to be. As in the case of the authentic mystics and the Prophets of Israel it is not because he was ill that he had visions; it is because he had visions that his body presented pathological symptoms.

"My heart was broken within me, all my bones trembled; I am like a drunken man because of the Lord and His holy words,' cried Jeremiah; and Amos, wrapped in his mantle, like Mahomet, speaks in the same tone.

"Neurotics, false mystics, and authentic visionaries present phenomena in common. The one is purely passive; the other active and creative. At the most we might say that a morbid tendency may facilitate trances which, in their turn, would increase the tendency. But one finds no traces, as it seems, of this pathological state in Mahomet. Until he was a middle-aged man his health was perfect and the attacks did not occur except for purpose of revelation.

"Aside from this and the illness which caused his death when he was about sixty, he suffered almost from a few headaches, induced by long marches in the sun, which were treated by cupping.

"The revelations assuredly caused him much suffering, and certain phenomena would then take place which he did not care to show in public. Abū Bakr one day commented in a melancholy way on the Prophet's beard, which had begun to turn white. . . .

"In the course of ten years Mahomet sent forth forty expeditions. This man who, when he is not represented as an adroit impostor, is often described as an epileptic visionary, personally took part in thirty campaigns and directed ten battles, not to mention the difficult negotiations he had to undertake. We know what qualities are required to support an expedition in Arabia . . . the physical endurance, the perseverance, the untiring diplomacy that must form part of the nature of every Arabian chief, whose power is always unstable, depends upon his ability to dominate personally. In this difficult and exhausting art Mahomet excelled."

"Great man that Mohammed was," says Mr. J. C. Archer in his *Mystical Elements in Mohammed* (London, 1924), "the full story of his life and work is not yet told. The outer facts are very generally —and, one may say, fairly accurately—known. Our knowledge of the inner state, however, leaves much to be desired." After discussing and finally discarding the theory that Muhammad was a psychopath, he gives the following estimate of the holy Prophet:

"We have seen in Mohammed a many-sided personality, one to whom many different types of men might appeal, and one to whom a diverse host have appealed. It is not surprising that interpretations of him vary. Extremists have found their roots in him, for example, the *faqir* (see THE QURAN 10: 63; 34: 32; 35: 16; and Krehl, *Sahih* 11, 105, 16 *f.*), the hermit, the dervish (cf. THE QURAN 24: 30), and the sūfi (cf. THE QURAN 2: 109; 18: 17), who have taken an attitude usually of utter 'dependence' upon God. But Mohammed was not altogether 'quietistic.' He displayed no exaggerated 'dependence' upon God. He was a practical prophet. He was not in the hands of God as the corpse is in the washer's hands (to use the words of Goldziher in his *Vorlesungen*). He was no mere 'child of the day' with no thought of the morrow. Nor was he indifferent to the things of the body, to sufferings and to buffetings. He had ends in view which demanded strength both of body and of spirit. He put his confidence in God, but did not neglect 'to tie the camel's leg.' He lamented the dishonesty and greed of his time, the indifference of his people to spiritual values, but he did not recommend as a cure for all this the denial of the world entirely. 'The dust of the actual' covered the way he trod, and prudence was a constant companion on the journey. . . . That he nevertheless did have so large and so effective a program of reform for this world is a matter of continuing wonder and admiration, not to be explained by any casual theory of the abnormal.

"Mohammed was an expert in things mystical who could, after all, occupy himself with the details of life (cf. THE QURAN 2: 180) without ignoring or losing the invisible world. Indeed, his administration of worldly affairs and the enduring success of his earthly mission were linked up with his insight into the invisible. Realizing this, he sought diligently to extend his limited knowledge of the invisible world."

I conclude this chapter with the words of Mr. E. E. Kellett, in his *A Short History of Religions* (London, 1933), p. 333. He says, ". . . There is no more astonishing career in history than that of the founder of this religion, and scarcely any man has more profoundly influenced the destinies of the world. He was, of course, favoured by circumstances, but he knew how to turn them to his purposes, and he faced adversity with the determination to wring success out of failure. While he could not have succeeded in another place or at another time, it is tolerably certain that no one could have succeeded at all."

CHAPTER 26

THE PERSONALITY AND CHARACTER OF MUHAMMAD

> "We have not sent thee but a
> Mercy to all the nations."—THE
> QURAN 21 : 10.

THE greatness of a man lies in the possession
of personality—"One of the indescribable mar-
vels of the world." A great personality is not only
an asset of itself but is also a thing of great and
lasting value to those in contact with it; it inspires
others with confidence and resolve, and urges them
to follow faithfully its trend to the highest point
of perfection. Among all the world's heroes, the
personality of the holy Prophet alone can be said
to be mighty and unique. The light of his personality
was like the sun—it dispelled darkness from every
corner whither it penetrated. So wonderful was it
that Christian writers have been compelled to
admit that "Muhammad must be remembered
among the greatest." Marvellous, indeed, it must
have been to have claimed and retained the love,
respect, and obedience of all followers. Of the first
few years, when persecution of the new Faith was
at its height, Mr. Marmaduke Pickthall writes,
"Listen to the answer which a follower of the holy
Prophet, when put to extreme torture, gave his
persecutors. They asked him, 'Don't you now wish

Muhammad was in your place?' Amidst his pain the sufferer cried out, 'I would not wish to be with my family, with my children and my wealth, on the condition that Muhammad was only to be pricked with thorn.' This is the accent of a personal love, and the same note of personal affection is evident in all the hundreds of reports concerning him. . . ." We do not see this kind of thing in the lives of others, even of Gods-Incarnate, and it is because they did not possess the greatness, the humaneness which is essential in a reformer and moulder of men. In the holy Prophet, on the other hand, we do find this ideal personality, which moulded the character of his fellow men, reformed them, revolutionized their thoughts, and elevated them to a higher plane.

The state of the people of Arabia when he was born, as well as at the time of his mission, is well known to all; irreligion, infanticide, immorality, infidelity, and corruption were rampant. As against it we know the wonderful change brought about by the personality of Muhammad. He was fully conscious of his mission, he felt the force of his convictions, and because he was the possessor of a great personality he went to the root cause of the evil instead of adopting half-measures and compromises. He had no pretensions and did not indulge in hyperbolical language, but straightforwardly said, "I am only a preacher of God's word, the bringer of God's message to mankind," and succeeded in his mission. The Arabs were extremely superstitious, and the holy Prophet could have claimed any sort of supernatural power, had he so wished. But instead we find in him a man, a reformer, a Prophet, a Messenger from God, who stripped himself of all the trappings popularly associated with those before him who came on a similar mission. His life's aim was his mission, for the purpose of which he was chosen. He chose to achieve it by a direct and simple method, putting aside all temptations to and chances of self-aggrandizement. That is why Muhammad's life is not crowded with miracles to achieve his object.

A prophet comes to act as a guide and exemplar and, as such, he must possess the highest personality, for to achieve lasting success he should work humanly, that is, adopt those means only that are within human reach. By this I do not mean that miracles are unnecessary; they are but to strengthen the conviction of, or drive home, certain truth. For example, Moses saved his people from the wrath of Pharaoh by miracles, whereas the holy Prophet saved his people in Medina by his heroic deeds. But Moses with all his miracles failed to instil that spirit of manliness which we see in the followers of the holy Prophet. Jesus Christ always complained of the lack of faith of his disciples, while the holy Prophet Muhammad had never to complain of any such thing.

"In the furnace of trial and persecution the ore of character becomes burnished gold. Adversity and hardships bring out what lies in man; they either make of him an everlasting character the light of which shines always and everywhere, or reduce him to nothingness and oblivion." It is a fact that nobody passed through so many vicissitudes of life as the holy Prophet, and in spite of all this he remained firm, and succeeded in his mission, simply because he possessed an unimpeachable and high character. The Meccans strove their hardest to impugn his title to the call, but found they could not call him liar or impostor. All that they could do was to invent such excuses as that he was a magician or sorcerer, but this did not appeal to the *intelligenzia* of Arabia, as is shown by a speech of Nazr bin Hārith to the Quraysh Assembly in which he said, "O Quraysh! you have not been able to devise any plan to get out of the difficulty which descended on you. Muhammad grew up from childhood to manhood before your eyes; you all know very well that he is the most honest, the most veracious, and the most charming of you all. And when his hair is growing grey, and when he has placed his ideas and claims before you, you cry with audacity, 'He is a magician, he is a sorcerer, he is mad, he is a poet'; by God, I have listened to what Muhammad says and preaches; Muhammad is neither a magician, nor a sorcerer, nor a poet, nor a madman. I believe some new calamity is about to befall you." Abū Jahal, the uncle and the enemy of the Prophet had said, "Muhammad, I do not say you are a liar, but whatever you preach is untrue." Another uncle, Abū Tālib, who when invited to join Islam said that he could not give up the religion of his fore-fathers, yet, when informed by his own son of his belief in the holy Prophet, said, "Well, my son, Muhammad will not call you to anything save that which is good; therefore, thou art free to cleave to him." All this points towards the one conclusion that the holy Prophet possessed an unimpeachable character, as well as a mighty personality. Once during the early messages to the Quraysh he assembled a gathering at the foot of Mount Safā, and addressed them thus: "O People of the Quraysh! If I were to tell you that behind this mountain there is lying hidden a large army, would you believe me?" And all of them replied: "Certainly, because to our knowledge you have never told a lie." Then he spoke to them of their wickedness, and warned them of the fate that had befallen those who strayed from the path of God, but the Quraysh did not pay heed to his words. He then started preaching to those who came from afar and the Quraysh, alarmed at this, one day sent 'Utba to the Prophet offering him riches, wealth, and women if he could but stop preaching, but Muhammad's character was far too high for these temptations. His faith in God and in his mission was great, and in spite of all odds he strove patiently towards the goal. Even a hostile writer like Sir William Muir was compelled to write, when he came to this part of his book on the *Life of Mahomet* that "Mahomet, thus holding his people at bay, waiting, in the still expectation of victory, to outward appearance defenceless, and with his little band, as it were, in the lion's mouth, yet trusting in His Almighty power Whose messenger he believed himself to be, resolute and unmoved, presents a spectacle of sublimity paralleled only in the sacred records by such scenes as that of the Prophet of Israel, when he complained to his Master, 'I, even I only, am left.' " It is a pity that Sir William Muir, true to his purpose, tries to belittle the holy Prophet by citing as a parallel case the vicissitudes of a Prophet of Israel, between whose trials and those of Muhammad can be traced no similarity whatever.

As in Mecca, his career at Medina is an essential link in the chain of his character. The only difference is that, persecution being left behind, it marks a new era in the life of the Prophet, as well as in the history of Islam. In Medina, the Prophet found people ready to help him, and eager to become his followers, which fact gave him the opportunity of practising what he had preached at Mecca. He enlarged and expanded the laws of Moses, and virtually brought on earth the "kingdom of Heaven" spoken of by Jesus Christ. There he succeeded in bringing to life the theories of Aristotle and Plato by establishing, so to say, for the first time in the history of the world, and administering a socialistic state. Thus the socialistic ideas of which Jesus Christ dreamed were materialized by the holy Prophet.

Soon the whole of Arabia was subjugated and Medina became the shrine of learning and government. The life of the Prophet there quickly dispelled the misgivings of those, if any there were, who still believed that earthly riches and a kingdom were his aim. Every action of his in Medina as well as in

271

Mecca clearly shows that he possessed a character unique in the annals of the world. There was one trait in him which proved that he had attained that height of character and morality which must be the final goal of human effort, where man begins to reflect the Divine morals.

He was the same in victory as in defeat; in power as in adversity; in affluence as in indigence. His life in Mecca had been a life of adversity, of trial and danger; in Medina it was a life of success and prosperity. But in the former as in the latter he remained the same man, and at times gave evidence of that magnanimity of soul, the equal of which the history of the world cannot produce.

CHAPTER 27

THE PERSONAL QUALITIES OF MUHAMMAD

> "And surely you conform your-
> self to sublime morality."—THE
> QURAN 68 : 14.

SINCE the personal qualities of the holy Prophet
were all of the highest, it will be interesting and
educative to study them in some detail so that we
may the better realize and understand the success
achieved by him.

To-day, when the world is lapsing into the
barbaric stage on account of the growth in material-
ism, sin, and ungodliness, there is a crying need
for one whose example will avail to guide human
beings back to the ideals of happiness and perfection.
Muhammad's personality is not only great but
perfect; it can be set as an example to the world
for the correction and reformation of all evils.

Of all men Muhammad was the kindest and
most gentle, the bravest, the meekest, the most
chaste, and the most generous. He was kind to
one and all alike, rich or poor, free man or slave.
One who had been in his service for over ten years
said that in all that time he was never once repri-
manded by the Prophet. If his servants did aught
amiss or went against his wishes in any way, he
would speak to them kindly and point out their

S

mistakes. He never kept slaves. If he was given a slave, he would at once set him free. From the time of his birth to his death he was never known to be harsh to anyone, or beat a servant or child.

The Prophet not only expounded the theory of the equality of the sexes, but also followed it in practice himself. The love and care with which he treated all his wives, in spite of the heavy duties imposed upon him as the Prophet of God, is a wonderful example, and should be a lesson to all. He was the perfection of justice, and the regard he had for the feeling of the ladies of his house amply proves it. And because he knew human psychology very well, he understood all the phases of the female character, and not only gave heed to them personally, but also advised his followers to do so. He often said, "Those of you are best who treat their wives and children kindly and lovingly." The private life of a person, in the seclusion of his home, is the true test of his character; for then he is his own self without formality or affectation and the life of the holy Prophet stands this test triumphantly.

Among his many beautiful qualities, that of appreciation of kindness or service is remarkable. Muhammad always appreciated any service, however small, done by a person to himself, to the nation, or the world at large. As God recognizes and appreciates the works of His creatures so did Muhammad, who was imbued with this attribute of God. It was his belief that he who did not recognize and encourage the endeavours of others could not appreciate the many mercies of God. And this belief he put in practice himself; for it was his custom to demonstrate to the world by practice what he or the Quran had said, so that there might not be any shadow or difference between example and precept.

The incidents recorded below show that not only did the holy Prophet appreciate and admire the deeds of the rich and great, but also of the lowly, the poor, and the simple. Bilāl and Salmān were of low birth. Zayd and 'Ammār, though Arabs, were very poor. But Muhammad appreciated their work as he would that of anyone else. Zayd was the purchased slave of Khadīja. She presented him to Muhammad, who gave him his freedom at once. But even after his manumission, Zayd insisted on staying with the Prophet. After a while the father and the relatives of Zayd came to the Prophet and begged him to allow Zayd to return to their native place with them. He at once gave his consent, but Zayd himself absolutely refused to go with them. He said, "The care that the holy Prophet takes of me, and the love and kindness with which he regards me, are greater than those of parents and relations." In token of this faithfulness Muhammad regarded Zayd as a member of his family, and married his own cousin Zaynab to him. His appreciation of Zayd's faithfulness did not end there; for later he was made commander-in-chief, and his son, 'Usāmah, the commander of an army. Furthermore, on the occasion of the victory of Mecca, 'Usāmah was given the honour of riding on the same camel as the holy Prophet.

Bilāl was a negro. Being a black man the fair Arabs hesitated to associate with him freely, but the Prophet put an end to this by making him *Mu'azzin* (the person who calls for prayers), and controller of his household. Further to elevate his status the Prophet said, "You will walk in front of me in Heaven." His treatment of strangers, and the poor and lowly, was ever marked by kindness and love; so that they would talk proudly, and boast of their relations with the Prophet, saying, "The Prophet sits with us, our bodies often touch his body."

Khadīja, the first wife of the holy Prophet, was a great help and companion to him, and long after she was dead and buried he would remember her and speak in praise of her; and would send presents, from time to time, to those who were her friends. 'Ā'isha, another wife of Muhammad, used to feel jealous at times. One day she spoke to the holy Prophet, asking why, since she herself was young and handsome, he was always remembering and talking of Khadīja, who was an old woman, and many years dead and buried. Muhammad replied, "Khadīja believed in me when I had no one to believe in me; she helped me with money and influence when I had no one to help me. She was always a great comfort to me." 'Ā'isha was ashamed of her jealousy. Thus his regard for his dead wife helped those round him to realize how he cherished the memory of those who had been kind to him.

It is recorded that not one of the Prophet's wives was ever dissatisfied with him. They all regarded him as the perfect and ideal husband.

According to the Arab custom, the holy Prophet's childhood was spent with his nurse, Halīma Sa'diya, whom he always called mother. Once some women of her tribe were captured as prisoners of war. She came in person to Muhammad to ask for their release. Those who did not know that she was the Prophet's foster-mother were surprised to see a Bedouin woman, covered with dust, go straight up to him and address him in these words, "Ay Muhammad! What have you done? You have taken your aunt's relatives prisoners." The holy Prophet at once released those who had been allotted to the Quraysh, and as for the others, he appealed to their possessors to liberate them, which they all promptly and willingly did. Once Shaymā, the daughter of Halīma, came to see him. In order that he should recognize her, she showed him his teeth marks on her back; for in childhood they used to play together, and once in play he had bitten her. When he saw the mark, he at once said, "Please stay with us, and we will do all we can to make you comfortable." When some visitors from Abyssinia came, they were received with due honour, and made most comfortable. He remembered how the few Muslims who had migrated to Abyssinia had been received with kindness by the Abyssinians. It was only right, he said, that now that the Abyssinians had come to visit them, they should be accorded a befitting welcome.

277

The courage of Khālid was always admired
and appreciated, and he was given the name of
Sayfullāh, which means the sword of God, and a
like appreciation was accorded to the trustworthi-
ness and wisdom of 'Ubayd, who was called Amīnu-
'l-'Ummat, that is to say the trustee of the nation.
In short, the services and deeds of all were recognized, appreciated, and encouraged by the Prophet;
the recognition accorded respectively to Abū Bakr,
'Omar, and 'Alī, is well known to students of
history. Of Abū Bakr, the Prophet always spoke
in praise, and was wont to say that he had served
him as a true friend, and helped him by his money,
power, and position. When 'Omar embraced Islam,
Muhammad felt very happy and proud, saying that
it was an event at which the Heavens fully rejoiced.
All his life he was treated by Muhammad as a
beloved brother; he often criticized certain policies,
but Muhammad never felt annoyed. In a similar
way were 'Osmān and 'Alī treated. If the Prophet
honoured Abū Bakr and 'Omar by marrying their
daughters, so did he honour 'Alī and 'Osmān by
marrying his daughters to them. Once, during a
battle, he said he was going to trust the standard
to one who was the beloved of God and Prophet,
and this honour was accorded to 'Alī.

'Abbās, an uncle of the Prophet, once came to
Medina as a prisoner of war. The Prophet felt
uneasy and unhappy about it. He could not bear
to see it. He therefore asked Takrār to loosen the
cords round him. 'Abbās had nothing to wear;
'Abdullāh bin Ubayy gave him a shirt. Muhammad

did not forget this act of kindness of 'Abdullāh. Later, when 'Abdullāh died, he gave him his own shirt to be used as a shroud for him. Muhammad was very grieved and upset when he heard the news of the martyrdom of his uncle, Hamza. He prayed for him and went to his funeral. Likewise, on the occasion of the death of Sa'd, he was very sad and shed tears, and said, "Even Heaven hath felt the death of Sa'd!"

These instances I have cited above show how Muhammad respected and appreciated the deeds of men and women, rich and poor, high and low, alike. As a nation is the sum-total of all individuals, he treated them all equally, which made them all faithful to him, and eager to do their best for Islam. All this was achieved because of his personal qualities. Had he treated them harshly, or shown no appreciation of their conduct, or tried to coerce them, he would never have succeeded in his mission.

In spite of his exalted position the holy Prophet was above all things humble. He did all his work with his own hands, and never allowed anything to be done for him that he could do himself. Daily he milked his own goats, washed and mended his own clothes, repaired his own shoes, and cleaned and swept his house. At the building of the "Mosque of the Prophet," he dug earth and laboured with others in the work of construction. When he had time he always helped his servants in their duties, and besides doing his own marketing did that of others as well, especially the old and feeble.

Once a Jew visited him and stayed the night.

279

The Prophet gave him food, gave him his own sheet to lie on, and asked him to sleep in his own room. During the night the Jew, who had either eaten too much or something which had disagreed with him, suffered from diarrhoea and fouled the room. In a panic he ran away and in his hurry left his sword behind. He decided to return for it. But when he came he was amazed to see the holy Prophet cleaning up the room himself. It is said also that once a Jew's son fell ill in Medina, and the Prophet made it his duty to go daily and inquire about his health.

Once during a journey all present decided to lend a hand with the cooking. Different tasks were allotted to each. The Prophet went into the fields to gather sticks to light the fire. His Companions remonstrated with him, but he set their minds at rest by pointing out that he did not like to have any advantage over the others, and that since all were willing to help in the cooking he saw no reason for exemption. At the battle of Badr, there were more men than there were animals to carry them, therefore three men must needs ride on one camel, and the Prophet choose two men to ride with him on his. The men were reluctant to ride on the same camel as the holy Prophet, and said that they would rather walk, but the Prophet said that if they walked he would also walk.

One day the holy Prophet was distributing the wealth from the national exchequer among the poor; he had a little stick in his hand, and in trying to keep the crowd aside the stick accidentally struck a person in the face and gave him a small bruise. The Prophet in remorse handed the stick to the man and asked him in justice to hit him back.

When the Prophet was returning from his "Farewell Pilgrimage" with his one hundred and forty thousand followers, the cloth on the camel he was riding had cost eighteen pence.

There was an old man who used to dust and sweep a mosque. One day he fell ill and the holy Prophet went to visit him. During that night the old man died, and the people buried him without any funeral prayers or obsequies. In the morning when the Prophet heard of this he was very angry and hied him to the grave of the poor old man and said the funeral prayers.

Fātima, the beloved daughter of the Prophet, used to do all the cooking and grinding of the corn herself. One day she asked her father to get her a help. The Prophet replied that he regretted not being in a position to comply with her wishes; for he had not finished with relief work to the orphans and widows of "the residents of Suffa."

Some, when they came before him, felt awed, but the Prophet always put them at their ease by saying, "Be not afraid of me; I am not a king, but the son of a simple woman who ate dried meat." When people rose at his approach he did not like it. He would ask them to remain seated; for he strongly objected to being treated with what he considered excess of respect. A Companion once addressed him thus, "O, our Master! the son of

our Master! . . ." and the holy Prophet said, "I
am but Muhammad, the son of 'Abdullāh, the
servant of God and His Apostle. I do not desire
that you should exceed that which God has con-
ferred on me." Again, a man once said to him,
"O the best of the world!" whereupon Muhammad
said, "That was Abraham, not I." It is no slight
thing for a great man to be meek and humble
amidst a host of friends and devoted admirers, who
are willing to lay down their very lives for him.
When he entered Mecca as a conqueror, there were
gathered round him over ten thousand followers and
admirers, yet, as the holy Prophet entered, he
bowed his head so low that it rested on the saddle.

The spirit of sacrifice is most prominent in the
character of the holy Prophet. If he possessed
anything that someone else needed, he would part
with it at once, although he might himself have
real need of it. For example, gardens in Arabia
are the most coveted form of property. Once the
holy Prophet was given seven beautiful gardens,
but instead of keeping them for himself he gave
them in charity, their produce being expended in
helping the poor. A man belonging to the Ghaffār
clan came to visit the Prophet, who himself had
had nothing to eat. All there was in the house was
a little milk and this he gave to his guest, himself
having to go hungry to bed. On one occasion all
the Prophet had in his house was a sack of flour.
A Companion of his was to be married, but he was
a poor man and had nothing to entertain his friends
with. The Prophet told him to go to his house and

ask his wife for the sack of flour. The sack was given and there was nothing left in the house of the Prophet for the meal.

A woman once offered the Prophet a beautiful cloth to cover himself with. As it was just the thing he badly needed, he accepted it; but a man standing near admired the cloth saying, "What a lovely cloth!" The Prophet, seeing that the man also needed it, gave it him at once.

The holy Prophet also had an abundant humour and a ready wit. Once a man asked for a ride, and the holy Prophet replied he would give him a baby camel to ride, whereat the man asked what use would the baby camel be. The Prophet replied that a camel gave birth to a camel, and that every camel was once a baby.

It is related that an old lady once paid a visit to the Prophet, who to tease her said that no old women would enter Heaven. Thereat the guest became upset and frightened, and begged the Prophet to tell her what sins she had committed to be thus excluded from Heaven even if she was old. He then told her that it seemed she had not read the Quran properly; for if she had she would have known that in it is stated that everyone would be made young again before entering Heaven. The old lady heaved a sigh of relief on hearing it, and went home with her mind made up to read the Quran through again most thoroughly on her return.

Zāhir bin Hazm, a villager, was very fond of hunting. Often he used to bring the Holy Prophet presents from his village. The Prophet, in giving him presents in return, used to tease him and say to others, "Zāhir is my village representative, and I am his town representative."

It is this goodness of nature together with charm of personality that made so many love the Prophet and become his willing followers.

Simplicity was the keynote of the character of the holy Prophet. All his actions were characterized by simplicity and sincerity; anything artificial was repugnant to him. He would eat whatever was put before him without fuss or question, nor did he mind with whom he took his meals, whether a slave or another.

In his dress, too, he was most simple; he would willingly wear an old patched garment and did not care where he went in it; he had no objection to clothes made out of thick coarse cloth; cleanliness, not the fabric, was the thing which mattered most. Nowadays in India *Khaddar* cloth is the fashion of the day, and more and more people are daily wearing it, but the underlying motive of this is not simplicity as some would have us believe, but a political motive to cripple another nation and force it to come to terms. Yet there are some who, though they clothe themselves in *Khaddar* cloth, adorn their wrists with costly watches, their pockets with expensive fountain-pens, their houses with all modern comforts; and these people, when they travel, have a reserved first class compartment; and when they go abroad they book the most comfortable first class, single-berthed cabin available; these people, when asked where is their simplicity, have no satisfactory reply to make because they cannot give an answer that would satisfy a normally intellectual being.

We Muslims thank God that we have in the person of the Prophet a complete pattern, so that it has taught us how to be truly simple without running the risk of being hypocritical. It has been a help to us at all times, and in all climes. He, for instance, by forbidding Muslims the use of silk and gold made it possible for them to dress neatly and with simplicity.

In regard to all other things, such as food, clothing, living, housing, and the like, the holy Prophet has preached moderation; he taught the Muslims to be simple in all things, and not pompous or foppish. And not only did he preach this but showed it by his perfect example. After the Prophet had breathed his last, his wife, 'Ā'isha, showed people the torn sheet and shirt in which he had died.

Had he so wished he could have lived in a gorgeous palace, surrounded with beautiful gardens, but what he chose for himself was a small house of small rooms; in his own room for furniture a bed made of palm leaf matting, and a jug of water. It is said that at times for months on end there would be no fire in the house. The Prophet never saw or ate roasted goat or loaf bread; very often he lived on nothing but dried dates and water—and, remember, it was not because he did not have the means that Muhammad lived like this. This mode of life was for choice. He loved simplicity, and this quality of his manifested itself in his Companions and followers as well; they lived in the same simple manner. Only once did 'Omar say to the Prophet, "O Prophet! pray for us Muslims; our condition is very bad compared to the people of Byzantium and Persia who, though unbelievers, have all the comforts and luxuries of life." Thereupon the holy Prophet replied, "Do you not agree that they should have the comforts of this life, and we the comforts and luxuries of the other life that is the life everlasting?" Bukhārī, in his *Sahīh*, states that seventy Companions known as Ashābus-Suffa (residents of Suffa) remained with the Prophet all day, and slept at the mosque all night. They did not have beds or bedsteads, but only sheets to cover themselves with. It was these people who succeeded in conquering lands—not only lands but hearts as well—and whose godliness became the proverb of the Muslim world and made them famous.

It was these semi-naked and half-fed men that not only planned conquests, sitting under the roofs of mosques that were neither protected from rain nor from the sun, but also succeeded in effecting them.

Among the qualities of the holy Prophet, neatness and cleanliness were blended with simplicity. He liked to see everything clean and tidy in the house and around him. He kept his body perfectly clean by bathing every day; several times daily he cleaned his teeth; and at least twice daily he would wash out and comb his beard and hair. He liked using a little scent. When out walking, he would always play with the little street children, and carry them up in his arms. Very often they would soil his clothes. But this never annoyed him. He would return home, would wash and change.

In doing justice the holy Prophet was most even-handed. He treated all alike, whether friend or foe, Muslim or non-Muslim. From his very child-hood he was noted for his honesty and fair dealing, and many would come to him to settle their disputes. A Jew once lent the Prophet some money. Three days before the time the loan fell due, he came demanding its payment from the Prophet. Not only did he address the Prophet in a very harsh and insolent manner, he also snatched away his sheet and abused him. 'Omar was greatly annoyed at the rude behaviour of the Jew, and rated him for it, upon which the Prophet rebuked 'Omar and said, "O 'Omar! you should not lose your temper; it is displeasing to God. It would have been better if you had advised us both; me, the debtor, to repay the debt soon, and him, the creditor, to ask for it in a more polite manner." He then paid the Jew more than was his due; paying the extra was be-cause of 'Omar's anger. The Jew was so impressed by the Prophet that he soon afterwards embraced Islam and became a devoted follower.

Once one of the uncles of the holy Prophet was taken a prisoner, the hands and legs of all the prisoners being tightly bound to prevent their escape. The uncle was an old man, and soon felt pain and started moaning. When the prophet heard him he was ill at ease. The Companions, sensing that it was causing the Prophet pain, went without telling him and loosened the cords of the uncle. But when it came to the knowledge of the Prophet he was displeased and told the Companions, that as they had loosened the cords of his uncle, the same consideration must be accorded to all the other prisoners, or else they must bind his uncle again.

At Medina he was accepted as the arbitrator by both the Jews and idolaters in all their disputes. In a case between a Jew and a Muslim which came before the Prophet, he decided in favour of the Jew because he said the Jew was more in the right. When a woman belonging to the tribe of Makhzūm was found guilty of theft, all her relations went to 'Usāmah bin Zayd, of whom the Prophet was very fond, begging him to intercede with the Prophet to set her free, but the Prophet refused, saying that it would not be justice, and added that if his own daughter, Fātima, had committed theft, she would have been punished in the very same manner.

He treated all in the same just way regardless of dignity or rank; slaves and free men were accorded the same treatment as those belonging to a rich and noble tribe. The Quraysh, when going on pilgrimage, were accustomed to stay at a place they had reserved for themselves because they thought it beneath their dignity to mix with the common people. This conduct of the Quraysh was repugnant to the Prophet who always put up at places frequented by the common and poor people. Sometimes at a halt the Companions would select a cool and shady place for him, but he would not use it, and would say, "Whoever gets here first has the prior claim to it."

Because of his generosity, the holy Prophet was always in debt. The Jews were the rich class of Medina, and it was from them that he usually had to borrow, but he always paid back in time and very often he would pay in return more than was due. He often said, "The best men are those who pay their debts honestly." He once borrowed a camel from a friend, and in its place returned a much better one. In the battle of Hunayn, the Prophet was forced to borrow of Safwān forty suits of armour. After the battle it was found that a few suits were missing. The Prophet went to Safwān and said, "Some suits of armour are missing, but here is the price of them."

A rich merchant named Sā'ib, who embraced Islam, was wont to say to his friend, "May my life be the Prophet's sacrifice! Among all men he has been in all transactions and dealings most straightforward and above reproach."

The generosity and kindness of heart of the holy Prophet was a household word. During the month of Ramazān he would give away so lavishly as to leave hardly anything for himself. Whatsoever he was asked for that he would give if he could. Once a man who had embraced Islam asked the Prophet for some goats and sheep. It happened at this time that the Prophet had recently been given great abundance of these animals, so he gave the man so many that they filled the space between two hills.

The Prophet was once given ninety thousand dirhams, which he began to distribute among the beggars. Soon the whole amount was exhausted. After all the beggars had departed an old man came and asked for alms. Muhammad had nothing left to give but he did not like to send the man away empty-handed. He therefore borrowed something from another and gave it to him. A very large sum of money was received as tribute from the province of Bahrayn, the which sum the Prophet ordered to be placed in the mosque. When he arrived he first said prayers and then began to distribute it. Everyone got something, and some who had been reduced to poverty got so much that they could hardly move with the weight. The Prophet did not leave the mosque until he had given it all away. He would never accept anything given in charity for himself or his family. Once his grandson accepted a date given in charity, and began to eat it. The Prophet saw him, rebuked him, and said, "The sons of Hāshim do not eat the things of charity," and made him spit it out.

One day the Prophet arrived home looking very worried, and on his wife inquiring what troubled him he said he had a few dinars which he intended giving to the poor, but had forgotten about them and left them on the bed. So he took them and gave them in charity, and then returned to the mosque to continue the prayers, which he had abruptly left on remembering the money. He never kept money with him overnight. If he had anything left, before nightfall he would give it to beggars. If he came across a beggar who was starving he would give him his meal and remain without anything himself.

It is said that the holy Prophet was more modest and bashful than a virgin. On the road he did not stare at the passers-by but kept his eyes cast down. To him modesty was part of his religion. He was careful to see after he was dressed that the cloth he wore covered him perfectly. The Arabs attached no importance to modesty; they delighted in bathing naked, and saw no harm in it. But to the Prophet this was something abhorrent; he used to say to them, "Do not bathe naked when you bathe in public baths." The women of the town of Homs in Syria used to frequent public bathing places; some of them on one occasion visited Umm Salmā, the wife of the Prophet. She asked them where they had come from, and they replied, "Homs." Whereupon she inquired, "Are you then the women who bathe in public baths?" And they asked, "Why, is it a thing to be condemned?" To which Salmā answered, "The Prophet has said that a woman who bathes in a public place is a disgrace to God."

The social manners of the Prophet are equally edifying. It was the custom of the holy Prophet to be the first to greet on meeting anyone, and in shaking hands he let his hand remain in that of the other person until he himself let it go. When anyone spoke to him in his ear, the Prophet never turned his head until the other had finished saying all he had to say. It was his custom when visiting to stand at the side of the door, call his greeting, and beg for admission. If the greeting was not answered he at once turned back. Once the holy Prophet went to the house of Sa'd bin 'Ubāda to pay him a visit, and, as usual, after the greeting called out for admission. Sa'd heard the greeting but replied in a very low voice, upon which his son Qays told him to answer louder as it was the Prophet who was waiting. Sa'd said he was aware it was the Prophet, but had purposely answered low so that the Prophet might call out many times; each time, he said, the Prophet called out would be a blessing on the house. The Prophet called out again and again Sa'd answered in a low tone. After the third call, the Prophet turned to go back home. When Sa'd saw the holy Prophet going away, he ran out and begged him to come in and explained that he had returned the greeting in a low voice so that the Prophet might repeat it many times, and that each time Sa'd would get a blessing. On hearing this the Prophet was very pleased, and prayed for Sa'd. As it was his custom to greet and asked for admission, he expected others to do the same. Once a member of the tribe of Banū 'Umayr called on the Prophet. The visitor only asked permission for admission and omitted the greeting. The Prophet, who was very particular about good form, told one of his disciples to go and teach him the proper way.

It was also his custom never to sit in an exalted

place or on anything expensive or grand. Once he went to see a friend, who took out a fine leather carpet and spread it for the Prophet to sit on, but the Prophet would have none of it and sat upon the bare floor.

In company the Prophet would never cut short another person's speech in order to speak himself. He never heeded anything that was said to hurt, but always ignored it. He accepted thanks only when thanks were due. He took part in all decent kinds of conversation, and would add to the humour by saying witty things himself. He never allowed or indulged in coarse and vulgar jokes. If a great man of any tribe paid him a visit he was accorded the respect due to him; for, the Prophet would say, "Respect all elders and great men of all tribes." He did not like anyone to remain seated while others stood up to receive a guest. He always asked everyone who visited him if he wished for anything or wanted anything done; he would ask his disciples to find out the needs of those who were not able to come to him, so that the needs of all might be fulfilled.

He did not like asking questions, and his advice to one and all was the same. Whether poor or rich, the Prophet always treated with respect and perfect politeness everyone who came to him. His house was very small, and its accommodation limited. Many a time there was no room therein to accommodate the late-comers. He would spread his own sheet for them to sit upon. Once at Mujrāna, when the Prophet was distributing meat to the poor, a lady arrived and went up to him. On seeing her approaching him he left everyone else and attended to her, and spread his sheet for her to sit on. People inquired who she was, and were told she was the Prophet's old nurse and foster-mother. The same thing happened once in Mecca, when his foster-father paid him a visit, and the Prophet spread a corner of his sheet for him to sit on. A little later his foster-mother came and he spread another corner of his sheet for her; a short time after his foster-sister arrived; the Prophet got up and let her sit on the rest of the sheet, and sat on the floor himself.

He met everybody with a smiling face. He would talk freely to all alike and never gave himself airs of superiority. He never spoke of himself, and was always punctilious in inquiring after his guest's health and needs. If any man was hungry, he would give him what there was in the house, even if he had to go hungry himself. When the holy Prophet made a promise, nothing could ever make him break it. "The believers are . . . those who are keepers of their covenants" (THE QURAN 23: 8). The world would have been better to-day if others had followed his perfect example. Governments of to-day think nothing of making and signing treaties almost every day which they do not respect nor keep. I will state a few instances, which, if taken as a lesson, would most decidedly help to make the world a different and better place. The Prophet regarded a treaty as a sacred document, not as a scrap of paper, as is the mode nowadays.

He entered into treaties with his enemies, and sometimes was forced to consent to terms which were far from favourable to his mission. But if he accepted them he kept to them under any circumstances. In the Truce of Hudaybiyya (627 A.C.), one of the stipulations agreed upon was that any Meccan who embraced Islam and fled to the Prophet for protection the Prophet was legally bound to return him to Mecca. As soon as the treaty was signed, Abū Jandal escaped from prison and fled to Medina. He told the Prophet all he had to suffer, and begged for protection. The Prophet was sad on hearing his tale but said "Abū Jandal! have patience, we have made a promise and cannot break it. God will create some way for you out of this difficulty." Once at the battle of Badr, when the strength of the Muslims was very small compared to that of the enemy, two of the Companions of the Prophet were left behind. The enemy overtook them and made them prisoners. They begged to be released. Their captors granted them their request on condition that they did not join the Prophet again. The promise having been taken they were allowed to go. Soon they reached the camp of the Prophet and told him how they had managed to escape. When the Prophet heard this story he straightway sent them back to the enemy, knowing full well that he could not spare either of them. A promise, he said, was never to be broken. Again at the time of the Truce of Hudaybiyya in 626 A.C., a number of Meccans came to Medina and embraced Islam. And as they were afraid to return to Mecca because of the persecutions by the Quraysh they implored the Prophet to protect them. The Prophet remained firm. He expressed his regret for not being in a position to give them his protection in contravention of the Truce of Hudaybiyya. Once a slave, Abū Rāfi', was sent to Medina by the Quraysh with a message. When the slave beheld the holy Prophet and heard his voice he embraced Islam and said, "O Prophet of God! I will not return to the unbelievers." But the Prophet said, "I have made a promise and cannot break it. You must go back now."

Meek and humble though the holy Prophet was, there was none braver than he. On the field of battle, it is said, he was, above all others, most warlike. In the thick of the fight, when both enemies fought hand to hand, the Prophet was always to the fore. In the battle of Hunayn, 8 A.H. (630 A.C.), the Muslims were far superior in strength to the enemy; showers of arrows descended upon the Prophet and his followers. The unfortunate Muslims were driven back and many ran for their lives. But the Prophet did not move from his place on the battlefield, though he was the chief target of the arrows. He was the only one who showed no sign of fear or trepidation. One of the Companions admitted, "I bear witness to the fact that we did run for our lives, and it was the holy Prophet alone who did not budge from his post, the one who stood by the side of the Prophet being counted the bravest of the men of Medina." Once rumour went abroad that the enemy was at the gates of

Medina. Everyone consequently began to make ready for the fray; but as soon as the holy Prophet heard the rumour he did not wait even to saddle his horse, but rode at once bare-back all alone to meet the enemy. On reaching the gates he discovered there was no cause for fear. He at once rode back to his people and gave them the good news to their great relief. This instance alone is proof sufficient of the Prophet's intrepidity; for had this rumour been true, he, being alone, would have suffered a most cruel death.

In his book, *Musnad*, Ibn Hanbal writes that in the battle of Badr the Muslims were only three hundred in number and the enemy over a thousand. When the Muslims saw how they were outnumbered, and how poorly armed they were in comparison to the enemy, they began to lose heart. They came, one and all, in a flurry to the Prophet, who alone was staunch and steadfast. He bade them not to fear; he encouraged them and cheered them. Thus in a short time their confidence was restored and they were brave again and ready for battle. It is related that once when returning from an expedition, the scorching heat of the sun was so strong that the holy Prophet and his companions halted under the shade of some trees, being unaware that the enemy was on the lookout for them. The Prophet went a little distance away, ungirdled his sword, and hung it on the tree before lying down, and was soon asleep. One of the enemy, a Bedouin, seeing that all the Companions were resting, took the opportunity of approaching the Prophet, and

297

quietly removed the sword from the tree. At that moment the holy Prophet awoke to find a man standing over him with a sword in his hand. The enemy, seeing him awake, said, "Muhammad, tell me, who can save you now?" The Prophet did not move and just replied, "God." His voice was so calm, without a trace of fear, that it had a miraculous effect on the Bedouin. He gazed at the Prophet in amazement and as though in a trance put the sword back in its place.

In civility, kindness, and affection the holy Prophet was his own example, and by his refulgent examples Muslims have been taught to treat all men kindly, regardless of what their religions and beliefs may be. They were forbidden to destroy or interfere with the places of worship, or lands and property belonging to those of different religions. He taught them never to hurt but always to heal. Worlds may be conquered by force, but hearts can only be won by kindness and love. This politeness and love was made the sheet-anchor of Islamic teachings, and it is this that has helped so largely the spread of Islam. Those who aver otherwise can only do so through ignorance and bigotry, hiding the true facts to suit their own ends. Carlyle, the great historian of Europe, contradicting these baseless falsehoods, rightly says, "The sword indeed! But where will you get your sword? Every new opinion, at its starting is precisely in a minority of one. In one man's head alone there it dwells as yet. One man alone in the whole world believes it; there is one man against all men. That he take a sword and try to propagate with that will do little for him. You must first get your sword!"

Before concluding this chapter on the perfect attributes of the holy Prophet, it will not be out of place to mention another aspect in his character—that of his great love of children. He would say, "Those who love their children and are kind to them and do their duty towards them, will be saved from the flames of Hell." Not only was the Prophet kind to his own children but he loved all the children of slaves and free men alike. I can say without fear of contradiction that he was the first person to inaugurate a Welfare League for children. He would spend as much time as possible every day in the affairs of children. Female children he treated with respect and taught others to do the same. He once said that all those who did not love children, or pity them and treat them with kindness, were not true Muslims. It was his habit, on meeting children, to wish them a "good day" first, and pat and play with them for a while. Often when going about the city he would pick up children, put them in his conveyance, and take them for a drive. When he went on a pilgrimage, the children of the Banū Hāshim ran out to receive him; he treated them kindly and played with them, and also took many away with him on his camel. During prayer time, if the holy Prophet saw many children in the congregation he would shorten the prayer so that they might not feel tired.

Abu Qatāda tells us that the holy Prophet loved his two grandsons exceedingly and came once to

299

the mosque with both of them perched on his shoulders, and performed the prayers with them near him, one on either side of him. Whenever he went to the house of his daughter, the first thing he would say after the salutation was, "Bring the children to me." There he would spend a long time in playing with them. Another important point to be remembered is that this kind treatment of the Prophet towards children was not confined to Muslim children only. He treated children of all other religions in exactly the same way. It is related that once a few children were accidentally killed in a battle. When the Prophet heard of this it might almost be said that his anger knew no bounds, and on someone observing that it did not matter much since all the children killed were children of the unbelievers, the Prophet retorted that whether they were children of unbelievers or not, the fact remained they were children; and he gave orders that no child was ever again to be killed, or hurt in any way.

People believed that for children to grow into good citizens they should be brought up very strictly and punished for the slightest offence. This sort of treatment did not commend itself to the holy Prophet and he strongly discouraged it. He taught mothers to be kind and loving, told them that their babies and children needed hugging and patting as much as they needed their nourishment, that it was as essential to them as is the sunshine to the plant.

CHAPTER 28

MUHAMMAD, THE WORLD'S GREATEST BENEFACTOR

> "This day have those who disbelieved despaired of your religion, so fear them not, and fear Me. This day I have perfected for you your religion and completed My favour on you and chosen for you Islam as a religion."—THE QURAN 5 : 3.

IN the history of the world the holy Prophet is regarded as the greatest of all benefactors, and this is a fact that even the greatest of commentators have had to acknowledge. The starting and basic point of all his teachings was, "There is no God but one God, and Muhammad is his Prophet."

The history of the world shows that from the time of the first religious person to the beginning of the new civilization the world has remained divided between two groups of people, the oppressor and the oppressed. One assumed superiority over the other; difference of birth, race, wealth, pomp, and power making it regard the other with contempt. The trouble to-day is the same. There is everlastingly some dispute raging over Imperialism, colour, and race. And there are the disputes between the rich and the poor, the employer and the employed, the landlord and the peasant, and the like;

for self-delusion and self-aggrandizement are still the cause, as they always were, of all human troubles and misunderstandings.

The only remedy for this state of things is the Book of God revealed to the holy Prophet 1,300 years ago. This book is so complete and sufficient, both as regards its language and spirit, that in spite of all the advances made in modern thought, the greatest thinkers of to-day cannot say a word against it. This book is so simple that it needs no priests to interpret it to the Muslims. It is so great a book that it is no wonder that a hardened critic like Professor D. S. Margoliouth was obliged, in the preface of the Translation of the Quran by Rodwell, to admit its greatness. The Quran, by its perfect teachings, has induced the Muslims to make themselves masters of all the sciences and arts of the world with the result that Muslim Spain became the University of Europe in the Middle Ages. Before the Prophet's coming the world was in a parlous state, but he changed everything, making all human beings equal, ending once and for all the question of superiority and inferiority.

Not only did he make an end of slavery, he repudiated all such ideas and notions as make one man despise another. It is the teachings of the Prophet that have given us our present Democratic institutions wherein the king rules by and with the advice and consent of the representatives of the people. These teach us to respect the opinion of another person, and a spirit is born which guides us to solve all the intricate problems of humanity.

And so the Prophet established a brotherhood which knows no restrictions of colour, race, wealth, and power, and under which all stand shoulder to shoulder to pray to the one and only God who is True and Real.

He taught us that birth was mere accident and that wealth could not be acquired without the help of others, and enjoined his followers to keep *Zakāt*—poor rate—separate as a share of the co-operation of others. Strength, he said, was the result of natural and physical conditions and that the education of the heart depended on self-culture. "The heart of mankind is the seat of wisdom; it leads a man either to Hell or Heaven."

It is a great pity that the world to-day puts things of no worth before that which can bring love and peace to humanity. It is high time we realized that world peace and harmonious international relations can only be achieved in following the principles of Islam. It is no mere assertion, for a time will surely come, sooner or later, as is foreseen by eminent thinkers of to-day, when the whole world will be forced to admit that the only means to end all its troubles is to follow the perfect teachings and examples of the holy Prophet. The world is drifting towards Islam. Mr. George Bernard Shaw puts the following words into the mouth of one of his characters in his *Getting Married*:

"It fits you to perfection; but it doesn't fit me. I happen, like Napoleon, to prefer Mahometanism. I believe the whole British Empire will adopt a reformed Mahometanism before the end of the century. The character of Mahomet is congenial to me. I admire him, and share his views of life to a considerable extent. That beats you, you see, Soames. Religion is a great force: the only real motive force in the world."

From time to time God sent prophets for the reform and guidance of people, and to bring to life their deadened feelings, by stirring in them a desire for spiritual attainment. Every prophet came with this mission. They were all builders of spirituality, and they discharged their duties with honour and credit and succeeded in their efforts. It is of course a different thing that later generations regarded their teachings as wrong or interpreted them wrongly, but it remains truth and a fact that these prophets were all messengers of one and the same God, and promulgators of the highest form of spirituality. They succeeded in leading the poor wanderers back to the true path; for only those who come from God can reform others and guide them back to God. Spirituality was the combined mission of all prophets, and the sole purpose of the creation of man. The holy Quran says, "I have not created the Jinn and the men but that they should serve Me" (51 : 57).

All religious teachers are equally agreed on the importance of the attainment of spirituality, and have made it the foundation of their respective religions, but their followers differed always in their concepts of the word. Some understood it to be renunciation of the world and severance of all human connections, others made celibacy a means for its attainment. Some regarded abstinence from delicious food and fine clothing to be spirituality, others the saying of supererogatory prayers and performances of all sorts of tiring rituals, litanies, and the like. Many and varied definitions have made of the word a mystery. All were eager for it, but none were agreed over the meaning of it. The holy Prophet Muhammad, at his coming, taught them all that their conceptions of spirituality were entirely warped; he taught and made them believe that spirituality is something above and beyond all religious practices.

The falsity of these conceptions becomes clear when it is recalled that God would have not created so many things in the world if it had been His purpose that human beings ought to abstain from, or renounce them. The very fact that God had created them is enough to show that He desired us to participate in them and by their aid to attain spirituality. I should say that the participation in all things created, except things forbidden, is essential for the attainment of spirituality. To renounce them is wrong and an act of sheer ingratitude to God. That is why those who followed the former policy have failed hopelessly in the attainment of spirituality. True spirituality consists in the method adopted together with the participation in the things created. God sent man, after showing him the difference between right and wrong, to adopt a course in practical life that would lead him back to Himself. If there was no wrong in the world, then right and goodness are

U   305

nothing and less than nothing. Spirituality is not to renounce the world in order to avoid wrong and attain good. Not only should wrong be shunned, but also fought with resolution and courage. True spirituality is to remain in the human world amidst all temptations, and to combat all evil and attain good. If a blind man says he is a good man because he did not look upon anyone of the opposite sex with lust, then he is wrong. He did not look because he could not see. Probably had he had sight he would have looked, but to be blessed with eyes and not to abuse them is a creditable act. Similarly, those who renounce the world cannot say that they are really good; for they shut themselves up in solitude, away from all worldly temptations, so that they cannot help being good. The beauty and greatness of what is good and what is right lie in the presence of their opposite qualities: then they become valuable. A person can only hope to attain true spirituality if he lives under the existing and natural conditions of life by respecting and discharging all obligations, both to God and his fellow men. As a matter of fact, those who renounce the world acknowledge their own weakness and prove they are not competent enough to fight temptation. Such people are often acclaimed religious or spiritual by the ignorant masses, but this system is wrong. God does not wish it, and no true religion of His demands from human beings the renunciation of the world or the non-participation in what has been especially created for them.

As people come by such views wrongly, the Quran

was revealed to repudiate them and show the correct perspective. It is not wrong to say that Islam changed the entire religious outlook by making it possible for human beings to attain spirituality together with participation in the good things of the world. Concerning celibacy and the priesthood of Christians, it is said in the Quran, "As for monkery they innovated it—We did not prescribe it to them—only to seek God's pleasure, but they did not observe it with its due observance" (57 : 27).

The Prophet says, "Islam does not recognize monkery." In the Quran there is much written concerning food, clothing, and the like. "Who has prohibited the embellishment of God, which He has brought forth for His servants, and the good provisions?" (7 : 32). This verse clearly shows that these are for the benefit of true believers in the life and that it is obligatory for them to participate in them. Once the Prophet advised a rich Muslim to wear handsome clothes, saying, "God wishes that human beings show their gratitude to Him by using the things He has given them." On the subject of marriage there are clear and simple rules in the Quran, and the words of the holy Prophet are, "To marry is to follow my example; one who avoids it is not of me." In all things the Prophet showed that spirituality does not mean just fasting and prayer or renunciation of the world; he defined it as the height attained by prayer and fasting along with the discharge of all worldly obligations. It was in this wise that the Prophet said that to maintain

307

a wife is a good act and a means to the attainment of spirituality. A group of Companions once wanted to renounce the world to this end but the holy Prophet forbade it, telling them to follow his own example which was to fulfil one's duty to God as well as to the world. The Quran says, "If you love God, then follow me, God will love you" (3: 30). Millions have succeeded in gaining spirituality by following the example and teachings of the holy Prophet; millions are succeeding and millions more, in time to come, will succeed in this way only.

The Quran was revealed to the holy Prophet as the final and complete Book of God for the benefit of humanity. The world at the advent of Muhammad was a lost world, a veritable sea of sin. Men had discarded all theories of the good and the spirituality. In the words of the Quran, "On land and sea moral degradation had settled" (30: 41). When the evil became universal, it was necessary to adopt a universal cure. The Quran says, "To-day your religion was made complete and perfect" (5: 3); which means that the religion that was inaugurated by God in the beginning of the world became complete on his sending the Quran through the holy Prophet Muhammad. As a child is taught his alphabet, so God taught religion to the world gradually and little by little by sending at different times and to different peoples His prophets to teach His religion. When the world had reached that stage of understanding, when it was ready for the final lesson, He sent the last and complete book through Muhammad, for the perfection of mankind, so that by following it men may attain to the goal of perfection.

It is right that the teacher of a religion so perfect should himself be a perfect man. God selected Muhammad to be the guide and reformer of the whole world. God's words concerning the Quran are, "And this Quran has been revealed to Muhammad that with it he may warn you and whensoever it reaches" (6: 19); "He is a warner to the nations" (2: 51). Because of this God granted him the title of *Khātamu 'n-Nabbiyyīn*, which means not only the "last of the Prophets," but also those things that go to prove that he was the greatest Prophet of God, and the benefactor of the world. One signification of the word *Khātam* is "ring." Thus the whole phrase *Khātamu 'n-Nabbiyyīn* means that the holy Prophet encompasses all prophets as the ring encompasses the finger. This also signifies that all the miracles performed by other prophets were given collectively to the holy Prophet Muhammad; that it was because of this that he was made Prophet of the whole world; and that the Book given to him was made to comprise the teachings of all the prophets. God Himself says, "All the teachings of all other prophets were thus secured" (THE QURAN 5: 48). The Quran comprises all other revealed books (THE QURAN 98: 3), and the holy Prophet all other prophets. The word *Khātam* also means an ornament, therefore the phrase may also signify that the holy Prophet is the ornament of all prophets. All blame fastened upon other prophets also disappears under this phrase.* The clearing of the characters of other prophets of false allegations was only achieved by the Prophet of Islam as the study of the Quran shows. Other books deny the presence of prophets among people other than themselves, but the Quran avers that God sent prophets to different peoples at different times for the uplifting of their souls and for their guidance and that it was incumbent upon the Muslims to believe in them all (THE QURAN 10: 47). The Prophet Muhammad in a tradition of his which reads, "All Prophets are brothers," connects all prophets in a bond of love.

When the holy Prophet attained prophethood and began his preaching, he was at first met with abuse and was booed and reviled. When he addressed the people thus, "I spent the greater part of my life among you before the Call; you all know that I never did wrong; but to-day you all find fault with my teachings," the people answered that it was true enough they had nothing against him, but even so they could not accept the religion he was preaching. They tried by all means in their power to put an end to his preachings; he was tortured, abused, and harassed, but never did he swerve from his duty towards God. When the people saw that all they did was of no avail, they sought to tempt him by offering riches, women, and position, but the holy Prophet gave rebuff to their offer with the remark that he would not desist from his duty even if they brought the sun to him and placed it in one hand and the moon in the other. Throughout he remained steadfast in spite of all threats and all temptations. Any other man would have fallen in the face of such temptation but he did not pay the slightest heed to the offers made him. Instead, by his example and teachings he showed disgust for all the frivolous things of life. He told his wives that if they hankered after the world and its luxuries he would give them as much wealth as they wanted, but in the event of such choice on their part he would have to part with them. Nevertheless, he was so much respected and loved by them all that they said that they would rather stay with him and live a poor and simple life than leave him and live a luxurious one. His examples of godliness and kindness were such that his most severe critics could find nothing to say against him. A man can, at a pinch, hide his true character before the world at large, but cannot play the hypocrite in his own home indefinitely. His real character is unmasked by stark familiarities of the home. The demeanour of the holy Prophet was so perfect that he was adored by all the members of his household. After his death his wives always remembered him and shed tears at the loss of such an ideal husband.

I have already mentioned that God gave to the holy Prophet the title of *Khātamu 'n-Nabbiyyīn*, and I could now add that the word *Khātam* besides meaning a ring, ornament, etc., also means "seal"; so that we can say that he was sent as "the seal of all the prophets," meaning that the prophethood of Muhammad was the last, that is to say, God would not send any more prophets after Muhammad.

The holy Prophet was a perfect example of poverty in riches. Later, when success brought plenty to Medina, he never partook of it. His was the heart that had only one image in it, and one purpose—that of God; there was no room in it for worldly things. He would often say, "A simple house to live in, clothes enough to cover one, and some bread to eat are quite enough for the sustenance of human life."

In discussing the things that the holy Prophet did for womanhood, I have remarked that before Islam woman was considered to be among the meanest creations of God. The followers of Jesus Christ had called her a "devil," and "the tool of the devil," because of the crucifixion of Jesus Christ who had to atone for the sin of Adam committed at the instigation of a woman. Hinduism, too, gives her no better place than that of a slave and a servant of man. Krishnā, who is often painted in the company of the "Gopies" (milkmaids), when he attained spirituality discarded them as beings unclean, but in the sixth century A.C. the benefactor of the world, Muhammad, changed the whole outlook about woman. From lowly and mean she became a being to be loved and respected. The holy Prophet would often say, "Paradise is beneath your mother's feet."

In spite of the nearness of God, in spite of being the greatest of all prophets, Muhammad used to say his prayers with as much zeal as though he was a lost soul seeking God. He would spend nights standing in prayer, regardless of physical pain.

But what was mere physical pain to one whose heart was filled with God? He was never properly at rest unless he was in communion with God. All people—men and women, young and old—were equally the recipients of his benefits, his kindness, and his love. Even his bitterest foe found in him a friend. At the battle of Uhud the holy Prophet was wounded and knew that the enemy was bent on taking his life, but still he prayed: "God forgive them, for they know not what they are doing." The people of Tā'if did all in their power to torture and harm him, and he in return prayed for them, "O God! forgive them, give them the privilege of joining Islam and send them as friends to Medina." The Arabs were the greatest of unbelievers but the kindness and the love of the holy Prophet succeeded in winning them over to Islam. And soon they were proud to submit themselves to the personality of the holy Prophet.

The love and respect which a person wins in the heart of another depend largely on the benefit which that other derives from him. The heart of man is so fashioned that he is bound to love and respect those that do him good or some kind service. As there are infallible laws of nature, so there are of humanity, and any deviation from them, such as blind love or blind hatred, does not last long. A being who by his example does good and uplifts the souls of others is bound to be loved and respected.

Reason and careful study will lead one and all to admit the very great obligation under which the world is labouring towards the holy Prophet. I do not say this because of my faith, but because of facts, and I do not think anyone in the world, whether Hindu or Christian, will deny it. The real benefactors of the world are those who dedicate their lives to the good of humanity. Such people are found in all nations, and universal love and respect should be their portion. The doers of good, be they Moses, Rama, Krishnā, Zoroaster, Buddha, or Jesus Christ, are, every one of them, to be respected. On the roll of benefactors the name of Muhammad the holy Prophet shines out as the greatest. What he did for Arabia and the world at large, in so short a time, has never been accomplished by any other prophet before him. Within the short space of twenty years what did he succeed in doing? He made the Arabs, who were the most ignorant, illiterate, and superstitious of nations, the greatest, the most learned, and most civilized nation of the world; he caused the disunited, scattered, and least-known nation of the world to establish empires and devise laws of government that spread all over the world. Small wonder, then, if the Christian historians of Europe should admit that of all the reformers and prophets of the world the holy Prophet was the most successful and the greatest. His intentions were great, and not restricted to one people or country as were those of the other prophets. Any nation, be it Afghan, Turk, or another, who sought for guidance, was helped and prospered. The brotherhood which he established comprised all races—black and white, weak and strong, great and small—all were made equal participants in the goods of the world. The white had a right to become famous and great, so had the black and the slaves. History records where slaves have become kings. No one before had ever conceived of such a brotherhood as this of the whole world. Muhammad, the greatest of God's prophets, not only conceived of it, but established it and thus removed all barriers of caste, colour, and race. It is, therefore, the duty of the whole world not merely to recognize but also to love and respect such a great and wonderful personality.

Muhammad came at a time when the world had extinguished all light given by other prophets, and was plunged in utter darkness and ignorance. Judaism, Hinduism, Zor astrianism, etc., had become religions only in name, their followers having completely forgotten every principle. The last religion of the world before Islam was Christianity; its principles were really true and great but they were never put into practice. The depth to which Christians had at that time fallen can best be stated in the words of a Christian writer, Sir William Muir, who writes, "Moreover, the Christianity of the seventh century was itself decrepit and corrupt. It was disabled by contending schisms and had substituted the puerilities of superstition for the pure and expansive faith of the early ages." And I am not guilty of over-enthusiasm if I say that the world would have remained ignorant and dark if Muhammad had not appeared at that time.

The words that the Quran uses to depict the condition of the then world in "Corruption had appeared in the land and the sea on account of what the hands of men had wrought" (THE QURAN 30: 41) years ago, are almost the same as those used by a scholar of to-day, writing in the light of modern historical research. Mr. J. H. Denison, discussing Islam in his book, *Emotion as the Basis of Civilization* (London, 1929), mentions the following facts. "In the fifth and sixth centuries A.D. the world was standing on the verge of darkness. Ancient thoughts, the basis of which are emotions and which have made the existence of the world possible by teaching love and respect, were dead, there was no new light to take its place. It looked as if the civilization that was built in four thousand years was on the point of destruction, and that the world was about to go back to the age of complete darkness and barbarism . . . civilization like a big tree, the branches of which had spread all over . . . looked as if it were going to give way from the very root by being eaten up. . . . Was there anything that could have saved civilization and the whole world from destruction by uniting and consolidating all the forces?" Answering his own question the author, in describing the Arabs, speaks of Muhammad, the Prophet of Islam, in these terms, "These were the people among whom was born a man who united the world from East to West in the unity of God, and saved the world from destruction." Is it not correct, then, to say that Muhammad kept civilization alive in the world? Colossal is the obligation under which humanity lies to him and greatly do

I pity those who, instead of love and respect for the one and only great benefactor of the world, have for him nothing but abuse, malice, and slander.

One of the principal ailments of the world to-day is that some nations are thrusting their greatness and superiority on others. Just because it happens to be of a particular land where the people are white, it regards itself as superior, and looks down on those who are dark, deeming coloured people to be inferior in intelligence, manners, and standards of life. The havoc and misery that this racial and coloured prejudice has caused and is still causing can be better understood by studying the conditions of the countries where this question is imminent. Take, for instance, the coloured people of Africa and America. They will tell a tale that shocks and scandalizes many. They will tell of the cruel treatment meted out to them by their "white masters" and how wealth and position cannot help them in any way. There was a man of colour and editor of a great newspaper in America. He married a white woman, but when he went to London on business no hotel would give him accommodation. Why? Simply because he belonged to a coloured race. He had wealth, money enough to stay at the best hotel, but that was not the point. One person in every ten of the great American Republic is a Negro, who, though a member of the Republic, does not enjoy full legal rights. In the Southern States of the Republic the right of the Negro to be called "Mister" is just being recognized. Formerly, in ordinary speech, in newspapers, and in shops,

317

and in addressing parcels, no Negro, no matter how wealthy, was styled Mister. In theory the Negro can vote, but in practice he can do no such thing because there is a clause that the voter must understand the constitution. If a Negro ventures to present himself at a poll he is asked to state the text of a certain amendment to the constitution. If he can do that he is asked to recite the whole constitution. No one can do that. In the Southern States the hospitals for whites and Negroes are still always separate. The hospital for a white is modern and good. The one for a Negro is a hovel. In many Southern cities if an ambulance finds that a street casualty is only a nigger it will drive away again and leave him in the road. Often you would come across notices, "No Negro washing taken." Once a West Indian was travelling on board a steamer. He was never seen to take his bath, and when questioned on the subject he said that he took baths daily, but he had to do it late at night. He dared not do so in the day-time. When pressed for the reason he explained further that a few weeks previously one of his countrymen who was on a voyage was seen using the baths and was very roughly treated by the white men on board, because they said he had the "audacity" to use the same baths as they. A friend of mine tells me that a short time ago he was staying in India at a certain big hotel, and that among the numerous people there was an Englishman who had a dog. This Englishman was on speaking terms with my friend, and although well aware that the latter was an

Indian he often would show his dislike and contempt and air his poor opinion of India and Indians. Once he said in the hearing of my friend, "Indians bark! This dog of mine has more intelligence than an Indian."

When you read the history of Islam you will realize what is meant when it is said that the holy Prophet removed all distinctions of colour and race between man and man, and brought them under one brotherhood of Islam. The coloured Muslims have no fear of being snubbed by the white men who have embraced Islam. The Islamic principles have secured them the right of absolute equality, and encouraged them to activities in all directions of human effort and co-operation. There is in Islam no such thing as inferiority complex; for Muslims are taught that all human beings are equal.

CHAPTER 29

POLYGAMY IN ISLAM AND THE HOLY PROPHET
MUHAMMAD

> "O Prophet! say to your wives,
> If you desire this world's life and
> its ornature then come, I will give
> you a provision and allow you to
> depart a goodly departure."
> THE QURAN 33: 28.

THE first marriage of the holy Prophet took place, when he was twenty-five years of age, with Khadīja bint Khuwailid, who was fifteen years his senior. She was carrying on an extensive business in many parts of Arabia. Before their marriage Muhammad used to act as her manager, and she was so deeply impressed by his truthfulness and integrity that she asked him to do her the honour of marrying her. All the children of Muhammad were born of this union, except one son named Ibrāhīm. Khadīja was the first woman to become Muslim. She died when Muhammad was fifty years of age. They lived happily together for twenty-five years. During her lifetime he did not marry, although it was the practice in Arabia in those days to have more than one wife at a time. She was always a great help and comfort to him, many a time in war as in peace. She proved herself a good friend and counsellor to him. Muhammad

320

was devoted to her and her death was a great sorrow.

His second wife was Sauda, an elderly widow of Mecca who, with her first husband, had embraced Islam. They emigrated to Abyssinia, and on their way back her husband died and she was left alone and destitute. For succour she went to the Prophet and his Companions; and after a while she asked the Prophet to marry her. He married her because he was loath to see the wife of a friend of his with no one to help her.

The third wife of the holy Prophet was 'Ā'isha, the daughter of Abū Bakr. At the time of their marriage she was very young, so she remained at her father's house until eight months after the Emigration. 'Ā'isha was the beloved of Muhammad. She, on account of her services to Islam, holds a very honoured position in the Muslim world.

After his death she was always consulted by both high and low alike on all matters of religion and policy. She is to this day called *'Ummu 'l-Muslimīn* which means "the mother of all Muslims." Muhammad often had revelations in her room and it was in her room that he breathed his last. She lived till about the last period of the fourth Caliphate. The marriage of Muhammad and 'Ā'isha was a perfectly happy one, except for this one incident—which I relate below—that marred their happiness for a brief time.

It happened that the Prophet, accompanied by his wife, 'Ā'isha, was returning from the expedition against Banū Mustaliq in the fifth year of the

Hegira (626 A.C.). 'Ā'isha had gone out on a private occasion but when she returned to the camp she perceived that she had lost her necklace and went back to search for it. In her absence the attendant, supposing her to be in her *howdah* (seat for two or more with a canopy on the back of a camel), started while it was yet dark. When she returned, finding the camel and the men gone, she sat down there and was brought to Medina by Safwān who was coming in the rear. Some mischievous persons from among the Hypocrites spread false reports, slandering her and some of the Muslims also associated themselves with the slander.

'Ā'isha protested her innocence, but Muhammad had an anxious time; for he did not know whether to believe her or not. At length her innocence was proved by the following revelation in the Quran, "Surely they who concocted the lie are a party from among you" (24: 11). Then the Prophet's mind was cleared of all doubt in the matter. The two chief slanderers, 'Abdullā bin Ubayy bin Salūl and the poet, Hassān bin Sābit, together with the rest who took part in accusing her, were severely punished.

Hafsa was the fourth wife of the holy Prophet, being the widow of Khunays who was slain in the battle of Badr. She was an excellent and pious lady and the Prophet married her in the third year of the Hegira (624 A.C.).

In the same year he married his fifth wife, who was also a widow, having been married to 'Abdullāh bin Jahsh, who fell in the battle of Uhud. Her name was Zaynab *Ummu 'l-Masākīn*—mother of the needy. She was given this cognomen for her generosity.

The Prophet also married Zaynab, a daughter of his aunt, 'Umayma. The holy Prophet did not desire this marriage, preferring that the girl should wed his own liberated slave, Zayd, but both she and her relations were against it, seeing that she was a lady of high birth and the proposed bridegroom but a freed man. They urged the Prophet to marry her himself, while the Prophet insisted that she should marry Zayd; but in the end they yielded and the marriage took place. It proved a most unhappy one. Things went from bad to worse and soon became intolerable. They were forced to separate and then divorced. Again, she and her relations brought pressure to bear on the Prophet to marry her, and he did so, because he had been responsible for bringing about her disastrous marriage with Zayd and he felt himself morally bound to grant their wishes. Zaynab was really a good woman; the chief point in her favour was her charitable nature and to this day she is known to Muslims as the "Mother of the Poor." She died soon after her marriage with the holy Prophet.

Umm Salma was another wife of Muhammad. She was a widow with four small children. The Prophet married her in order to afford her protection and to give her children a good upbringing and education. She lived to a ripe old age and died many years after her noble husband.

After the battle of Banū Mustaliq (626 A.C.) a number of male and female prisoners were taken by the Muslims, among whom were the Arab Chief, Hāris, with his daughter, Juwayriya, and his two sons. All of them embraced Islam. Juwayriya's husband had died. Her father offered her hand to the Prophet, who accepted it. As a consequence of this marriage all the prisoners of Banū Mustaliq could be released. About a hundred families were released from prison, because the Muslims said that the tribe that had been given the honour of the Prophet's relationship could not remain in prison.

Umm Habība was another wife of the holy Prophet. She was the daughter of Abū Sufyān, an Arab chief. She and her husband emigrated to Abyssinia where her husband became a Christian, but she remained staunch to her own faith and never wavered from Islam. After her husband's death the holy Prophet married her in the seventh year of the Hegira (628 A.C.).

Muhammad also married Safiyya, the daughter of a Jewish chieftain, after the battle of Khaybar in which her husband was slain. The Jews at that time were an endless source of trouble to the Muslims, so it seemed to the holy Prophet that by marrying the daughter of the Jewish chief this might put an end to the tension.

Not long afterwards the holy Prophet married Maria, a Christian sent him by Mukoukas, the King of Egypt. She was the mother of Ibrāhīm. In the same year he married another widow named Maymūna. After her husband's death she offered her hand to the Prophet and he accepted.

All of the wives of the Prophet lived till after his

death except two, Khadīja and Zaynab, who died during his lifetime. At his demise nine wives survived him.

Many people, mostly non-Moslims, criticize the married life of the holy Prophet, and say a prophet should not have so many wives. Such critics are apt to overlook certain important considerations. For example, Muhammad married at twenty-five, and for another twenty-five years and more lived only with one wife who was his senior by fifteen years. At her death he was between fifty-three and fifty-four, an age when one has outgrown the passions of youth, and only then did he consider marrying again. To have more than one wife was common and a custom among famous saintly persons in the olden days. Abraham, Jacob, Moses, and David all had more than one wife, and as for Solomon, tradition ascribes to him hundreds. Jesus Christ is the only one who did not have even one. Had the holy Prophet Muhammad so wished he could, from an early age, have had more wives than one, for during that period, owing to the attrition of constant warfare, the female population was very much greater than the male. It is well known that up to the age of twenty-five he had led a perfectly chaste life and that, notwithstanding the corrupt state of Arabia at that time, his purity was a household word. He married one wife, a widow, and lived with her alone until he was over fifty. That fact alone brings us to the conclusion that Muhammad was proof against lust and passion, and no sane person can ever accuse him of sensuality. It is true that after the death of his first wife he took other wives, but there were many reasons, political and otherwise, which, as I will explain in due course, led to these later marriages.

Another important fact is that all Muhammad's wives except one were widows or divorced women. Now if the holy Prophet's motive in marrying many times was merely to gratify his passions, it must be borne in mind that if had so desired he could have married virgins, as many or more even than Solomon did. I shall be inclined to think that any sensible man would rather have a virgin than an elderly widow or a divorced woman for a wife, and many a father would have felt honoured and only too willing to give his virgin daughter in marriage to the holy Prophet. But the object of his plural marriages was a good and noble one. The widows he married, five in number (their husbands having been slain in battle), had to be protected and their children provided for. Here, again, it must be remembered that food is not all that is required. The holy Prophet considered the sex requirements of women, and he was more careful and concerned about their chastity than their physical needs. That is why it became necessary to sanction polygamy and the reason why Muhammad married these widows in the Medina period. Also, in those times it was very hard for widowed women to remarry, as is shown in the case of Hafsa, the widow of Khunays who was slain in battle. Her father, who was a man of position and influence, tried in vain to get her married to two or three men, but they would not consent. In the end the holy Prophet himself married her, to set an example and show that it was better to marry widows than to leave them unprotected. So it can be seen that the moral safety of Muslims in those days lay in polygamy. Now, in the case of the divorced woman, at that time such were despised and given no chance to remarry. The Prophet married them to set an example and rehabilitate them in the eyes of society. Zaynab, a lady of high birth and a relation of the holy Prophet, was married to and divorced by his liberated slave, Zayd; and later the Prophet married her. Some allege that the Prophet saw Zaynab and was attracted by her, and that Zayd was forced by the Prophet to divorce her for that reason. This is as untrue as it is absurd. Had there been any truth in it, Zayd would never have remained, as he did, faithful and devoted to the Prophet or to Islam to the end of his days; for he was as deeply attached to the holy Prophet after as he was before his divorce. Consider, too, that the Prophet and Zaynab were cousins and been constantly together since childhood. Her relations wished the Prophet to marry her and she wished it herself. If he had been attracted by her, there was absolutely nothing to prevent him from marrying her when she was a virgin. But he married her to his liberated slave in the hope of abolishing all distinctions of birth and class. The marriage was a failure, as I have stated before, and when Zayd decided that divorce was the only remedy, he came to the holy Prophet

327

who did his best to dissuade him. But in the end a divorce was absolutely necessary. The Prophet married her after she had been divorced and as such lowered in general estimation. Refusal of her hand in the first place and acceptance in the second is enough to show that his motive in marriage was anything but self-gratification. It was, indeed, nothing else but the elevation of the divorced woman in the eyes of society.

The holy Prophet's marriage with Juwayriya was for a political reason; for she belonged to the tribe of Banū Mustaliq which hated the Muslims. This marriage proved a great success, for it ended all enmity and made the Banū Mustaliq staunch friends of the Muslims. But that with Safiyya, the daughter of the Jewish Chief, which took place also for a political reason, was not a success at all. Although the holy Prophet had married one of their tribe, the Jews still remained the deadliest enemies of the Muslims, the Prophet doing all in his power to be on friendly terms with them, but to no purpose. The Jewish malice proved too strong for conciliatory measures of the Prophet.

Quite other was his motive in espousing Maria, the Copt. She was an Egyptian, and to show that he had the same regard for other nationalities as for his own, when she was sent from Egypt by Mukoukas, the King of Egypt, he married her and treated her in the same way as he treated his Arab wives.

It must be admitted that lust and passion so common in human nature were not to be found

328

in the case of the holy Prophet. Every one of his marriages was for a noble reason. He was simple and sincere all his life. From a poor orphan he became a king, but his mode of living was always the same. In Medina, when the Muslims had prospered and come to live in ease and luxury, Muhammad continued in the same humble way. He could have lived like a king, amidst pomp and circumstance, but he did not. Often there was not enough in the house for a meal and the whole family would live merely on dates and water, and once the Prophet's wives, seeing other Muslim families living in comfort, went to the Prophet and begged him to let them do so too. He told them that if they wanted such ease and comfort he would give them all they needed, but they must forfeit the honour of being his wives. That answer shows his character clearly enough. A sensual man would never have disregarded the wishes of his wives, but would, on the contrary, have sought to gratify every whim of theirs. The object of his marriage was a noble one and altogether remote from self-indulgence. He was willing to part with them all rather than encourage them to turn to worldly things, yet for all his wives he had a great regard and sincere affection and would often say, "The best of you is he who treats his wife best."

The Prophet's wives were a great help to him in his mission, for there are many things in the Islamic code that need explaining, and points which the Prophet could not explain to women himself he could expound through his wives.

There are instances on record of women seeking information on certain matters pertaining to their sex who would go to one of the Prophet's wives and get the necessary enlightenment.

The holy Prophet Muhammad brought about an entire change in the institution of marriage. He elevated and ennobled it. From the place of a mere worldly convenience he made it a means for the development of the noble side of man and life. He imbued it with the spirit of sacrifice, with the thought that a man is made to live for his family, for his wife and his children. He taught us to feel and do for others what we feel and do for ourselves. In this connection it may be well for me to deal with the absurd charge of polygamy levelled at Islam. I say "absurd" on purpose, because it is nothing but that. Monogamy is not a Christian gift, for polygamy was practised in Christendom itself centuries ago. What is more, all religions and social systems allow it. Jesus Christ himself followed the Mosaic law, and insisted on its observance. All he tried to do was to check the excessive indulgence of his people in this respect. It was left for the Roman Emperor Justinian to legislate about monogamy. When asked by the Grand Duke Philip of Hesse, Martin Luther, than whom no one could understand the Bible better, held polygamy lawful. Therefore, monogamy should not be taken as a Christian verity. It was in vogue in Christendom only a few centuries ago not only among the laity but the clergy also.

"Islam came to reform the abuses of the world

330

POLYGAMY IN ISLAM AND THE HOLY PROPHET

at large, and took notice of polygamy as well. It brought it under drastic restrictions and made it next to an impossibility in ordinary cases. The institution, as such, was not without its use under special circumstances. A house with no children is a graveyard. The first marriage may prove barren for years, and if the wife is responsible for the misfortune a second marriage would be the only thing in requisition in the case of those whose happiness remains incomplete without children. In India, such marriages take place often at the instance of the first wife herself. It was to meet such contingencies of an exceptional character that polygamy received countenance in Islam. If the females sometimes outnumber the males—and this occurs in and after a period of war—it furnishes another argument for bringing more than one wife under one roof, to ward off evil in its most heinous form. It was in the days of wars, when the number of women had increased in Medina, that the Quranic verses allowing polygamy under certain restrictions were revealed. The sexual instinct is, after all, a life tendency, and cannot become extinct. The curbing of the passions is unhealthy, and the institution of celibacy has always and everywhere created a spirit of moral leprosy. Men and women are entitled, under the demands of nature, to claim companionship of each other in lawful wedlock, but promiscuous intermixture is pernicious to society. Is not polygamy—carried on, of course, with Muslim restriction—the only remedy under such circumstances? We do not advocate it—we resort to it only by way of remedy; and Islam can dispense with it without affecting its tenets.

"Europe has, since the war, been facing the same problem. The war has left women outnumbering men in the West to an appalling extent. Unmarried life is unnatural and unhealthy. It is a sin, if sin means anything and everything that is damaging to human progress.

"But has Christendom been purged of polygamy? Marriage, in its bald form, is, after all, a connection of man and woman. Our interest in the coming generation and the consciousness of paternity gives sanctity to the institution of marriage. Take it in its initial form, and the Christian in the West would appear to be more of a polygamist than the Muslim anywhere. The latter, in very rare cases (and, moreover, in a legalized form), does that which the former does unscrupulously and in an illegal form. But what an irony of fate! The former action, so healthy in its consequences, is branded as an offence which the law calls bigamy, while the latter, so flagrant and shameless in its methods, is practised with impunity, and the law takes no cognizance of it. Legislation should not succumb to sentimentality; its mission should be the betterment of human society and to contribute to the happiness of that society. There are two evils which the world, from the beginning, has never been able to remedy—the uncontrolled brutality of man under the excitement of his passions, and the weakness of a woman when she has become a victim thereto; and what is the result? Bastardy for the child, misery and shame for the mother. Has religion or civilization, in this matter, schemed out anything to remedy this double evil? Muslim lands are free from it. Why should the innocent children who were not consulted by their parents as to their being brought into this world to a life of infamy, be debarred from inheriting the name and property of their fathers? England had, in a manner, to recognize 'war babies' and thus give indirect countenance to polygamy. But that was a temporary measure. Humanitarian principles have come forward to provide 'Houses of Rescue' and 'Foundling Hospitals' to save these innocent victims of human depravity from misery and indigence, but what about the ignominy that stigmatizes their whole life and leaves their mothers in the lurch? Could they not have been saved from all this, if the mothers had been allowed by the law to hold the honourable position of a second wife, where the first marriage, for various reasons, could not accomplish the matrimonial purpose?

"Polygamy was observed indiscriminately before Islam, as I said before, and there was no restriction as to the number of a man's wives. He could have as many as he wished. Islam regulated the number if special circumstances did unavoidably necessitate plurality of wives. There are certain contingencies in life where polygamy alone can check incontinence. The Muslim conception of evil is very vast. Islam regards it from various angles, and one of them is the hygienic angle. In connubial life, there arise occasions when man and woman should separate

333

from each other for hygienic reasons. For instance, woman labours under certain disabilities for a week in every month. The days of pregnancy, and the time of suckling a child are further disabilities that would last at least for eighteen months. In the interest of the health of the child and of the mother Islam strongly recommends that husband and wife should not share beds under these conditions. In this respect Muhammad advised us to exercise control over our passions and suggested various ways which might help us, of which fasting was one. But in no case would he leave any loophole for misconduct. He would rather allow the husband to have the company of another wife than violate hygienic laws or pursue the course of incontinence; and if we observe these injunctions strictly, the number of wives will come to four.

"An advocate of equality between man and woman would demand polyandry—plurality of husbands. Apart from the fact that woman, and not man, labours under the disability aforesaid, there are other reasons for prohibiting polyandry, hygienic as well as such as will help to proper bringing up of children. For example, the ascertaining of parentage is essential on each birth, to ensure the performance of natural obligations as the rearing of children. In polygamy we can ascertain maternity and paternity both, but in the case of polyandry we cannot ascertain the latter.

"Moreover, all kinds of venereal disease follow polyandric connection. Some of the hilly districts in the Himalayan mountains, where polyandry is

334

observed, are notorious homes for such diseases. It is now an established fact that these maladies come from woman. She, and not man, becomes the first victim of it. Connection with more than one man brings disease to the female sex." Khwaja Kamal-ud-Din, *The Ideal Prophet* (Woking, 1925).

Napoleon has some very interesting and thought-provoking observations to make on the attitude of the holy Prophet Muhammad towards polygamy. Napoleon says (*vide Bonaparte et l'Islam*, by Christian Cherfils, Paris, 1914):

"Muhammad reduced the number of women which one could marry; before him it was indefinite: the rich used to marry a large number of women. He thus restricted polygamy. Women are not born more in number than men; why then is this permission to man to have more women and why has not Muhammad adopted the law of Jesus in this matter? In Europe the legislators of nations, whether Greek or German, Roman or Gaul, Spanish or British, have never permitted but one wife. Never in the West was polygamy authorized. In the East, on the contrary, it has been always authorized. Since historic times all men, Jews or Assyrians, Arabs or Persians, Tartars or Africans, could have more wives than one. Some have attributed this difference to geographical conditions. Asia and Africa are inhabited by men of various complexions; polygamy is the only effective means to blend them together, so that the white may not persecute the black, nor the black the white. Polygamy makes them born of the same mother or of the same father; the black

335

and the white, being brothers, sit and see each other at the same table. In the East, also, colour does not give one superiority to another. But to fulfil this object Muhammad thought that four wives were sufficient. One may ask how it is possible to permit four wives when there are not more women than men. As a matter of fact, polygamy does not exist except among the wealthy class. As it is this class which forms the opinion, the mixture of the colours in these families is sufficient to maintain the union among them.

"If we should like our colonies to give liberty to the black and to get rid of the colour prejudice obtaining in them, our legislators will have to allow polygamy."

CHAPTER 30

THE CONCEPTION OF THE BROTHERHOOD OF MAN
IN ISLAM

> "O you men! We have created
> you male and female, and have
> made you nations and tribes that
> you may know one another. Lo!
> the noblest of you, in the sight of
> God, is the best in conduct."—
> THE QURAN 49: 10.

SINCE the days of the holy Prophet the world
has made progress in all departments of life;
Islam, too, the seed of which was seen by the holy
Prophet, has made great progress. The philosophers
and learned men that it has produced are second
to none in their achievements. It is a well-known
fact that in the last few centuries the non-Muslim
world, especially the European part of it, has
derived more benefit from Islam than have the
Muslims themselves, especially in such branches of
knowledge as politics, philosophy, medicine, organization, economics, and the like. It is, therefore,
high time for Europeans to realize their obligation
to the great Prophet of Islam, seeing that he it
was who inaugurated the new era, whose activities
produced the wealth of knowledge that made
it possible for them to become the great ones of
to-day. The teachings of the holy Prophet are

Y

such that all the world can benefit by them for their worldly advancement; for those who wish to find God, the same personality guides them to the path that leads to God. No doubt there were true worshippers in the world before the holy Prophet, as well as many who worshipped one God. To-day there are many people and many nations who, though not followers of the holy Prophet, yet believe in one God. They see no difference between the God they worship and the God whom the Prophet of Islam preached and asked people to worship. God is described in the Quran in the following words: Nothing is like a likeness of Him. Vision does not comprehend Him; He is Merciful, Beneficent, Kind, and Great; He is Creator and Master; He is the Lord of all the worlds; He is also Wrathful, Omnipotent, and Just; He neither sleeps nor is subjected to human frailties, nor has He any defect; His knowledge and power are unlimited; He is First, He is last, He is everywhere; He is a Being beyond human comprehension. Instead of mere metaphorical belief, if one wishes to have a complete and absolute belief in such a God, there is no way other than of following the prophets of God and, above all, the holy Prophet Muhammad, whose life was "imbued with Divine attributes."

The Prophet may be said himself to have been the living personification of the qualities of God. There is no other personality who is so well known, or whose life is so widely read. No book in the world has revealed as much as has the Quran; no person in the world has prayed so much to God for the world as has the Prophet Muhammad. In everything he remembered God; everything in the world presented to him a glimpse of God; no one had such true belief, trust, and faith in God as Muhammad. He was the personification of the mercy, or, as the Christians say, the love of God. There was none who did not benefit by his mercy. Everyone—orphan, poor, young, old, rich—all benefited by him; his greatest mercy of all was that he opened the gates of Heaven to one and all. What perfect justice. There had been much controversy in the Christian world over the question of the souls of those good men who were in the world before Christ, and those who are not baptized, and also of the little ones who die without baptism, and the verdict of the Christian Church was that they could not be saved and admitted into Heaven, but must go to hell. Against this Islam teaches that no good deed, however small, will go without reward. Everyone, whatever his religion be, will get a just reward for his deeds, if the good deeds in a person's life are more than the bad. If, on the whole, his life has been a good one, he will then most certainly go to Heaven. From this it is clear that virtuous men and women before Muhammad were saved; and also those now living will be saved if their deeds so far justify it. This is what Islam teaches. The gates of Heaven are open to all. It is the reward of those who lead good lives. None need fear; for all are the creation of the same God who is Beneficent and most Merciful, and who loves all more than they are loved by their mothers, and whose law is the same for all. Take the opening chapter of the Quran. It says: "All praise is due to God, Who is the Lord of the worlds" (1 : 1). It does not say that he is the Lord of Muslims alone.

Muhammad is the incarnation of the mercy of God, but some critics say that if Muhammad showed all these qualities of God he also showed the qualities of very ordinary human being, by marrying, and waging war, and like pursuits. It is true he did. If he had not, he could have been called "God" instead of the personification of God's qualities. Such criticism, however, can hardly be called genuine; for other religions give human attributes to their deities. The Prophet Jesus himself said that he had not come to send peace but sword; and as to marriage, Jesus, too, regarded it as a sacred union. The Hindu deities each have a spouse or more, as can be seen in their scriptures. The Hindus worship stones, trees, rivers, and other things, believing them to be the incarnation of God.

The Prophet himself says, "I am but a human being like you" (16: 110). He did not, like Jesus or Buddha, attempt to strangle all human feelings or renounce the world. Like them, in his early life, he sought seclusion, to meditate and pray to God, but when he discovered the real purpose of existence he included worldly affairs also in his life. He gave up meditation and prayer in the jungles and in caves, and, instead, prayed and meditated in the house, amidst family relations and other humanities, thus showing by his example that God created a person to discharge both his obligation to God and his obligation to the world. What entitles him to be called a perfect man, a being to be praised, and a guide to others, is the fact that he became the personification of the qualities of God.

The holy Prophet contemplated the Kingdom of Heaven and Nirwānā, but, unlike Jesus and Buddha, saw therein not the renunciation of the world, but something in the world and with the world. If the purpose of creation is Nirwānā, and if it is only to be attained by denying oneself of all pleasures, then it could very easily be attained. One has only to shut oneself up away from the rest of the world, meditate and pray, and when one dies, Heaven is reached immediately. If that was so, why did God create so many things in the world for mankind's delight? Because he wished mankind to carry out its duty to him without renouncing the world, and thus attain Heaven. The holy Prophet succeeded in this. He showed them it was possible to reach Heaven without renouncing the world. It was also because of this that he succeeded in reforming the manners and training the mentality of men and also in leaving a code of law for national advancement, by following which a nation may become great in all respects and expand its territories far and wide.

"The main purpose of the Quran is to awaken in man the higher consciousness of his manifold relations with God and the universe. It is in view of this essential aspect of the Quranic teaching that Goethe, while making a general review of Islam as

341

an educaional force, said to Eckermann: 'You see this teaching never fails; with all our systems we cannot go, and generally speaking no man can go, farther than that.' The problem of Islam was really suggested by the mutual conflict, and at the same time mutual attraction, presented by the two forces of religion and civilization. The same problem confronted early Christianity. The great point in Christianity is the search for an independent content for spiritual life which, according to the insight of its founder, could be elevated, not by the forces of a world external to the soul of man, but by the revelation of a new world within his soul. Islam fully agrees with this insight and supplements it by the further insight that the illumination of the new world thus revealed is not something foreign to the world of matter but permeates it through and through.

"Thus the affirmation of spirit sought by Christianity would come not by the renunciation of external forces which are already permeated by the illumination of spirit, but by a proper adjustment of man's relation to these forces in view of the light received from the world within. It is the mysterious touch of the ideal that animates and sustains the real, and through it alone we can discover and affirm the ideal. With Islam the ideal and the real are not two opposing forces which cannot be reconciled. The life of the ideal consists, not in a total breach with the real which would tend to shatter the organic wholeness of life into painful oppositions, but in the perpetual endeavour

342

of the ideal to appropriate the real with a view eventually to absorb it, to convert it into itself and to illuminate its whole being. It is the sharp opposition between the subject and the object, the mathematical without and the biological within, that impressed Christianity. Islam, however, faces the opposition with a view to overcome it. This essential difference in looking at a fundamental relation determines the respective attitudes of these great religions towards the problem of human life in its present surroundings. Both demand the affirmation of the spiritual self in man, with this difference only, that Islam, recognizing the contact of the ideal with the real, says 'yes' to the world of matter and points the way to master it with a view to discover a basis for a realistic regulation of life." Sir Mohammad Iqbāl, *The Reconstruction of Religious Thought in Islam* (London, 1934).

There are many things from the teachings of the holy Prophet which the non-Muslim civilized nations of to-day are adopting, such as the prohibition of intoxicating liquor in America—though as an experiment this cannot be said to have been altogether successful—and restriction on the rate of interest in Russia: these and many other problems that the holy Prophet solved for Muslims 1,350 years ago. The questions of capital and labour, of equal opportunities for all, and the like, are all things first taught by the Prophet when he drew up a civic constitution for the conduct of the Muslim civic affairs, which was strictly adhered to by the Companions of the holy Prophet and more especially 'Omar. To-day the first step towards the achievement of internationalism is considered to be universal education. This, like most other things, the holy Prophet made not only universal, but compulsory for Muslims, male and female. In the world of to-day, industries occupy a large proportion of the time of national Governments. On that subject the words of the Prophet 1,300 years ago are, "A labourer is a friend of God." The world owes a great gratitude to Islam, for there is not a science to-day that was not first started by Islam through the teachings of the holy Prophet. In the Middle Ages the Europeans who wished to gain knowledge were forced to go to Muslim Spain to learn science and philosophy, for those studies were at that time tabu in Christian Europe.

It is not so long ago since feminism became something of a craze among Western nations. Women, after the war, started their agitation in favour of the equality of the sexes, and since then they acquired considerable civic status, but before that they had no life outside the narrow boundaries of their homes. The very first injunctions touching the respect due to women, especially mothers, were given by the Prophet of Islam, and he has left a tradition which is still the wonder of many. "Paradise lies under the feet of your mother," says Muhammad.

It is much to be deplored that the Muslims of to-day seem to have forgotten all the great things which their forefathers invented and discovered. The present state of the Muslims has not come about

344

because they were always backward and ignorant; it is the fault of the present generation who have not made the most of the teachings of their fore-fathers.

What is the purpose underlying the division of the world into families, clans, societies, and nations? Hindu Shāstrās and European political theorists may say what they please, but Islamic teaching is that they are only for the smooth running of the affairs of the world. Mere appellations and styles mean no superiority. This was not only theorized and taught, the followers of Islam trans-lated it into practice. The life of Muhammad is a grand example of this, as also are the lives of his Companions. The Quran 49 : 13 reads, "O you men! We have created you of a male and a female, and made you tribes and families that you may know each other. . . ."

I will give a few instances that will show how greatly the holy Prophet believed in the theory of equality, and emphasized it on his followers. 'Omar, a Companion, afterwards the Caliph, after the victory of 'Irāq, made Abū 'Ubaydah the com-mander of a battalion. Some of the other Compan-ions of Muhammad objected to this because after all he was not one of them, but when they spoke to 'Omar he replied, "The honour you had was on account of your valour and courage, which you have now lost, and that being the case it is impossible not to promote and honour those who have proved their capability." Abū 'Ubaydah himself was a brave and noble man. Once, when he was commander, the Persians after their defeat in the battle of Qādisia had sent delicacies of food to him by way of an offering. He asked them if what they had sent was for the whole army or for himself alone; they replied that as it had to be prepared in haste, they were only able to bring it for him alone. Abū 'Ubaydah then thanked them, and declined the food, for he said he could not accept it as it was not enough for his men as well, and as there was no distinction between anyone in Islam, and as his men could not partake of it with him, he could not take it himself.

After the capture of Jerusalem, Bilāl, whose duty it was to give the call for prayer, reported to 'Omar that the officers ate good food and plenty of it while the men hardly got enough. At this 'Omar was very angry. He sent for the officers and spoke to them severely. They replied that as the things were very cheap they could afford to buy the dishes, at which 'Omar had, for this time, to be silent. But the next day he gave the order that the men should be given better food and more pay to buy any extras they wanted themselves.

Islam has given individual freedom to all, and the modern cry of "Freedom is our birthright," which we hear a good deal from our leaders, is one that was first uttered by 'Omar. It is related that once the son of a governor for no reason beat a poor defenceless man; 'Omar heard of this, and in a public gathering ordered the same poor man to give the son of the governor a beating. He said to the governor and his son, "Since when have you made human beings slaves? Do you not know that everyone is born a free man?"

An incident which occurred during the Caliphate of 'Omar shows the absolute equality of all men in Islam. Jabala, king of the Ghassan, having embraced the faith, had proceeded to Medina to pay his homage to the Commander of the Faithful. He had entered the city with great pomp and circumstance, and been received with much consideration. Whilst performing the *tawāf* or circumambulation of the Ka'ba, a humble pilgrim engaged in the same sacred duties accidentally dropped a piece of his pilgrim's dress over the royal shoulders. Jabala turned round furiously and struck him a blow which knocked out the poor man's teeth. The rest of this episode must be told in the memorable words of 'Omar himself to Abū 'Ubaydah, commanding the Muslim troops in Syria. "The poor man came to me," writes the Caliph, "and prayed for redress; I sent for Jabala, and when he came before me I asked him why he had so ill-treated a brother Muslim. He answered that the man had insulted him, and that were it not for the sanctity of the place he would have killed him on the spot. I answered that his words added to the gravity of his offence, and that unless he obtained the pardon of the injured man he would have to submit to the usual penalty of the law. Jabala replied, 'I am a king and the other is only a common man.' 'King or no king, both of you are Muslims and both of you are equal in the eye of the law.' He asked that the penalty might be

347

delayed until the next day; and, on the consent of the injured, I accorded the delay. In the night Jabala escaped. . . .

"This letter was read by Abū 'Ubaydah at the head of his troops. These communications appear to have been frequent under the early caliphate. No person in the camp or in the city was a stranger to public affairs. Every Friday after Divine service the Commander of the Faithful mentioned to the assembly the important nominations and events of the day. The prefects in their provinces followed the example. No one was excluded from these general assemblies of the public. It was the reign of democracy in its best form. The Pontiff of Islam, the Commander of the Faithful, was not hedged round by any divinity. He was responsible for the administration of the state of his subjects. The stern devotion of the early Caliphs to the well-being of the people, and the austere simplicity of their lives, were in strict accordance with the example of the Prophet Muhammad. They preached and prayed in the mosque like the Prophet; received in their homes the poor and oppressed and failed not to give a hearing to the meanest. Without cortège, without pomp or ceremony they ruled the hearts of men by the force of their character. 'Omar travelled to Syria to receive the capitulation of Jerusalem, accompanied by a single slave. Abū Bakr on his death-bed left only a suit of clothes, a camel, and a slave to his heir. Every Friday 'Alī distributed his own allowance from the public treasury among the distressed and suffering; and

348

set an example to the people by his respect for the ordinary tribunals. Whilst the Republic founded by Muhammad lasted, none of the Caliphs could alter, or act contrary to, the judgment of the constituted courts of justice." Ameer Alī, *The Spirit of Islam* (London, 1922.)

I will give you another incident to illustrate the principles of equality in Islam. The chief of the Quraysh, Abū Sufyān, called one day to see 'Omar, and found waiting there Bilāl, Shu'ayb, and 'Ammār; all of whom had once been slaves. As these three had come before the others, when 'Omar began receiving his visitors they were called the first; which thing Abū Sufyān, the leader of the Quraysh, took as a great insult, and protested. But one of the Companions present told him that Islam called everyone with the same voice, and that there was no distinction between man and man, and as the three men who had been slaves had called first they were entitled to be seen first, and those who came later had to wait.

This is the true teaching of Islam, in which caste and creed have no part. Those only are entitled to honour and position who follow Islam truly and rightly and fulfil their duty to God and to humanity. Islam has made slaves wear the crowns, and raised the ordinary average man to become one of the great. Bilāl, who was once a poor slave, gained so much honour by his righteousness and true Islamic sincerity that 'Omar, the Second Caliph, always addressed him as "My Lord."

After the capture of Jerusalem, when the Muslim army was entering the city, 'Omar, their leader, was on foot and in most ordinary clothes. His officers were greatly concerned at this; for they thought that the Christians would not think much of their leader if he entered the city in that poor condition. So they chose a splendid horse and some magnificent clothes and took them all to 'Omar, who thanked them but declined to accept, explaining that the honour he had was because of Islam, and that the honour alone was quite sufficient for all occasions; there was no need of fine clothes or fine horses.

The incidents I have related above show that in Islam properly speaking nothing worldly can make a person great or honoured. The only thing that counts is the goodness of a person and his sincere adherence to all the teachings of Islam. True greatness does not mean to be born a Mogul, Afghan, Arab, Englishman, or Turk, but to be a good and true Muslim. These, then, are the teachings of Islam, and those who go against them need hope for no honour or greatness; for such cannot truly be theirs. This equality of Islam had abolished slavery from Muslim countries.

"Zaid, the freedman of the Prophet, was often entrusted with the command of troops, and the noblest captains served under him without demur; and his son Osama was honoured with the leadership of the expedition sent by Abū Bakr against the Greeks. Kutb-ud-din, the first king of Delhi, and the true founder, therefore, of the Musulman empire in India, was a slave. The slavery which was allowed in Islam had, in fact, nothing in common with that which was in vogue in Christendom until recent times, or with American slavery, until the holy war of 1865 put an end to that curse.

"In Islam the slave of to-day is the grand vizier of to-morrow. He may marry, without discredit, his master's daughter, and become the head of the family. Slaves have ruled kingdoms and founded dynasties. The father of Mahmūd of Ghaznī was a slave. Can Christianity point to such records as these? Can Christianity show, in the pages of history, as clear, as humane an account of her treatment of slaves as this?

"The Koran always speaks of slaves as 'those whom your right hands have acquired,' indicating thus the only means of acquisition of bondsmen or bondswomen. It recognized, in fact, only one kind of slavery—the servitude of men made captives in *bona fide* lawful warfare. . . . Among all barbarous nations the captives are spared from a motive of selfishness alone, in order to add to the wealth of the individual captor, or of the collective nation, by their sale-money or by their labour. Like other nations of antiquity, the Arab of the pre-Islamic period spared the lives of his captives for the sake of profiting by them. Mohammed found this custom existing among his people. Instead of theorizing, or dealing in vague platitudes, he laid down strict rules for their guidance, enjoining that those only may be held in bond who were taken in *bona fide* legal war until they were ransomed,

351

or the captive bought his or her own liberty by the wages of service. But even when these means failed, an appeal to the pious feelings of the Moslem, combined with the onerous responsibilities attached to the possession of a slave, was often enough to secure the eventual enfranchisement of the latter. Slave lifting and slave dealing, patronized by dominant Christianity, and sanctified by Judaism, were utterly reprobated and condemned. The man who dealt in slaves was declared the outcast of humanity. Enfranchisement of slaves was pronounced to be a noble act of virtue. It was forbidden in absolute terms to reduce Moslems to slavery. To the lasting disgrace of a large number of professed Moslems it must be said, however, that, whilst observing, or trying to observe the letter, they have utterly ignored the spirit of the Teacher's precepts, and allowed slavery to flourish (in direct contravention of the injunctions of the Prophet) by purchase and other means. The possession of a slave, by the Koranic laws, was conditional on a *bona fide* struggle, in self-defence, against unbelieving and idolatrous aggressors, and its permission was a guarantee for the safety and preservation of the captives. The cessation of the state of war, in which the Moslem community was at first involved, from the animosity of the surrounding tribes and nations, would have brought about the extinction of slavery by a natural process—the stoppage of future acquisition and the enfranchisement of those in bondage. However, whether from contact with the demoralized nations of the East and the West and

352

the wild races of the North, or from the fact that the baneful institution was deeply rooted among all classes of society, many Moslems, like the Christians and the Jews, recognized slavery, and to some extent do so even now. But the wild Turkoman, or the African Arab, who glories in slave-lifting, is no more a representative of Islam than is the barbarous Guacho, who revels on the savage prairies of South America, of Christianity." Ameer Alī, *The Spirit of Islam* (London, 1922).

"Mr. Joseph Thompson, the well-known African traveller, in a letter to the London *Times* of 14th of November, 1887, thus writes on the subject of slavery in East Africa: 'I unhesitatingly affirm, and I speak from a wider experience of Eastern Central Africa than any of your correspondents possess, that if the slave trade thrives it is because Islam has not been introduced in these regions, and for the strongest of all reasons, that the spread of Mahommedanism would have meant the concomitant suppression of the slave trade.' His account of 'the peaceful and unassuming agencies' by which Islam has been spread in Western Africa and Central Sudan deserves the attention of every reader. 'Here,' he says, 'we have Islam as a living, active force, full of the fire and energy of its early days, proselytizing too with much of the marvellous success which characterized its early days.' " Ameer Alī, *The Spirit of Islam* (London, 1922), in a footnote on p. 266.

What the world needs to-day is a brotherhood of human beings, and no better example of human brotherhood or internationalism can the world

z

present than the brotherhood of Islam, which binds all in one. ". . . we cannot deny that the conception of brotherhood in Islam transcends all barriers of race and nationality, a feature which does not characterize any other religion," says Sir S. Radhakrishnan, the eminent Hindu philosopher and a student of Comparative Religion in his *East and West in Religion* (London, 1933).

The fact that the Helpers of Medina were not only eager to take the emigrants as their brothers, but were also willing to allow them to share in their property, gives a true example of the brotherhood that the teachings of the holy Prophet inspired. Even to-day, in any Muslim country, one will see all, rich and poor, standing side by side, shoulder to shoulder, black and white, king and subject, nobleman and servant. The teaching of the holy Prophet killed the narrow outlook of nationalism by making all, whether Indian or Arab, Turk or Mogul, Englishman or African, equal and one before God. Muslims may be living poles asunder, but they are all united in one brotherhood. Prayers for all were prescribed in Arabic, so that all should at least know one language in which to converse and communicate with each other. To strengthen this international relation Hajj—the pilgrimage to Mecca—was made obligatory on all those who have a certain amount of money. This theory of equality taught by the holy Prophet is a great thing, and if only other nations of the world follow it, it would indeed be of incalculable benefit to all.

CHAPTER 31

AL-ISLAM, THE TEACHINGS OF MUHAMMAD

"Surely the true religion with
God is Islam."—THE QURAN 3: 18.

NO book on that great personality would be
complete without a word concerning the
religion he preached, in addition to glimpses of it
one gets in the discussion of his personality.

Islam, the religion preached by the holy Prophet,
means submission to God. If we look on the universe
around us, we shall see many things all in certain
stages of progress; evolution is going on, for every
step in nature is onward and upward. The law of
nature, which is observed by every atom of nature,
is actually the law of God; for everything depends
on the strict observance of this law for its creation,
existence, and upbringing. This is Islam—the
observance of, and the submission to, the law of
God, as in the words of the Quran: "Do these
people seek for themselves any other religion but
the religion of God? Do they not see that the
whole Nature around them, everything which is
in Heaven or earth, gives submission to God for
its very existence?" (3: 82).

In these words the Quran gives us the religion
of nature. And man being the highest product of
nature, and the finest handiwork of God, it is

355

essential that he followed the religion of God. From the very beginning man has had some sort of dim idea about God, and what has seemed to him to be the controller of events becomes the object of his adoration. As objects of worship, the sun, fire, rivers, trees, etc., are but imperfect manifestations of God imagined by mere human beings, for there is a Power, beyond and above all these things, which controls all. These things are but manifestations of God as is man himself, and not God, or gods in themselves as their worshippers believe. It was to show people the True God, and to make them worship Him and Him alone, that prophets were raised up by God, and they on their part explained to humanity what God is. But through flaws or imperfections of intelligence, human beings strayed from the true course to the worship, in many cases, of the expounders of creeds themselves, as Gods or sons of Gods; as, for example, in Hinduism and Christianity. It is, therefore, vouchsafed to the holy Prophet of Arabia to expound the theory of God in such a way as to make it impossible of misunderstanding or misrepresentation, and this is so because he found God, as the testimony of a truthful, though Christian, writer (Major A. G. Leonard) shows, when he says: "If ever a man on this earth found God, if ever a man devoted his life to God's service with a good and great motive, it is certain that the Prophet of Arabia is that man." Having found God, the same writer continues: "The Quran was the immediate consequence of his concentration and communion with Nature, and the God of Nature: Islam the natural result."

The main theme, therefore, in Islam is God; not God the Personal Being, but God the Maker of the Universe and of all mankind. As the Quran in 2: 255 says: "God is He besides Whom there is no God, the Ever-Living, the Self-Subsisting." Thus the conception of God in Islam is much too exalted and much too divine for the belief in the fatherhood of God.

Having explained the conception of God in Islam, I proceed to another important question: What is the purpose of religion? The Quran, having described religion thus, "The Nature made by God in which He has made men that is the true religion. . . ." (30: 30), explains the purpose of religion in the following words: "Who believes in that which has been revealed to you, and that which was revealed before you, and they are sure of the hereafter" (2: 4). This means that the purpose of religion is submission to God: submission to God in the sense that it should be the observance of the laws of nature—Islam—which ultimately unites mankind with its Creator. Religion is, therefore, a means to an end, an end that is the purpose of Creation—it should be revealed to all. God is the God of all nations and all races, and when He is not partial to any particular nation or race, as far as physical sustenance is concerned, then He will not be partial to any one race alone by revealing to it alone the purpose of Creation. If there be any doubt in the minds of the people, the Quran dispels

357

it in the following words: ". . . Their apostles had come to them with clear arguments, and with scriptures, and with the illuminating book" (35:25), yet people took other religions as coming from anything but God, the result of which has been bigotry, hatred, and discord, that have separated brother from brother, and torn to pieces the fabric of universal brotherhood. The Quran or Islam, for the first time, showed the fact that God is not a tribal God, but the God of all races and of all nations.

Religion, as I have said above, is a means to an end. Before Islam, every religion believed in and had a different means of its own for obtaining the end or purpose of Creation. Most of those religions considered religion and ordinary life to be two different entities divergent and conflicting in purpose as well as action, and in consequence preached that to attain one the other must necessarily be renounced. To attain God by renouncing the world is to attain nothing, for God is the world—the true World, the Natural and the Inexorable. The severance of all worldly connections preached by Buddha for the attainment of "Nirvāna," or the celibacy, meekness, and poverty preached by Jesus Christ are not the means to the end God has made. The very fact that the world was created with human beings, I may say, intellectual human beings to utilize its other creations, and to fulfil their obligations to one another, would be a negative one if we take renunciation of the world as the means to the end. Humanity, which is a part of nature, is progressive like Nature, and not retrospective and stationary; and if we accept the theory of renunciation we shall have to admit that there could be no progress in the world. In spite of these teachings the progress of the world shows that the means preached by Islam are the only true ones, for they are consistent with nature. Islam demands that a person should discharge both his duties as a human being to human beings and as the created to his Creator. In fact, one leads to the other naturally. It is, therefore, a religion which is human. Major Leonard, from his personal experiences, writes: "One of the first thoughts that a very careful perusal of the Quran brings home to me is the intense humanity of Muhammad and his work," which means that Islam is a human representation of the Unity and Supremacy of the One and Only God.

The principles of Islam are given in the Quran, and they are five, which are divided into three main points of belief and four of practice. The points of belief are (1) The belief in God; (2) The belief in Divine revelation; and (3) The belief in the life to come. Of the three, the first, Belief in God, has already been discussed in the above paragraphs and shown to be the basic and cardinal point of Islam. The second, that of Belief in Divine revelation, does not imply only belief in the Quran, but also in the truth of all the divine revelations of all the ages and to all the nations on earth. The third, that of Belief in the life to come, is as expressed

359

and defined by Islam, a comprehensive one; for it is an advance on all previous theories expounded by other religions. The Quran, with reference to this, first points out that the life after death is only a continuation of this life; for on the day of resurrection it will bring the hidden realities. The gulf that is generally interposed between this life and the life after death is the great obstacle in the solution of the mystery of the hereafter. Islam makes that gulf disappear altogether: it makes the next life only a continuation of the present one. On this point the holy Quran is explicit. It says: "And We have made every man's actions to cling to his neck, and We will bring forth to him on the resurrection day a book which he will find wide open" (17: 13). And again it says: "And whoever is blind in this, he shall also be blind in the hereafter" (17: 22). And elsewhere we have: "O soul that art at rest! return to your Lord, well pleased with Him, well pleasing Him; so enter among My servants and enter into My garden" (89: 27–30). The first of these three verses makes it clear that the great facts which will be brought to light on the day of resurrection will not be anything new, but only a manifestation of what is here hidden from the physical eye. The life after death is, therefore, not a new life, but only a continuance of this life, bringing its hidden realities to light. The other two quotations show that a hellish and a heavenly life both begin in this world. The blindness of the next life is surely hell, but according to the verse quoted only those who are blind

here shall be blind hereafter, thus making it clear
that the spiritual blindness of this life is the real
hell, and from here it is taken to the next life.
Similarly, it is the soul that has found perfect
peace and rest that is made to enter into paradise at
death, thus showing that the paradise of the next
life is only a continuation of the peace and rest which
a man enjoys spiritually in this life. Thus it is clear
that, according to the holy Quran, the next life
is a continuation of this, and death is not an inter-
ruption but a connecting link, a door that opens
upon the hidden realities of this life.

Islam also makes it clear that the state after
death is a complete representation of the spiritual
state in this life. In this connection the other point
on which Islam throws light is that man is destined
to make infinite progress in that life, which means
that the development of human faculties that takes
place in this world is not limited to this world.
Having thus enumerated the beliefs, I would like
to add that belief according to Islam is not only
a conviction of the truth of a given proposition, but
also the acceptance of a proposition as a basis for
action.

The practical side of Islam, as I have said
before, involves the observance of four principles:
they are, (1) Salāt or Prayer; (2) Fasting; (3) Zakāt
or Poor-rate; and (4) Pilgrimage. Prayer, according
to Islam, is the outpouring of the heart's sentiment
and a devout supplication to God. Describing the
ethics of Prayer, the Quran says: "Recite that
which has been revealed to you of the Book, and

361

keep up prayer. Surely prayer keeps one away from indecency and evil, and certainly the remembrance of God is the greatest" (29: 45), which means that prayer is something like a spiritual diet, which one takes five times a day. The founder of Christianity has himself emphasized this, "Man shall not live by bread alone, but by every word that proceedeth out of the mouth of God" (Matt. iv: 4).

What Islam requires is that a Muslim, however busy he may be, should disengage himself from all occupations to pray to God when the appointed time comes. There is no need to speak of the Islamic prayers in detail, except to say that by its means Islam has made communion with God possible.

Fasting is one of those institutions which was given a new birth and a new meaning after the advent of Islam. Before Islam, fasting was generally resorted to with sorrow and affliction, but in Islam it is enjoined as a food for moral elevation. The Quran says, "Fasting is prescribed for you, as for those before you, so that you may guard against evil" (2: 133). Thus fasting, like prayer, is for the purification and cleansing of the soul. Islam is a religion that teaches one to shun all evil, and fasting, like prayer and other practices, is a means to this end, and as such does not mean mere abstinence from food, but from evil of every sort. In fact, it is a species of training; by learning to abstain from what is unlawful. Fasting is compulsory for all adults. But those who cannot keep the fasts because of long illness, old age, physical debility, pregnancy, and the like are exempted. In these cases if the

362

persons concerned can afford, they are recommended to give away the measure of one man's food to a poor man every day during the whole month.

The third principle of practice is "Zakāt," or Poor-rate. All religions have preached charity, but it has been left to Islam only to regulate it and make of it a living institution. It has made charity obligatory and binding upon all. A rich man can enter the brotherhood of Islam if he is prepared to part with a fixed proportion of his wealth for the poor. He is not faced with the insurmountable difficulty propounded by Christianity, that it is easier for a camel to pass through the eye of a needle than for a rich man to enter into the Kingdom of Heaven. The poor-rate is payable only on money that is saved or hoarded, and exemption is granted when the amount is below four pounds at the end of a year. For all sums above that, one-fortieth is payable every year, and in the case of immovable property it is paid from the income or rent derived therefrom. This "Zakāt" should be given or used for the poor, the needy, those in debt, the ransoming of captives, and for wayfaring men, for the officials appointed for the collection and disbursement of Zakāt, for propagation of the faith of Islam, and in the way of God. The fourth and last form of practice that is incumbent on every Muslim but once in a lifetime provided he or she has the means, is the performance of the pilgrimage to Mecca. This is good in many ways for Islam, for the closer intercourse of all the different nations embracing Islam, so as to make the brotherhood real, for the discussing and deciding of differences. It is, in short, a spiritual and political institution.

"On the Pilgrimage to Mecca," says Sir Thomas Arnold, in his *Preaching of Islam* (London, 1913), p. 416, "it ordains a yearly gathering of believers of all nations and languages brought together from all parts of the world to pray in that sacred place, towards which their faces are set in every hour of private worship in their distant homes. No touch of religious genius could have conceived a better expedient for impressing on the minds of the faithful a sense of their common life, and of their brotherhood in the bonds of faith. Here, in a supreme act of common worship, the negro of the west coast of Africa meets the Chinaman from the distant East: the courtly and polished Ottoman recognizing his brother Muslim in the wild islander from the farthest end of the Malayan Sea. At the same time, throughout the whole Muhammadan world, the hearts of the believers are lifted up in sympathy with their more fortunate brethren gathered together in the Sacred City, as in their own homes they celebrate the festival of 'Id 'ul-Azha. . . . Whatever be the race, colour, or antecedents of the worshipper, he is received into the brotherhood of the believers, and takes his place as an equal among equals. Islam is a great political power, whose effects the world will feel more and more in proportion as the ends of the earth are brought closer and closer together.

"Islam, which claims the allegiance of three

364

hundred million souls, is the only solution for all the ills of the world. This is no idle boast on my part. Events are proving it. Every thoughtful observer of what is going on in Western Asia and in Africa can appreciate its truth. For it is in Islam only that the idea of a real material league of nations has been approached in the right and practicable way." "The ideal of a league of Human races," observes Prof. Snouck Hurgronje in the *Moslem World of To-day* (London, 1926), "has indeed been approached by Islam more nearly than by any other: for the league of nations founded on the basis of Muhammad's religion takes the principal of the equality of all human races so seriously as to put other communities to shame." Islam is the only religion which has attempted to cope with this aspect of human life—an aspect which is growing in importance every day—the only religion which has succeeded to an almost incredible extent in actually establishing a real world-brotherhood.

We see, then, that prayers and other practices and beliefs of a religion are to make a human being understand God, and it is a conception of God so formed that has much to do with the moulding of a man's character. The conception of God before the advent of Jesus Christ was such that it could not inspire man with love for him, for "He was understood to be an implacable ruler, whose anger demanded some sort of sacrifice for its pacification." Jesus Christ, when he came, gave a more lovable conception of God: "Our Father in Heaven" was the epithet he gave to the Creator

365

and Ruler of the Universe. Thus it was the revelation of the father and the son, and not that of the ruled and the ruler, which he preached. He always spoke of God as your Father and my Father, and not as his Father alone. It was after him that St. Paul, to accommodate the new faith to Greek and Roman predilections, developed the theory of reconciling the angered deity by means of sacrificial atonement, and brought about the necessity of the blood of the Son to pacify the anger of the Father in order to wash out the sins of the world. As shown above, the holy Prophet put an end to all such misconceptions; and of all beautiful attributes of God the one that will make the Muslim conception of God most clear is that of *Rabb*, an Arabic used in the first verse of the opening chapter of the Quran and which means the fosterer of a thing in such a manner as to make it attain one condition after another until it reaches its goal of completion. Hence *Rabb* is the Author of all existence, Who has not only given to the whole creation its means of nourishment but has also beforehand ordained for each a sphere of capacity and within that sphere provided the means by which it continues to attain gradually to its goal of perfection. It will thus be seen that the word *Rabb* conveys a far nobler and grander idea than the Arabic word *ab* (father), which has comparatively a very limited significance. Another peculiarity regarding this attribute may be noted here. It is never used absolutely but always as my *Rabb* or our *Rabb* or your *Rabb*, or thy *Rabb* or *Rabb* of the world. The reason is plain. The Nourisher or Sustainer can only be spoken of in relation to something which he nourishes or sustains. And He is spoken of repeatedly as the *Rabb* (or Sustainer) of believers as well as unbelievers, of the Muslims as well as their opponents, which is a clear evidence of the broadness of the conception of God in Islam.

This, then, is Islam, a simple, pure, and natural creed, that proves that the most natural way leads one to God. It is not a new creed, for all prophets preached the same religion, but it is certainly unique in the sense that while all religions have wandered from the natural path, Islam and its followers still adhere to it, and this is because the expounder of this religion found God.

CHAPTER 32

THE QURAN

> "Surely We have revealed the Reminder and We will most surely be its guardian."—THE QURAN 15: 9.
>
> "And this Quran is not such as could be forged by those besides God, but it is a verification of that which is before it and a clear explanation of the book, there is no doubt in it."—THE QURAN 10: 37.

HAVING described Islam briefly in the previous chapter, I will now say something about the Quran, the Book of the Muslims, in which are given the main points and principles of Islam, together with a religious history of bygone days. In describing Islam I said that faith in Divine revelation is one of the fundamental principles of Islam —faith not only in the Quran but in all previous revelations of God as well. Divine revelation is the basis of all revealed religions, but this simple fact was overlooked by the religions before Islam, and some of them went so far as to close the door of revelation after a certain time. Islam, on the other hand, came to assert that there is no limit of time, space, or boundary to Divine revelation.

Another aspect of this belief is that a Muslim refuses to believe or acknowledge the incarnation of a Divine Being. The ideal of every religion is the communion of man with God, and while Islam does not bring down God to man in the sense of incarnation, it strives to raise him by spiritual progress and purification, so that he may attain to that communion. Again, the holy Quran was not meant only for one people, or for one age; it is for all people and for all ages, for it is the complete Law of God.

Not being able to understand the apparent incongruous arrangement of the verses in the holy Quran, non-Muslims who are not conversant with the Quran and, as a rule, are new to it, have rushed to advance the theory that the Quran is amorphous, ill-assorted, chaotic, and devoid of cohesion. Thus Mr. Sale, a translator of the Quran, writes: "After the new passages had been, from the Prophet's mouth, taken down in writing by his scribe, they were published to his followers. Several of them took copies for their private use, and the original was then put into a chest." Mr. Palmer, another translator of the Quran, writes: "The individual portions of the Quran were not always written down immediately after the revelation." He again says: "And lastly, many odd verses appear to have been inserted into various suras for no other reason than that they suit the rhyme." I cannot, by way of a reply to these critics, resist the temptation of giving a somewhat lengthy quotation from Dr. Steingass as quoted in the

Dictionary of Islam, by Hughes: "But if we consider the variety and heterogeneousness of the topics on which the Quran touches, uniformity of style and diction can scarcely be expected; on the contrary, it would appear to be strangely out of place. Let us not forget that in the book, as Muhammad's newest biographer, Ludolf Krehl expresses it, 'there is given a complete code of creeds and morals, as well as of the law based thereupon. There are also the foundations laid for every institution of an extensive commonwealth, for instruction for the administration of justice, for military organization, for the finances, for a most careful legislation for the poor: all built up on the belief in the One God, who holds man's destinies in His Hand.' Where so many important objects are concerned, the standard of excellence by which we have to gauge the composition of the Quran as a whole must needs vary with the matter treated upon in each particular case. Sublime and chaste, where the supreme truth of God's unity is to be proclaimed; appealing in high-pitched strains to the imagination of a poetically gifted people where the eternal consequences of man's submission to God's holy will, or of rebellion against it, are pictured: touching in its simple, almost crude, earnestness, when it seeks again and again encouragement or consolation for God's messenger and a solemn warning for those to whom he has been sent, in the histories of the prophets of old: the language of the Quran adapts itself to the exigencies of everyday life, where this everyday life, in its private and public bearings,

370

is to be brought in harmony with the fundamental principles of the new dispensation.

"Here, therefore, its merits as a literary production should, perhaps, not be measured by some preconceived maxims of subjective and aesthetic taste, but by the effects which it produced in Muhammad's contemporaries and fellow-countrymen. If it spoke so powerfully and convincingly to the hearts of his hearers as to weld hitherto centrifugal and antagonistic elements into one compact and well-organized body, animated by ideas far beyond those which had until now ruled the Arabian mind, then its eloquence was perfect, simply because it created a civilized nation out of savage tribes, and shot a fresh woof into the old warp of history."

These critics also forget that the chronological order of any book would be different from its arrangement according to subject matter. Now the arrangement according to subject matter came about in this wise. The whole of the Quran was committed to memory and written down in the lifetime of the holy Prophet; and the verses in each chapter and the chapters themselves were arranged in his lifetime—and under his direction. The "collection" of the Quran by order of Abū Bakr was no more than the collection of different writings into one volume. That this is so there is abundant proof. That the Quran was reduced to writing as revealed under the direction of the holy Prophet is shown by the evidence of Muslims and non-Muslims, as well as by the Quran itself.

Sir William Muir, a very hostile critic of Islam, felt constrained to write: "But there is good reason for believing that many fragmentary copies, embracing among them the whole Quran or nearly the whole, were, during his lifetime, made by the followers of the Prophet. Writing was, without doubt, generally known at Mecca long before Muhammad assumed the Prophetical office." 'Usmān, the third Caliph, once explained: "It was customary with the Messenger of God that when portions of different chapters were revealed to him, or when any verse was revealed, to call one of those who used to write the holy Quran, and say to him, 'Write these verses in the chapter where such and such a verse occurred.' " Of other reports of high authority Bukhārī says: "When the verse 4: 95 was revealed, the Prophet (may peace and the blessing of God be upon him!) said, 'Bring Zayd to me and let him bring the tablet and the ink-stand,' and when Zayd came, the Prophet said, 'Write it down.' " Thus it is clear that the preparation of the Quran under the orders of Abū Bakr was but the gathering together into one volume of verses already written, arranged, and preserved. Zayd, who did the whole work, remembered two verses as being part of the Quran; but they were not permitted to be written down until those already written in the same context had been found. Not only this, but at every step in the compilation of the Quran, Zayd was assisted by many who had committed the whole Book to memory. Arabs are famous for their retentive memories. Inasmuch as the reciting of the Quran is made a part of religion, it was not at all a difficult test for them to memorize it. For example, even to-day, not only in Arabia but all over the Muslim world men can be found in thousands who know the holy Quran by heart, word for word. Therefore, even if it had never been actually committed to writing, not a single verse of it would have been lost.

I trust I have made it clear that the Quran was both written and committed to memory during the lifetime of the Prophet. As to the arrangement of verses and chapters there is conclusive proof to show that this also was done in the lifetime of the holy Prophet and under his direction. God speaks thus in the Quran: "Surely on Us devolves the collecting of it, and the reciting of it, therefore, when We have recited it, follow its recitation." (75: 17, 18.) This shows that the collection of the Quran, its arrangement, and all things connected with it, were brought about by the guidance of Divine revelation. History bears ample testimony to the fact that the holy Prophet at his death left the complete Quran with the same arrangement of verses and chapters as we have now. It is true that arrangement of the verses, as it stands to-day, is not in accordance with the order of revelation, but there is not a shred of evidence in the history of the Quran to show that any change was made in the arrangement of the verses at any time; and the conclusion must necessarily be that the present arrangement, being that followed by the holy Prophet, is correct. Had this not been so, then it

373

would have been the duty of the Companions to do the arrangements in their own way; and if this had been the case, it would not have passed without some mention of it being made in the mass of books written on the subject. Had there been any difference in the arrangement of the verses of the Quran as compiled by order of 'Usmān, then the Companions would have raised objections. 'Alī had a copy of the Quran arranged by himself in chronological order, and he was well aware that it was different from the arrangement made by the holy Prophet.

Seeing that he had himself co-operated in the work of compilation ordered by 'Usmān, we are forced to the conclusion that the arrangement of the verses made by 'Usmān was recognized by all Companions, without a single exception, to be the arrangement ordered by the Prophet. If 'Alī had in any way doubted the authenticity of this arrangement he, when he became the Caliph, could have authorized his own arrangement.

Now there might rise a natural question: If the whole of the Quran was preserved both in writing and in memory, with verses and chapters duly arranged, then what is meant by the "Collection of the Quran" in the time of the first and third Caliphs? As remarked, the primary work of the collection of the holy Quran was done by the holy Prophet himself under the guidance of Divine revelation. To this the holy Book itself refers in the following words: "Surely on Us devolves the collecting of it and the recital of it; and when We

374

have recited it, follow its recitation." (75: 17, 18.) On another occasion the objection of the unbelievers to the gradual revelation of the holy Quran is thus met: "And those who disbelieve say: Why is not the Quran revealed unto him all at once? Thus that We may strengthen thy heart therewith, and We have arranged it in right order" (25: 32). But we have seen that such collection was needed only by those who wished to commit the whole of the Quran to memory, and that it was in reciting the whole that the arrangement of chapters was needed. Hence, though the whole Quran existed in a complete and arranged form in the memories of the Companions, it did not exist in a single volume in a written form. Every verse and every chapter was, no doubt, committed to writing as soon as it was revealed, but so long as the recipient of the Divine revelation lived, the whole could not be written in a single volume. At any time a verse might be revealed which it was necessary to place in the middle of a chapter, and hence the very circumstances of the case made the existence of a complete volume impossible. Hence a collection of the Quran in a volume was needed, after the death of the holy Prophet, which should be in accordance with the collection made by the holy Prophet, as existing in the memories of his Companions. Such a collection was also needed to facilitate reference to and circulation of the holy Word, and to give it a more permanent form than was secured to it in being consigned to memory. Such was the object with which the collection of the holy Quran was taken in hand by Abū Bakr and 'Omar. Later, the collection of all the writings into one single volume became a necessity, and it was this task that the two Caliphs performed. There was also the constant danger of the Quran being lost, for every war waged by the Muslims took toll of the lives of some of the reciters, who had learnt the whole of the Quran by heart.

The last question that remains to be proved is: Did the collection of Zayd agree in every way with the Quran as stored and collected in the memories of the Companions? There is not the slightest reason to believe that it did not, if we take the united testimony afforded by the mass of writings dealing with the subject. Yet, in spite of all this we see absurd charges levelled against the Quran, such as that the fact of certain passages being in fragmentary form may have led to the loss of some of them; that certain passages might not have been intended by the holy Prophet for permanent insertion in the Quran, and that the Shias believe that the Quran is not complete, etc., etc. The first of these charges is entirely illogical; for to say that because certain passages appear fragmentary to a person, therefore some portion must have been lost, is to make an unreasonable assumption, especially when there is the strongest historical evidence to show that nothing is lost of the Quran. The collection of the Quran was made by Zayd from the mass of transcriptions in which the assistance of those who had committed it to memory was taken, so that nothing of it might be left out. To say that Ubbay and Ibn Mas'ūd had different texts of the Quran is also wrong, for it is a proven fact that their copies of the Quran tallied with that of Zayd. Ibn Mas'ūd was the only one to oppose the introduction of 'Usmān's Quran because of two chapters, but all evidence goes to show that these two chapters were well known to the Companions as being part of the Divine revelation.

As to the second charge against the Quran, to wit, that certain passages may not have been intended by the holy Prophet for permanent insertion, there is this to be said. The Quran contains all the revelations of the holy Prophet, as shown above. Each and every verse was revealed on some occasion and for some purpose, wherefore it stands to reason that all were intended for inclusion in the holy Quran.

With regard to the third charge, that the Shias believed that the holy Quran was not complete, let me point out first that the Imām of the Shias, when the work was being done, found no objection to it. In later times the Shias insinuated that 'Usmān omitted certain verses in the Quran that were in favour of 'Alī. There is no truth whatever in this; for at the time 'Usmān was preparing his work there was no enmity between the Omeyyads and 'Ālyites. Again, as I have said, there were thousands who knew every word of the holy Quran by heart as they had heard it delivered by the holy Prophet, and if passages concerning 'Alī were left out by 'Usmān, surely there would have been found some among the multitude to protest.

377

Moreover, at 'Usmān's death, when the followers of 'Alī raised him to the Caliphate, there would have been no need for 'Alī and his party to tolerate an incomplete Quran, specially as that incompleteness would have been due only to the omission of passages concerning 'Alī himself. Nevertheless, they continued to use the same Quran, and found no preterition to repair.

As a matter of fact, it is the ignorant among the Shias who believe the Quran to be incomplete. The learned admit that the Book has been handed down to us without any alteration whatever in the pure form in which it was revealed to the holy Prophet thirteen hundred years ago. The learned Shia, Mullā Muhsin, the author of *Tafsīr Sāfī*, writes: "Certain men among us . . . have asserted that the Quran has suffered loss and alteration. But the true belief of our friends is against this, and this is the belief of the vast majority. For the Quran is a miracle of the holy Prophet and the source of all knowledge relating to law and all religious injunctions, and the learned Muslims have taken the utmost pains for its protection. . . . With such strong measures of protection and such faithful preservation of the holy Book by the Muslims it cannot be supposed that any alteration or loss could take place." Again he writes: "Surely the Quran was collected and arranged in the lifetime of the holy Prophet exactly as it is in our hands. . . ."

Besides Mullā Muhsin, several other famous and highly respected men of the Shia world voice their opinion in the following words: "The Quran, as sent down by God to His Prophet, is exactly what is now between the two boards (the written volume) and in the hands of the people." This is sufficient to show that the third charge against the holy Quran is also without foundation.

This chapter will, I trust, convince my readers that Islam's title to be the perfect and final manifestation of Divine will is amply justified. This is a position to which no other religion lays claim except Islam, and its teachings in their scope and conception make it clear that it is justified in its claim. But with all this it must still be borne in mind that Islam does not deny the appearance of previous prophets: it recognizes them and their pure teachings. Islam only claims to have come to perfect the one religion which from the beginning God intended mankind to follow, and the first instalment of which Adam brought into the world. From Adam to Jesus Christ each prophet brought an instalment, which was completed and merged into the final whole by Islam.

CHAPTER 33

THE HOLY PROPHET MUHAMMAD FORETOLD IN ANCIENT
SCRIPTURES

ACCORDING to the injunctions of the holy Quran we Muslims believe that the advent of our Prophet Muhammad was expressly foretold in all the sacred books of the religions.

The holy Quran represents: "And when God made a covenant through the prophets: Certainly what I have given you of book and wisdom—then an apostle comes to you verifying that which is with you, you must believe in him and you must aid him. He said: Do you affirm and accept My compact in this (matter?). They said: We do affirm" (3 : 80).

The claim is advanced here that all the prophets had prophesied the advent of a world Prophet who should verify the truth of all the prophets who had appeared in the World.

PROPHECIES IN THE OLD TESTAMENT

There are many prophecies regarding the holy Prophet both in the Old and the New Testaments. Deut. xviii: 15–18 speaks very clearly of the rising of a prophet (who shall be the like of Moses) from among the brethren of Israelites, i.e. the Ishmaelites or the Arabs. The passage in question reads:

380

ORIGINAL HEBREW TEXT

נָבִיא מִקִּרְבְּךָ מֵאַחֶיךָ טו ׃

16 כָּמֹנִי יָקִים לְךָ יְהוָה אֱלֹהֶיךָ אֵלָיו תִּשְׁמָעוּן ׃ כְּכֹל אֲשֶׁר־
שָׁאַלְתָּ מֵעִם יְהוָה אֱלֹהֶיךָ בְּחֹרֵב בְּיוֹם הַקָּהָל לֵאמֹר
לֹא אֹסֵף לִשְׁמֹעַ אֶת־קוֹל יְהוָה אֱלֹהָי וְאֶת־הָאֵשׁ הַגְּדֹלָה
17 הַזֹּאת לֹא־אֶרְאֶה עוֹד וְלֹא אָמוּת ׃ וַיֹּאמֶר יְהוָה אֵלָי
18 הֵיטִיבוּ אֲשֶׁר דִּבֵּרוּ ׃ נָבִיא אָקִים לָהֶם מִקֶּרֶב אֲחֵיהֶם
כָּמוֹךָ וְנָתַתִּי דְבָרַי בְּפִיו וְדִבֶּר אֲלֵיהֶם אֵת כָּל־אֲשֶׁר
אֲצַוֶּנּוּ ׃

Deute XVIII, 15-18

TRANSLATION

"15. The Lord thy God will raise up unto thee a prophet from the midst of thee, of thy brethren, like unto me; unto him ye shall hearken. 16. According to all that thou desiredst of the Lord thy God in Horeb in the day of assembly, saying, Let me not hear again the voice of the Lord my God, neither let me see this great fire any more, that I die not. 17. And the Lord said unto me, They have well said that which they have spoken. 18. I will raise them up a prophet from among their brethren, like unto thee, and I will put my words in his mouth; and he shall speak unto them all that I shall command him."

In the above-quoted passages our Prophet is evidently foretold. For God declared to all the Israelites that He would raise up a Prophet from among their brethren. Now we hesitate not to affirm that it is impossible that the phrase "brethren of Israel," could have any other meaning than that of Ishmaelites, and these never had any prophet but Muhammad. It is admitted both by Jews and Christians that revelations to the Israelit-ish Prophets were not made in the very words as given in the Scriptures, but only their purport, which they afterwards delivered to the people in their own language. But the holy Quran, on the contrary, revealed to our prophet word by word as it now is a fact which makes the expression "and will put my words in his mouth" inapplicable to anyone except Muhammad.

In promising to raise up a prophet God tells Moses that "I will raise up a prophet from among their brethren." But we find in Deut. 34: 10 that there arose not a prophet since in Israel like unto Moses. There cannot then remain a single doubt but that the promised prophet must have been from among the Ishmaelites, the brethren of the Israelites.

ANOTHER PROPHECY OF THE PROPHET ISAIAH
ORIGINAL HEBREW TEXT

685   JESAIA CAP. 21. 22.   כא כב

וַיַּרְא רֶכֶב 7

צֶמֶד פָּרָשִׁים רֶכֶב חֲמוֹר רֶכֶב גָּמָל וְהִקְשִׁיב קֶשֶׁב רַב־
קָשֶׁב:

Isaiah XXI, 7.

TRANSLATION

"He saw two riders one of them was a rider upon an ass and the other a rider upon a camel, he hearkened diligently with much heed" (Isaiah xxi: 7).

Isaiah saw in a vision two riders, one of them was a rider upon an ass and the other rider upon a camel. In our opinion the above passage is the faithful rendering of the original Hebrew. In the English Bible, however, it is thus translated: "He saw a chariot of asses and a chariot of camels, etc."

The Vulgate has it as follows: "He saw a chariot

of two horsemen, a rider upon an ass and a rider upon a camel, etc."

There can be no doubt that of the two riders represented by the Prophet Isaiah, as being the restorers of the true worship of the Godhead, the rider upon the ass is Jesus Christ, because he so made his entry into Jerusalem, and that by the rider of a camel is meant the prophet of Arabia, of which country the camel is characteristic of conveyance.

PROPHECIES IN THE NEW TESTAMENT
The Ahmad of Messiah
ORIGINAL GREEK TEXT

15 'Εὰν
ἀγαπᾶτέ με, τὰς ἐντολὰς τὰς ἐμὰς τηρήσετε.
16 κἀγὼ ἐρωτήσω τὸν Πατέρα καὶ ἄλλον Παράκλητον
17 δώσει ὑμῖν ἵνα ᾖ μεθ' ὑμῶν εἰς τὸν αἰῶνα,

Ταῦτα λελάληκα ὑμῖν παρ' ὑμῖν 25
μένων· ὁ δὲ Παράκλητος, τὸ Πνεῦμα τὸ Ἅγιον 26
ὃ πέμψει ὁ Πατὴρ ἐν τῷ ὀνόματί μου, ἐκεῖνος
ὑμᾶς διδάξει πάντα καὶ ὑπομνήσει ὑμᾶς πάντα
ἃ εἶπον ὑμῖν ἐγώ.

7   ἀλλ' ἐγὼ τὴν ἀλή-
θειαν λέγω ὑμῖν, συμφέρει ὑμῖν ἵνα ἐγὼ ἀπέλθω.
ἐὰν γὰρ μὴ ἀπέλθω, ὁ Παράκλητος οὐ μὴ ἔλθῃ
πρὸς ὑμᾶς· ἐὰν δὲ πορευθῶ, πέμψω αὐτὸν πρὸς
8 ὑμᾶς. καὶ ἐλθὼν ἐκεῖνος ἐλέγξει τὸν κόσμον
περὶ ἁμαρτίας καὶ περὶ δικαιοσύνης καὶ περὶ
9 κρίσεως· περὶ ἁμαρτίας μέν, ὅτι οὐ πιστεύουσιν
10 εἰς ἐμέ· περὶ δικαιοσύνης δέ, ὅτι πρὸς τὸν Πατέρα·
11 ὑπάγω καὶ οὐκέτι θεωρεῖτέ με· περὶ δὲ κρίσεως,
12 ὅτι ὁ ἄρχων τοῦ κόσμου τούτου κέκριται. Ἔτι
πολλὰ ἔχω ὑμῖν λέγειν, ἀλλ' οὐ δύνασθε βαστά-
13 ζειν ἄρτι· ὅταν δὲ ἔλθῃ ἐκεῖνος, τὸ Πνεῦμα τῆς
ἀληθείας, ὁδηγήσει ὑμᾶς εἰς τὴν ἀλήθειαν πᾶσαν·
οὐ γὰρ λαλήσει ἀφ' ἑαυτοῦ, ἀλλ' ὅσα ἀκούει λα-
14 λήσει, καὶ τὰ ἐρχόμενα ἀναγγελεῖ ὑμῖν.

TRANSLATION

John 14: 15.—"If ye love me ye will keep my commandments. v.16. And I will pray the Father and he shall give you another Parakletos [Comforter] that he may be with you for ever. v.25. These things have I spoken unto you while yet abiding with you. v.26. But the Comforter [Parakletos] which is the spirit of truth whom the Father will send in my name he shall teach you all things and bring all things to your remembrance, whatsoever I said unto you."

John 16: 7.—"Nevertheless I tell you the truth. It is expedient for you that I go away, for if I go not away, the Comforter [Parakletos] will not come unto you, but if I go, I will send him unto you. v.8. And he, when he is come, will convict the world in respect of sin and of righteousness and of judgment. v.12. I have yet many things to say unto you, but ye cannot bear them now. v.13. Howbeit when he, the Spirit of Truth is come, he shall guide you into all the truth for he shall not speak from himself, but what things soever he shall hear, these shall he speak and he shall declare unto you the things that are to come."

We have not the least doubt that the word "Perikalutas" rendered in English as "Comforter" was not the one uttered by Jesus Christ, but that it was "Parakletos" meaning "illustrious" or "renowned" answering in every respect to the Arabic word "Ahmad." Sir William Muir says that the word Ahmad must "have been erroneously employed as a translation of Perikalutas in some

Arabic version of the New Testament," and that Parakletos (illustrious) for "Perikalutas" was forged by some ignorant or designing monk in Muhammad's time (Muir, *Life of Mahomet*).

It is a well-known fact that a person was expected by a great number of Christians in accordance with the prophecy from a very early period, which shows that the construction put on the passage in the Acts by the Roman Church and by Protestants was not general.

Of this Montanus in the second century earlier than Tertullian furnishes an example. He was considered by his followers to be the promised person.

PROPHECIES IN HINDU SCRIPTURES

Likewise in Hindu scriptures too there are a good many prophecies about the Holy Prophet Muhammad. A few of these are in the Puranas. The one in the Bhavishya Purana is the clearest of all. The fifth word from left to right is the name of our holy Prophet. It gives even the name of the country of the prophet "Marusthalnivasinan" denizen of the desert (Arabia). For this reason the Arya Samaj has tried to cast doubt on the authenticity of this Purana. Their argument is that it contains a reference to the Prophet. According to Sanatanist Pandits and the vast bulk of Hindus, nevertheless, it is considered very authentic. The prophecy runs as follows:

ORIGINAL SANSKRIT TEXT

पुनर्मिन्नन्तरे महेच्छ आचार्येण समन्वित: ॥ महामद इति ख्यात: शिष्यशाखासमन्वित: ॥ ५ ॥ नृपश्चैव महादेव मरुस्थलनिवासिनम् ॥ गंगाजलैश्च संस्नाप्य पंचगव्यसमन्वित: ॥ चंदनादिभिरभ्यर्च्य तुष्टाव मनसा हरम् ॥ ६ ॥ ॐ नमस्ते गिरिजानाथ मरुस्थलनिवासिने ॥ त्रिपुरासुरनाशाय बहुमायाप्रवर्तिने ॥ ७ ॥ म्लेच्छेर्गुप्ताय शुद्धाय सच्चिदानन्दरूपिणे ॥ त्वं मां हि किंकरं विद्धि शरणार्थं मुपागतम् ॥ ८ ॥

TRANSLATION

5. "Just then an illiterate man with the epithet Teacher, Mahamad by name, came along with his companions.
6. Raja (Bhoja in a vision) to that Great Deva, the denizen of Arabia, purifying with the Ganges water and with the five things of cow offered sandal wood and pay worship to him. 7. O denizen of Arabia and Lord of the Holies to thee is my adoration. O, thou who hast found many ways and means to destroy all the devils of the world. 8. O pure one from among the illiterates, O sinless one, the spirit of truth and absolute master, to thee is my adoration. Accept me at thy feet."

Bhavishya Purana Parv 3, Khand 3, Adhya 3, Shalok 5–8.

ORIGINAL SANSKRIT TEXT

॥ ऋग्वेदे २० । १२७ ॥

॥ ऋग कुन्तापसूक्रानि ॥

इदं जना उप श्रुत नाराशंस स्तविष्यते ।
षष्टिं सहस्रा नवतिं च कौरम ट्रा रुशमेषु दद्महे ॥ १ ॥ ॥ १२७

उष्ट्रा यस्य प्रवाहिणो वधूमन्तो द्विर्दश ।
वर्ष्मा रथस्य नि जिहीपते दिव ईषमाण उपस्पृशः ॥ २ ॥
एष च्छवेष मामहे शतं निष्कान्दश स्रजः ।
त्रीणि शतान्यर्वतां सहस्रा दश गोनाम् ॥ ३ ॥ (१)

For translation see opposite page.

TRANSLATION

" O people, listen this emphatically! the man of praise [Muhammad] will be raised among the people. We take the emigrant in our shelter from sixty thousand and ninety enemies whose conveyances are twenty camels and she camels, whose loftiness of position touches the heaven and lowers it.

He gave to Mamah Rishi hundred of gold coins ten circles, three hundred Arab horses and ten thousand cows." *Atharva Veda, Kanda* 20. *Sukta* 127, *Mantra* 1–3.

PROPHECY IN THE PARSI SCRIPTURE

The Parsi religion is one of the oldest religions in the world, perhaps as old as if not older than the Hindu religion. It has two collections of Scriptures —the Dasātīr and the Zand Avasta, which may be called respectively the Old and the New Testaments of the Parsi religion. In Dasātīr, No. 14, which is associated with the name of Sasānll, there is not only a corroboration of the Doctrines and the Teachings of Islam, but a clear prophecy as to the Advent of the Prophet Muhammad. The Prophecy is made in the clearest terms, and is preceded by a vision of a state of extreme disorder and demoralization in Persia. It runs thus:

ORIGINAL PAHLAVI

چم چیم کا جام کند ہر فوار جیام ور تاه ہتال ہو د بوہار سا مام ہو ہمیرناک

دیر ناک و سمراک و امیراک اسرویم ارند ۞ وہو ند ہ رور کتام نؤدام ۞

بیرن فذ ثای نہار و سیمار کسوار آبادی جوار ہ ہ یوستا ۞

و تدرا ہند ثای سیمارام مدیر دانؤرام ہام ونیؤد و یؤاک و ثایام انمناد ۞

MUHAMMAD: "A MERCY TO ALL THE NATIONS"

MODERN PERSIAN

چون چنین کارها کننه از تازیان مردمے پیدا شودکه از پیروان او دیہیم٘دلختدرکشور
وآئین همه برافند و شونده.سرکشان زیردستان—بینند بجائے پیکرگاه و آتش کده خانه آباد
بے پیکر شده نماز برون سو......دباز ستا نند جا و آتش کده ها مدائ ئن و کردها و آن و
توس و بلخ و جاها بزرگ پس انفند هرهم دائ یان ا یران و د یگران درایشان در روند.

TRANSLATION

"When the Persians should sink so low in morality, a man will
be born in Arabia whose followers will upset their throne, religion
and everything. The mighty stiff-necked ones of Persia will be overpowered. The house which was built (referring to Abraham building
the Kaaba) and in which many idols have been placed will be
purged of idols, and people will say their prayers facing towards it.
His followers will capture the towns of the Parsis and Taus and
Balkh and other big places round about. People will embroil with
one another. The wise men of Persia and others will join his
followers."

This prophecy is contained in a book which has
ever been in the hands of the Parsis, and its words
do not admit of two interpretations. The coming
man is to be an Arab. The Persians would join
his faith. Fire temples would be destroyed. Idols
would be removed. People would say their prayers
facing towards the Ka'ba. Can this prophecy fit
in with any person other than Muhammad?

CONCLUSION

Thus if, on the one hand, the holy Prophet
Muhammad testified to the truth of all the other
Prophets, belonging to all the different nations of
the world, and made it a part of his religion, on the
other hand, the Scriptures of these previous Prophets

388

are found to contain clear prophecies about the advent of our holy Prophet Muhammad (the Peace and the Blessings of God be upon him). This mutual corroboration, by furnishing a great evidence of the spiritual providence of God for humanity, strengthens people's faith in religion in general, and in the religion of Islam in particular.

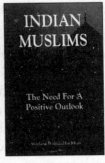

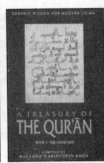

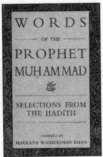

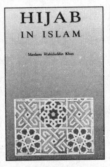

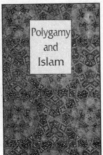

The Basic Concepts in the Quran

HARUN YAHYA

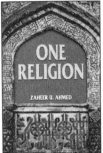

ONE RELIGION

ZAHEER U. AHMED

Heart of the Koran

Lex Hixon

MY DISCOVERY OF ISLAM

MUHAMMAD ASAD

BASIC THEMES OF THE QURAN

MAULANA ABUL KALAM AZAD

THE HAJJ PILGRIMAGE

BURTON

GCSE ISLAM

The Do-It-Yourself Guide

Ruqaiyyah Waris Maqsood

THE HADITH FOR BEGINNERS

Dr. MUHAMMAD ZABAYR SIDDIQUI

The Caliphate

Sir Thomas Arnold

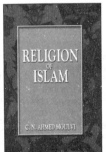

RELIGION OF ISLAM

C. N. AHMED MOLLVI

The Beloved Prophet

Ruqaiyyah Waris Maqsood

THE MUSLIM PRAYER ENCYCLOPAEDIA

A COMPLETE GUIDE TO PRAYERS AS TAUGHT BY THE PROPHET MUHAMMAD

Ruqaiyyah Waris Maqsood

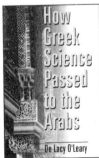

How Greek Science Passed to the Arabs

De Lacy O'Leary

ARABIC ENGLISH DICTIONARY FOR ADVANCED LEARNERS

J.G. HAVA

MUHAMMAD
A PROPHET FOR ALL HUMANITY

MAULANA WAHIDUDDIN KHAN

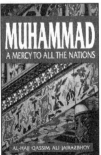

MUHAMMAD
A MERCY TO ALL THE NATIONS

AL-HAJI QASSIM ALI JAIRAZBHOY

Goodword Books

Tell Me About the Prophet Muhammad (HB)
Tell Me About the Prophet Muhammad (PB)
Tell Me About the Prophet Musa (HB)
Tell Me About Hajj (HB)
Tell Me About Hajj (PB)
Tell Me About the Creation
Honeybees that Build Perfect Combs
The World of Our Little Friends, the Ants
Life Begins: Quran Stories for Little Hearts (PB)
The Ark of Nuh (HB)
The Ark of Nuh (PB)
The First Man (HB)
The First Man (PB)
The Two Brothers (HB)
The Two Brothers (PB)
The Brave Boy
The Queen and the Bird
Allah's Best Friend
Tale of A Fish (PB)
The Travels of the Prophet Ibrahim (PB)
The Origin of Life (Colouring Book)
The First Man on the Earth (Colouring Book)
The Two Sons of Adam (Colouring Book)
The Ark of Nuh and the Animals (Colouring Book)
The Brave Boy (Colouring Book)
Allah's Best Friend (Colouring Book)
The Travels of the Prophet Ibrahim (Colouring Book)
The Ark of Nuh and the Great Flood (Sticker Book)
The Story of the Prophet Nuh (HB)
The Story of the Prophet Nuh (PB)
The Blessings of Ramadan (PB)
The Story of Prophet Yusuf (PB)
The Holy Quran (PB)
The Holy Quran (HB)
Islam Rediscovered
A Dictionary of Muslim Names
The Most Beautiful Names of Allah (HB)
The Most Beautiful Names of Allah (PB)
The Pilgrimage to Makkah
Arabic-English Dictionary for Advanced Learners
The Spread of Islam in the World
A Handbook of Muslim Belief
The Muslims in Spain
The Moriscos of Spain

The Story of Islamic Spain (PB)
Spanish Islam (A History of the Muslims in Spain)
A Simple Guide to Muslim Prayer
A Simple Guide to Islam
A Simple Guide to Islam's Contribution to Science
Islamic Medicine
Islam and the Divine Comedy
The Travels of Ibn Jubayr
The Travels of Ibn Battuta
Humayun Nama
The Arabs in History
Decisive Moments in the History of Islam
My Discovery of Islam
Islam At the Crossroads
The Spread of Islam in France
The Islamic Art and Architecture
The Islamic Art of Persia
The Hadith for Beginners
How Greek Science Passed to Arabs
Islamic Thought and its Place in History
Muhammad: The Hero As Prophet
A History of Arabian Music
A History of Arabic Literature
The Qur'an for Astronomy
Islamic Economics
The Quran
Selections from the Noble Reading
The Koran
Heart of the Koran
Muhammad: A Mercy to All the Nations
The Sayings of Muhammad
The Beautiful Commands of Allah
Allah is Known Through Reason
The Miracle in the Ant
The Miracle in the Immune System
The Miracle in the Spider
Eternity Has Already Begun
Timelessness and the Reality of Fate
Ever Thought About the Truth?
Crude Understanding of Disbelief
Quick Grasp of Faith
Death Resurrection Hell
The Basic Concepts in the Quran
The Moral Values of the Quran
The Beautiful Promises of Allah
The Muslim Prayer Encyclopaedia
After Death, Life!
Living Islam: Treading the Path of Ideal
A Basic Dictionary of Islam
The Muslim Marriage Guide

GCSE Islam–The Do-It-Yourself Guide
A Treasury of the Quran
The Quran for All Humanity
The Quran: An Abiding Wonder
The Call of the Qur'an
Muhammad: A Prophet for All Humanity
Words of the Prophet Muhamm
An Islamic Treasury of Virtues
Islam and Peace
Introducing Islam
The Moral Vision
Principles of Islam
Indian Muslims
God Arises
Islam: The Voice of Human Nat
Islam: Creator of the Modern A
Woman Between Islam and Western Society
Woman in Islamic Shari'ah
Islam As It Is
Religion and Science
Tabligh Movement
The Soul of the Quran
Presenting the Quran
The Wonderful Universe of Alla
The Life of the Prophet Muhamm
History of the Prophet Muhamm
A-Z Steps to Leadership
The Essential Arabic
One Religion
The Way to Find God
The Teachings of Islam
The Good Life
The Garden of Paradise
The Fire of Hell
Islam and the Modern Man
Uniform Civil Code
Man Know Thyself
Muhammad: The Ideal Charac
Polygamy and Islam
Hijab in Islam
Concerning Divorce
Search for Truth
The Concept of God
The Creation Plan of God
The Man Islam Builds
Non-Violence and Islam
Islamic Fundamentalism
The Shariah and Its Applicatio
Spirituality in Islam
Islamic Activism
Islam Stands the Test of Histo
The Revolutionary Role of Isl
Islam in History
Conversion: An Intellectual Transformation
A Case of Discovery
Manifesto of Peace